CW00558574

BENEATH WHOSE HAND

THE
AUTOBIOGRAPHY
OF R.M. WILLIAMS

WITH OLAF RUHEN

SUN
AUSTRALIA

First published 1984 by The Macmillan Company of Australia
Published in paperback in 1986 by Sun Books
This edition published by Pan Macmillan Australia Pty Limited
St Martins Tower, 31 Market Street, Sydney

Reprinted 1986, 1989, 1991, 1992, 1994 (twice)

National Library of Australia
cataloguing-in-publication data:

Williams, R.M. (Reginald Murray), 1908-
Beneath whose hand.

ISBN 0 7251 0511 9 (Pbk.)

1. Williams, R.M. (Reginald Murray), 1908-
2. Leather industry and trade – Australia – Biography.
3. Ranchers – Australia – Biography. I. Ruhen, Olaf. 1911-1989. II. Title.

338.7'685'0924

Typeset in Times by Abb-Typesetting Pty Ltd
Printed in Malaysia

Beneath whose awful Hand we hold
Dominion over palm and pine

Kipling, 'Recessional'

Chapter One

More than a personal history, this book is a story of adventure: the adventure that might be encountered in any life that keeps as guidelines the rules governing the human spirit. It represents also a search for those rules, a seeking after knowledge. It expounds a way by which a poor boy might capture wealth and power, and explores too his desire for the understanding of women. As to its success or failure, no man can judge before the end.

Perhaps it will be instructive to those who will bear my name. They will be many, for I have six sons. I leave it to my three daughters to write if they will for the generations of women that will also expect guidance from the past—something that most of us would have liked to find set out for them by their ancestors.

For uncounted centuries my mother's people lived, died and were buried in Cornwall's Penzance, where there were pirates no doubt in the family tree. A haunting perception tells me that this must have been so. My father's people were Welsh, and the oppression of the burdened miners also shaped my genes. Rebels from those forgotten ages shout down the corridors of time, accompanied by a polyphony of misery wailing at the doors of mercy to be set free. Somewhere there were gardeners to implant an irresistible urge to dig in the earth when it rains. Among the silent multitude of the dead there must have been one who prayed for the generations to follow, for the burden of that prayer lives on.

My conscience fortunately expanded to accommodate the exigencies that the poverty of my early youth created, so that this account is not just the boring story of a just man. Expediency has marked the road down which I have walked to dubious success, and always the pirate, the rebel, has shouted his advice over my shoulder while the faintest of lights pointed out a dim way. Whoever rejects this advice from the past (though he is barely conscious of it) ignores the mysterious ways of the spirit. A man must look to the muddy pit wherefrom was taken the clay that moulds him.

My father made his home at Belalie North, an insignificant settlement about 200 kilometres north of Adelaide, in the shadow of the Flinders Ranges and just south of the Goyder Line. To a South Australian that is almost a sufficient description: Surveyor-General George Woodroffe Goyder established the line after the searing drought of 1864–66 to mark the northern limit of viable wheat-growing. North of that an annual rainfall of less than 350 millimetres made agriculture hazardous, and this dry area spreads through the Flinders Ranges and thence out into the desert round Lake Eyre. These hills are intensely cold in winter and hot in summer. South of the Line the closer settlement (more efficiently established in South Australia than in any other of the colonies) assured a reasonable prosperity.

Belalie North, on the boundary, shared in this most years, though its pastures under the sun were more often gold than green. It is nearly 600 metres above sea-level, in the Jamestown district, the Northern Highlands of the State. Its long swathes of wild oats and buttongrass carry a light sprinkling of eucalypts and casuarinas, and a good many of those grass-trees (*Xanthorrhoea*) here known as yaccas or yuccas, and in Western Australia as blackboys. Their presence is usually accepted as indicative of poor infertile soils, or soils with a trace-element deficiency of copper, cobalt and zinc. Rigid grass-like leaves spring in a dense tuft from the crown which is carried on a short trunk often as slow-growing as a cycad's. A spike of white flowers rises like a carried spear from their midst. Yaccas grow about 30 centimetres a century and none are more than 2.4–2.7 metres high.

I was born here on 24 May 1908, in the coldest part of the State, at the start of a particularly cold winter that registered ten heavy snowfalls between June and September. My sister Effie was then two. My maternal grandfather Richard Mitchell, a Cornishman from Clare, had taken up a selection here, but Dad's home was more of a depot for his operations than a farm or a station. His life was centred on the horse business. He stabled his horses in a long open-fronted building with pillars. There were no stalls for them, just a long trough at the back where the stable was attached to the barn. The horses found their own places as horses do—each has a favourite place. Just like cattle. Or just like people. The barn was huge, a big service area that would carry many tons of chaff.

He used to buy hay and cut his own chaff. We had a big chaff-cutter on the place, a massive piece of machinery all noise and dust and vibration. That's where my grandfather Richard Mitchell lost his hand; he used to get around with a steel hook in its place.

Life, as I came to know it, revolved round feeding the horses, preparing them for work and making the implements they were to haul. Horses pulled wagons; they hauled the wool and the wheat and the merchandise. They had to be shod, and the harness and other equipment kept in repair. Father's work comprised being a horseman, the carting and cutting of food and, at the anvil, the making of steel parts for the wagons, the 'S' hooks for the collars and the chains, and the making and fitting of shoes. The smithy was also used for welding. Everything was hot-welded in those days; there was no such process as oxy-welding.

Buggy pairs, clattering down the unmade roads attached to their elegant buggies or their working vehicles, provided the chief means of personal transport in those days, and Dad supplied the market. Doctors, lawyers, parsons, even the mighty of the land sat behind horses. Near population centres the roads bore a cavalcade of the wealthy with their uniformed drivers, and the poor behind their shabbier animals. The parade was impressive on Saturdays, show days, sale days and sometimes when the church bells rang.

Occasionally on Saturdays my mother would take her eggs and other produce, such as home-made butter, to market. The roads were dusty with the traffic, every traveller flaunting his wealth or exposing his poverty as illustrated by the horse he drove or the rig that carried him.

In those days if you came by landau with four horses and a coachman you were royalty. Two horses pulling a carriage of sorts proclaimed you gentry. By buggy and pair you were landed folk. By single harness and sulky no bells announced you but at least you were not walking. The long-shafter brake my father drove was the mark of a horseman but not easily classified. As a small child I sat proud with my parents in that parade.

Dad had a passion for prancing, matched pairs of light horses—buying them, matching them, training them and then selling them to people who could afford them. The stock he drove was nearly always in the process of being trained. That was his business—and for some reason it was his pleasure to have my apprehensive, nervous mother hold the reins while he would call on the baker or the grocer, or make his last visit to the pub. She occupied the hard seat in constant trepidation. She would sit there in charge outside the local store while Dad loitered over purchases and be glad to hand over the reins and the footbrake when he returned.

'Oh Joe!' she would protest, as the buggy lurched into wild motion and Dad casually settled into his seat. 'Oh Joe!' We kids in the back would listen to the words and know we were away, to round the corner and hit the country road.

In return, Sunday was her day, and Joe my father chose to hold the reins while she bent a pious knee in the tiny country church. Dad always managed to have a pair of truculent horses for those days when Mother went to church. He could have tied them up, but he never did.

I was two years old when Dr Aitken drove into the district in his new Renault, the first automobile in the district. It was a reasonably prosperous locality. Land was bringing six shillings an acre, travelling dentists charged a shilling an extraction—but in nearby Caltowie the

3

local draper pulled them out as a free service to customers.

A dictate prohibited any work on Sunday, any work whatsoever. Did not the Good Book say that Sunday should be a day of rest? But in his own way Dad did manage to stop the waste of a day. He would make church day the day for taking out the colts, and I noticed that he always washed them down carefully and handled them before he put them away. On Sundays the buggy too had a cleaning that other days did not warrant.

He was a man of another age, really, holding a set of values that differed in essence from those that most men hold today. The son of a pioneer settler, he grew up believing along with most of the men of his world that a man's physical strength was his measure. And the life demanded strength. Hay had to be carried from the fields, heavy horses broken to harness, heavy wheels had to be mended and tyred with steel. Any wagon wheel weighed enough to need four men to lift it. Any four-bushel bag of wheat weighed more than two hundredweight (100 kg). Men of his breed worshipped strength.

As a heritage from his life at the forge and in the field my father had hands like a giant. As a child I had small slender fingers, and it was my ambition to develop hands like my father's. Artists have lately expressed the wish to paint my hands, so somewhere along the way I must have achieved my wish. But my father could carry two bags of wheat, one under each arm, up a ladder, and such a Herculean triumph of thews and sinews was ever beyond me.

With all this he was essentially a quiet man, a man who never wrote letters. He would sit quietly smoking his pipe, seemingly for hours on end, and I often wondered what he used to think about, what interested him most.

Teams being the main source of Dad's income he had numbers of the big quiet horses with their great heavy feet and their long silken manes. They were fed and groomed and cared for the year around, taken to their plodding work and returned to stable, taught to take their places in the teams and taught their names. They were driven by word of mouth, sometimes assisted by light reins. A sharp word was like the crack of a whip. Big, obedient, patient Clydesdales. I loved them.

Dad provided replacements for road transport and the like as a major part of his business. He dealt in teams, which had to be developed, and the training of a team was a serious matter. Some horses could not be trained for the lead; others were naturals for either the near-side or the off-side lead. Perhaps most of the transport animals were absorbed in the wool-carting trade, but other teams in large numbers were used to dig out earth tanks and dams, sometimes dozens of the ten- and twelve-horse teams together. Haulage of one sort or another was the biggest business of the time. Dad also met the demand for the medium-heavy horse largely used in deliveries and private farm transport. The brood mares were kept separate from the other stock and were serviced by travelling stallions to ensure the change of blood.

Dad trained his horses meticulously and bred them carefully. He loved the animals and I remember what a tragedy it was for him when one day lightning struck his team as he led it from the wagon, ten horses in two rows, joined by light chains. The storm came up and caught him; the lightning struck one of the horses and ran through the team, leaving them all dead together. Dad was not hurt, but the death of such a proud team took something from him.

On another day my mother escaped a storm by tying her horse to a rail and hurrying inside. When she came out she found her horse fallen where she had left it. It was dead, and a hole was drilled through the centre of the saddle. Lightning was greatly to be feared. On a much later day an Aboriginal stockman and I were sitting our horses beneath a large mallee box tree when lightning split the tree and knocked us from our horses, hurting neither of us but implanting unforgettable fright. Much later still, about 1960, I was telling my son John of these matters as we were driving cattle down a fence at the Auburn River when a tree behind us exploded, lightning scattering shards of wood over several hundred metres. I have seen lightning light fires in the long grass ahead of me as I have ridden. No wonder the Aborigines tremble when the sky rumbles!

Mother never felt happy about Dad driving young horses on social occasions but she never evaded the Sunday dash to church, one of those single-roomed and lonely structures far out in the bush. I fancy now that sitting behind two young horses pulling a hard spring brake on a road-less, bumpy track was quite a price to pay for sixty minutes of prayer and preaching. Dad never entered a church and an unexpressed tension lay behind their union. I was never christened into any church but I did learn to sing some of the hymns, nostalgic tunes now—'Rock of Ages' and Kipling's 'Recessional', which was a favourite with all the old-time preachers. I believe they saw themselves as heading the hosts of God's Executioners:

> God of our fathers, known of old,
>   Lord of our far-flung battle line,
> Beneath whose awful Hand we hold
> Dominion over palm and pine—
> Lord God of Hosts, be with us yet,
> Lest we forget—lest we forget.

Mother was born about 1880, and died in 1984 at the age of 103. She coped with the horse-and-buggy days most of her life. Her experience centred round wild horses, a blacksmithing horse-breaking husband and the eternal round of cooking for the men on the teams. She grew up to the sound of the ringing anvil, neighing horses, crowing roosters and cackling hens, this being the music to which all of our family marched.

Days started early before the sun rose, and chores for women and children continued long after dark: water to carry, eggs to gather, cream to churn, horses to feed. Without power or refrigeration women wore out early under the constant burden of the cooking stove and the wash-tub. Mending and ironing, the milking of house cows, the baking of bread came in the constant round. My mother was typical: a product of the nineteenth century, brought up without major interests beyond those which kept her busy as a child. It would have been better for her if she had taken more interest in the world at large, because as the world changed she had little in common with its new directions.

One of the modern philosophers has said, 'The traditions of the past weigh like an Alp upon the mind of the living'—and how true this is! I have felt its truth throughout my life as I encountered varying principles, different tenets of faith and different behaviour. My parents had a narrow suspicion of and anger towards those 'outside' people who tilled no earth and grew no crop. We are all prisoners in the moral judgments of those around us, and few of us escape these bars.

One of my earliest recollections is of a horde of Aborigines sitting outside our home, waiting for some word from my mother. A lifetime of familiarity with these people has made me conscious of the awful price we have paid for the fulfilment of our ambition to be civilized. The Aborigines, who walked the secret ways of the human spirit, lived in wonder at the marvels of those times, and I think perhaps we have lost this talent for wonder. We pay a heavy price for having left the simple world of such people as my mother and father. The few years of child-hood are the years to gather memories to last a lifetime; we spend the few years that follow gathering wisdom.

Aborigines believed that the mysteries which surrounded them belonged to another dimension—the world of the spirits. While nearly everyone sees plainly enough that we cannot contest the laws which govern matter, few of us learn to cherish the primitive's knowledge that we cannot outwit the laws that govern the human spirit. This is the world of the Aborigine.

They were not 'the good old days', and it is well to remember the things that we did not have and the things that have been replaced. The kerosene lights. The smelly outside dunnies. The lack of hot water, in fact the lack of running water. Metal pipe had been in use for centuries. Was the lack of it because people were too poor to buy? Or were they like the subjects that Thomas Gray found in his country churchyard:

> But knowledge to their eyes her ample page,
> Rich with the spoils of time did ne'er unroll;

Chill penury repressed their noble rage
And froze the genial current of the soul.

From the moment we are born we are conscious of problems with our environment, problems of heat, cold, hunger, annoyances and needs. It's a law of life, and some of us survive to become adjusted. My first memories are of cold, frostbite, crying for hot water to bring aching fingers back to life, and the pain before the relief. Ours was a small house, a pioneer's cottage with room for extras only on the verandah. As a second child I came into that category and slept on the exposed east side where blankets were never enough to keep out the below-freezing cold. Very early I determined not to spend my life in that cold place where the water in the dam froze deep enough to carry a heavy vehicle and the taps remained iced all day. Summer temperatures were over the century day after day and summer dust-storms would send Mum scurrying to paper over the cracks under the doors and the holes in the window.

We may have rested near the base of the social pyramid but one memory that has followed me is that of the old black-fellow who sat on the woodheap and ate on the ground, lacking tribe or status, and I 'weep for the loss and the loneliness there'. Even our own Australian people were then emerging from the gloom engendered by ignorance, poor education and lack of communications, an age when great literature was available to very few. Bigotry was the order of the day. Women's rights were in the hands of suffragettes. All the battles may not yet be won nor all the lamps yet lit.

Stoicism is born of one's inability to change the environment. I have always tried to change the environment, sometimes with success, but there are always problems in the hostile world around. I have tried getting on top of that world with money, only to find the burden of wealth too much. I have fled to the wilderness only to find that living alone or separate is never enough. Putting one's hand into the Hand of God and claiming son-ship is comforting, but that Father has laid down some harsh rules for His children, and none escape their allocated destiny.

Despite the hardship of that early life it had its compensations: the happiness of watching my father at the forge, listening to the music of his hammer as he beat out the horseshoes and made the tools for the machines and the metal parts for the wagons, and breathing the aroma of the red-hot iron. Out in the yard I watched the breaking of horses with an admiring fascination, or joined in what I could of the gathering of fodder.

All these things were magic to a child. But I moved on very early to the processes of a formal education.

My sister, Effie, was six, and I was only four, but she was not allowed to travel by herself in a horsedrawn vehicle. So early each morning we would harness the horse to a battered sulky and drive several kilometres to a small one-teacher school. The schooling proved a continuing disaster, but the drives there and back were much to our liking. As we neared our destination we could see others coming in from different directions, all driving or riding, and Effie would ply the whip to make the pony pick up her feet and reach the cross-roads first. There was always the exhilaration of a race, and a meeting. All roads leading to school were raceways and the children away from their parents had this heady moment of freedom and power, so ponies were whipped into a lather of sweat when rivals were converging.

The elderly Scots woman Miss McNeil also arrived from several kilometres away in a horsedrawn sulky, and we children shared the responsibility of tending the animal. The school itself was a small stone building, big enough to seat about twenty people. The dozen pupils ranged from beginners like us to those in Grade Five, the top. Education was by rote, memory being assisted with a tune. We had a song for the alphabet, a song for the months of the year, still another for the arithmetic tables. If a word proved a stumbling block (as most did to me) our brilliant educator devised a suitable tune for the spelling.

These essential rhythmic drills have stood me in good stead for a lifetime. This small basis of schooling with its musical mumbles has been all I needed to lead me on to read for myself. It provides instant recall. There's no need to look at a machine to find what is twelve times twelve. The answer is indelibly there.

I learned the formula of adding and subtracting, learned about the dictionary, and knew that the information to solve any problem was to be found somewhere. But I was bottom of the class all the way—not because I did not like Miss McNeil, but because I could not handle the required standards. The dear lady would keep me sitting by the hour to establish the way a word like 'altogether' was sounded and spelt.

In 1914, just before the beginning of the First World War, a great drought came to its peak. Crops failed, the grass withered and blew away, the haystacks were all eaten and my father came close to desperation. Gloom reigned. The atmosphere of the house was gloomy and dust pervaded everywhere. Water was low in the dams and all normal activities had ceased. Rumours of grass in the north persuaded my father to migrate his horses. The 'promised land' was at the southern end of the Birdsville Track where it takes off for Queensland, and we found green grass and herbage on the wide plains to the east of the railway near Marree.

Rain fell in the latter part of 1914 and the war began. Germany became a symbol of evil. The unrestricted fervour of a small town caught up in the fever of patriotism illustrated the ease with which a pogrom can be unleashed anywhere the human race has taken root. The patriots hanged the Kaiser in effigy, changed the names of streets and towns, harassed their fellows who had German names and quickly metamorphosed from peaceful rustics to a frenzied mob at war with people they had never seen and probably never thought of before. The hatred was something I did not believe could happen. The propaganda was fierce. The drums of war beat loud in 1914 and the cacophony of martial music calling young men to arms was something to hear.

I remember my uncle, sitting on the platform in the local hall listening to the speeches of farewell from the patriotic urgers, the priests and the parsons pressing the claims of battle, and the glory of dying for God and Empire. Go they did. Many did not return. I watched my aunties' sorrow through their long lives, weeping always for what might have been and the men who did not come back. I was six when the war started, ten when the Armistice ended the slaughter. The best of our horses had gone to pull guns, and the pony that I loved so much had been taken to pull a wagon of war. Thus early I learned of man's inhumanity to man.

Mother did not intend to lay down her life to the constant round of chores forever. She also knew that children educated in a one-teacher school would become like herself and all the housewives round her, semi-literate. I do not blame her for seeing a faint light at the end of a lengthy tunnel when she uprooted the whole family and transplanted us to the suburb of Prospect, in Adelaide. Muscular rheumatism was taking a toll of my father, interfering with the enjoyment and efficiency of his work. My sister Effie had reached the limits of what Belalie could teach her and had to go on to higher education. I could see no place for myself in the halls of learning; all I wanted to do was get back to the land. Perhaps my semi-literate father, separated now from the reins and the anvil, influenced me; to watch him at this time induced something of the feeling one has watching caged lions.

The transfer to more sophisticated learning left me stranded, floundering in the shallows of bewilderment. My new teachers were not sympathetic and tried to beat education into me with a cane. This of course did not work and I degenerated. I became antagonistic and failed to make any progress. I cut classes and learned to lie. Before I was fourteen I planned to leave school for ever, and trust to fortune to get an education. At that time it did not occur to me that I would need to study the English language and acquire a knowledge of geography, history and other subjects so necessary to understanding the modern world. That was to come many years later.

The Hero at the shrine where Mother worshipped had been a carpenter. Attempting to do something for me, she consulted a builder with the idea of guiding me into that vocation, and I started as soon as I had left school. I felt at once that the job was not for me, and stayed in it less than a week. It introduced me, however, to a man I knew only as Peter the Dane, who had contracted to burn lime for the erection of buildings including a church at Underbool, a town in north-western Victoria. I joined him, and my mother packed a Bible with my clothes.

The job took six months and I learned it thoroughly. A kiln is carefully built up of alternate layers of wood fuel and limestone and covered in such a way that it can be burnt under control, a process occupying about two weeks. The resultant quicklime is mixed with a larger quantity of sand and aggregate to form a cement, and while this is being used another kiln is prepared and burnt.

These fairly arduous processes gave me a sound training in the more elementary processes of building. The timber had to be cut and stacked, the limestone selected and broken; and when I was not employed thus I was given plenty of work carrying bricks in a hod to the builders. When the job was finished six months later I went home again; but I knew that more of the same work was available to me at a place called Laverton in Western Australia, on the edge of the desert north of Kalgoorlie.

There was still resentment in me that my mother had persuaded my father to leave the life with the anvil and the reins to take up what I considered to be a useless retirement. Dad was sitting, as was his custom, quietly smoking. He had a favourite spot on the back verandah, and no doubt he also spent long hours with his cronies, talking about the days when people tied their horses to a rail. He was probably just as nostalgic for the bush life as I was.

I presented myself before the stool where he sat alone and put my case.

'I'm going bush,' I said.

He was quiet for a while. Although I felt he had approved when I went to burn lime in the bushland of Victoria, this was different. He knew that by 'bush' I meant the back of beyond. I had heard about the vast lands, still unsettled and almost unknown, and these were calling me.

'You are too young,' he said. 'You had better stay a bit until you are ready to go bush on your own. Besides, your mother will not like it.'

I must have looked a bit sullen, because he threw a piece of heavy artillery at me.

'Don't you know the Fifth Commandment: "Honour your father and your mother"?' he asked.

That produced a heavy silence. Then I said, 'I will always be an honour to you, Dad.' That silenced him. He had not interpreted the commandment that way.

I pulled out while the silence held because I doubted that I could have disobeyed a direct instruction to stay. So I packed a few things I valued and left. I took with me two blankets and a piece of canvas that were to constitute my home for many days. I wandered, worked and married, but I did not go home again until I was supporting myself and my family.

The boys that stay at school and home until they are grown miss many elementary lessons that the working world loves to teach its newcomers. I quickly learned that a stockman's home is a piece of canvas three metres by two and a half metres, plus a blanket and two stout straps; nothing fancy, for 'th'apparel oft proclaims the man'. Indeed, the way a man rolls his swag tells the discerning much about him. It must be rolled to fit a pack-saddle, the right length, not too bulky, neatly strapped and the canvas clean of burrs. A man becomes very proud of his swag, for in a new camp it is his mark of identification.

For many years after I left home the swag and a campfire were enough, and that was how it was when I married a bush girl who knew all about campfires, swags and camp ovens. The centre of Australia is a land almost without dew, therefore comfortable, and, in spite of its dry bull-dust, clean to those who know how to keep clean in it.

The urge to get out and go it alone must be strong in most people, for the spirit of man answers to the blood of his ancestors. When a head is bowed before me the urge to kill is very strong. When it rains, the feeling for the soil and the urge to plant is powerful. The Celts who were my ancestors running before the Romans were beaten but not bowed. Who is there who has never cried to an unknown god, never answered the ghost call of generations of long-dead ancestors? Indeed we contain our past. Unknown it might be, but it persists alive and urging. We are sculptures in the making, just begun by the great Artist; not yet formed but indicative of what is to come.

Chapter Two

In the few weeks I spent in Adelaide before I left for the bush I had met Thelma in the eating-house where she served at table, a meeting that made a considerable impact on both of us and shaped the course of both our lives, though I was not yet sixteen and she about the same. Our acquaintance rapidly developed to the point of an agreement that, if I waited for her after work, she would take me out.

'Out' was to the old Exhibition building in North Terrace where the internationally famed revivalist Gipsy Smith was telling the story of his life, a story remarkable enough. His message sticks in my mind even now: 'The world marches to the tune of sobs and sighs.' I can hear the thunder of the spellbinder's voice. Accompanying him was a choir of singers whose music also stays with me; I still have a battered copy of his songs.

Thelma lived in a very old single-fronted building in a slum neighbourhood. She had never known anything but grinding poverty, but it was brightened for her by the romantic light in which she saw her father, a father she had not seen after he enlisted for service in the war. He had left his family of six children in their mother's care. A tall old eagle of a man who quoted poetry, he had been able to inspire his children with proud and glowing memories. And with love and little else her mother held that family together and under her guardianship they became without exception fine cultured people.

The father had been a shearer, a ringer in every shed he entered. Looked up to by his fellows, he became a leader also in the shearers' strike of 1891. This and the maritime strike that preceded it broke new ground, for the union membership consisted of unskilled and semi-skilled workers who could be replaced, unlike the skilled artisans who constituted the membership of earlier unions. Therefore it was fought with great bitterness, a condition enhanced by government use of troops and an excited press coverage.

At the opening of the 1891 season the Queensland pastoralists, supported later by those in New South Wales and Victoria, introduced an agreement that stipulated freedom of contract between themselves and individual shearers, and began to recruit non-union labour. In retaliation shearers, especially along the Darling River, formed camps to intercept these non-union shearers as they travelled to their jobs. These confrontations ended in compromise, but in 1894 the Pastoralists' Union repudiated the contract and a fresh strike developed. Camps of union shearers all along the Darling tried to intercept the non-union labour; and they kept a special watch on the crack river-steamer *Rodney*, which under stiff opposition had loaded forty-five non-union shearers at Echuca for Tolarno station, upriver.

On Sunday, 26 August, *Rodney* was within a day's journey from Tolarno and tied up in the middle of a swamp for the night with steam up and moorings ready to slip. A party of unionists boarded the craft, dumped the non-unionists in the swamp, transferred the crew to a barge and set fire to her. Earlier plans had been to sink her in the channel to stop following traffic, but *Rodney's* remains grounded in the swamp, immovable.

Thelma's father was a ring-leader of the attacking party. Eight men were captured and came to trial but the jury found them not guilty. Thelma's father, however, was on the run from that time. He continued to work under a variety of names; Thelma had been brought up under the name Cummings (or sometimes Davenport).

When I left Adelaide to go bush we kept up a correspondence. I knew where I was going. At Underbool a casual passerby had asked me if I would be prepared to burn some lime for people in Laverton, a small (and diminishing) town on the Mount Margaret goldfield on the western edge of the Great Victoria Desert. His name was Rod Schenk, and his project was to establish a mission to the Aborigines who in that quarter, he told me, were among the last native people living a tribal life. He wanted me to teach him to burn lime and build a large concrete tank, as water was his prime concern. That district has about 220 millimetres annual rainfall in good years.

The journey proved quite an adventure. I travelled on the 'Transcontinental Express' from Port Augusta to Kalgoorlie, and then north on a spur line to Laverton. Schenk demonstrated the job and gave me the services of a half-caste lad named Sandy. Limestone was close at hand, but the timber for burning it had to come from a stand of mulga about eight kilometres out, and each day we would walk the eight kilometres, cut the timber and stack it ready for carting, and then walk home again.

I had had very little experience with the axe, and I discovered that Sandy was a much better man than I was, and could cut nearly twice as much wood. He demonstrated to me that though people of a black skin may not be equal to whites in some ways, in others they were far better. They were better axemen, they were better bushmen and in many ways they were better men. Remember that I was then living in a physical world and consequently I was judging them by their physical attributes. The mulga posts were thick and Sandy could cut and trim a log while I was still clearing away the branches. Now how could that be? I was a white man and he was black. The lesson stuck through life that a man's a man whatever his colour or creed.

Sandy taught me much about bushcraft. He showed me how to

recognize the almost indistinguishable looseness of surface earth beneath which, a couple of feet down, a burrowing frog could be recovered. This frog (*Cyclorana platycephalus*), on the approach of dry weather, fills itself with water until it is like a ball and burrows deep into the mud of a claypan, waiting for the next rains. It is an emergency source of water; the supply under its almost transparent skin can be squeezed directly into the mouth. Sandy showed me how to detect the presence of grubs in the wood of small bushes, by the sound of tapping. They were very acceptable food. He taught me how to track lizards and other bush animals and to know them by their tracks. He showed me how to make fire, and how to find roots of the water tree. I discovered that all education does not come from schools and universities, but that a vast amount of knowledge is stored in the minds of people in the bush. This was a more useful education than any I had received at school.

With the timber cut, we had to bring it to the kiln-site in an old cart pulled by a decrepit horse—a day's task for each load. Then came the digging of the pit, the breaking of the stone and the building of the fire. This last was a simple process of laying large logs, then a heap of limestone, another layer of logs, another heap of limestone, till we reached the necessary height. We did this in an enclosed place in the back of a creek, and then stoned it up, completely surrounding the pile and putting a tin cover over the top so that it could be closed off when the fire was well under way. It took about two weeks to burn the lime.

When that was done, Schenk gave me the job of building a tank of lime-based concrete. We raked stones up on the hills to get the aggregate, brought sand from the creek and mixed these with the lime and water to form concrete. Apparently our building was successful for sixty years later it was still in use. It was then that I received a cassette tape from old Mrs Mysie Schenk about the tank still standing monument to the wood-cutting, the lime-burning and the mixing of concrete. Her voice was ancient, and the recording not the best, but I clearly heard its main message:

'Dear Reg: It's been a tremendous thrill to see in the *West Australian* last week a report of your achievement. It brought back a memory of many happy days. However, one thing they didn't mention, and what I think is your greatest achievement, is the burning of the lime for the limestone tank down at the Kings Well on Mount Margaret Mission. I remember how you spent nights and nights and nights working on that, burning that lime, chopping that wood and all the work you went to.

'It was a tremendous effort, tremendous, and for sure it has been a tremendous help to many people, the water of life to many Aborigines and white people. That tank you built was so strong it was a great disappointment to have found a week later that there was a leak in it and I can see you today—to this day—with two of them holding each of your legs while you hung over the side and mended the leak. Nothing has gone wrong with that tank ever since. It has been one hundred per cent. It was your greatest achievement, I reckon, and I want to thank you for it.

'Dear Reg, we did miss your fellowship when you left and we long to see you back in that fellowship with the Lord Jesus. I'm not very clear in my speech just now because I'm eighty-two and I'm on my deathbed . . .'

There was an exhortation for me to turn back to the arms of the Lord. 'Trust Him and learn to lean on Him. He is the water of life and the water of life means more to our native people than anything else. They all here admire your shirts and trousers and boots and hats but I want to tell the story of your well but I never will. I pray you will get the victory fruit of your service here at the Lord's Glory.'

A letter from her son accompanied the tape:

Dear Mr Williams:
My mother who knew you at Mount Margaret has just recently passed away. Sparked by your photo in the *West Australian* she taped a message specifically for you just before she passed away and I forward the tape at her request. After she taped the message to you she said, 'I feel my life work is over now', and I trust that her memories of you are encouraging.
Warmest greetings,
Rod Schenk.

The message had come from the grave. I stood bowed with tears for the pathos of that last word. It broke a barrier somewhere and across the far horizons of the years I saw a great figure, one person standing with her arms outstretched, pleading with the world she was leaving, letting it know: 'How often would I have gathered you in but you would not hear.'

About the time that I received it I passed by the church at Underbool and watched briefly as the good people entered it to attend their service. I thought of all the good fellows who built the church—all dead now. 'For them no more the blazing hearth shall burn, Or busy housewife ply her evening care.' Perhaps they look on from another dimension; if not, as Thomas Gray suggests, their ancient efforts still have puissance.

Lallie, the sister of young Sandy who helped me with the lime-burning, later went to live with an Afghan hawker who travelled in the area. Servants of the Native Affairs Commissioner discovered that the couple were not married, and they took Lallie to an institution in Perth. After her child was born they separated them.

Akbar, the hawker, went to Perth, discovered where they were and with an old truck transported them to Adelaide. He came to me later and told me the authorities were hunting him because he had stolen the girl, whom he had since married. I suggested that the best thing he could do

15

would be to settle down in some place where he was not known, and I helped him establish a small business at Renmark, in South Australia.

Many many years later I had a call from several of the children of that union. Lallie had told them that if they ever wanted to know the story of their beginnings they should contact me, and I was happy to tell them where they came from and the story of their parents.

At Laverton I first made contact with a tribe of really wild blacks. They had come in from the Gibson Desert to the north and east for their annual meeting with the tribes of the Laverton district. During this contact their ceremonies would introduce the boys to manhood and initiate the young girls. The people would settle their differences and discuss all the events of the year.

Their numbers were considerable. They were scattered over a large area of the plain, including the section where I was cutting mulga posts. Some of the tribal elders were fierce old men who very much resented the intrusion of white people. In the light of acquired experience I recognize them now to have been the doctors or the medicine men or, if you like, the keepers of the tribal secrets. Other leaders of the tribe were quite friendly, and one told me that if I were interested in Aboriginal affairs I should make an effort to hear something of a corroboree, the music of which is inspiring to the native soul. The rhythms created by people in their hundreds are unforgettable, particularly the sound produced by the women beating the earth with their heavy digging sticks in perfect time to accompany the men's singing.

Warned to keep my distance from these very secret ceremonies, I chose a night when the moon had gone down to go carefully and quietly towards the concerted sounds. When I was several hundred metres from my objective a team of spear-carrying men accosted me, and I would have proceeded at the risk of my life. They warned me in their own language to leave immediately, and I understood it enough to do so.

Half-castes like Sandy and others with whom I had working relations first told me the details of Aboriginal ceremonies. They had been in contact with white people over a long period, but they had grown up in the camps with the Aboriginal mothers and had taken part in the ceremonies. Some of them had been initiated and were treated exactly as if they had been members of the tribe. From them I learned of the way in which young men were initiated, and that the tribal initiation marks on their chests indicated to which totem they belonged. Most of the women also were scarred across the chest between the breasts, or sometimes on their backs and bellies, the marks indicating their totems and the nature of their availability as marriage partners. No more permanent brands than these keloid markings could have been devised. Cut deep into the skin with a stone and filled with wood ashes, they resulted in distinct ridges, clearly visible from a good distance.

This particular tribe had great skill with the returning boomerang, and I learned from them the ways in which boomerangs were used in hunting and in fighting. Not all Aborigines in Australia used the returning boomerang, and still less were skilled in its use; but these desert men were specialists. They could do things that I have not seen duplicated by men of other tribes or by white people who have taken up the art. Some of them could make the weapon course through two complete circles, or touch the ground and then rise again to complete its circuit. This is a skilful exercise, requiring great judgment.

I suppose that it was at Laverton that I took the first tenuous steps on the long journey towards literacy. I had the Bible that my mother had put in my pack, and for filial reasons I kept the battered volume throughout my travels, sometimes in sheer boredom looking over the pages which someone had marked. I spelled out these passages, and I remembered many of them through life. Becoming literate did not mean that I turned to the classics, or even that I learned to spell, but these early steps represented a great advance on not being able to remember a single address, or not having read a single book.

To read was a necessity in dealing with people. I always had a friend handy who could explain what was what, but under the pressure of needing to know I became conversant with the meaning of words, and the wonder of the printed page slowly opened up a new and exciting world. Years passed before I could claim to have read a book purely for pleasure; but the conviction that I must read or forever remain in a dark and clouded world led me slowly into what I now know to be the best thing in life. Reading is a window to the world or, to use a better metaphor, a deep well from which comes the water that lets the flowers of knowledge flourish.

The development took years, but once I began the climb out of darkness nothing could stop me. I acquired a dictionary and wrote down the new words, learning the meaning of what was written and said. In the back of every book I wrote out the unknown words, and still do. I read slowly, but with a desperate need to understand. Many people think that it is easy to read, but with me the study of the simplest story took time. It became easier as I went, and nothing can stop me now from reading everything that seems worthwhile. I have read the Bible, Karl Marx, the works of Chairman Mao. My library is overflowing.

If someone were to ask me, 'What should I read?' I would reply, 'Whatever interests you enough to keep you reading.' I had a son who did not read and showed no interest in books. I had sent him droving, which is a world without books, and expected that he might finish up much as I was at that age. Someone gave him a pile of books that looked vaguely pornographic, and son Kerry became a student overnight. Years later I was amazed to find him reading Tolstoy's *War and Peace.*

Truly any road that leads to Rome is worth taking. Without reading no one can know the infinitely interesting variety of this world. The greatest educational project is to learn to read; the rest can follow.

About the time the tank was finished the offer came to all such men as Rod Schenk to volunteer to explore the Aboriginal lands east of Laverton and west of Oodnadatta, to make a rough count of the Aboriginal population within a vast area of about a million square miles (2 590 000 km^2) of almost unknown bush. A man called Bill Wade got the job and he asked me to accompany him as camel driver, a job of which I had very little knowledge. This was an exciting project after the six months I had spent at Laverton, and bearing in mind my growing interest in the wild Aborigines I left for Oodnadatta almost at once, with an authorization to buy a string of camels.

From 1891 Oodnadatta had been the railhead of a line from Port Augusta. All stations north of it had to be supplied by camel. All the necessities of Alice Springs and beyond, including the buildings, were carried more than 500 kilometres from the railhead on the backs of camels. The supplies for the fledgling mining township of Tennant Creek, another 300 kilometres further on, were brought the same way. Some teams even supplied Newcastle Waters, 1300 kilometres from the railhead. A 'Ghan town' with a mosque developed at Oodnadatta, as well as at Marree, Lyndhurst, Farina and Hergott Springs.

Between Oodnadatta and the Finke River, thousands of square kilometres of gibber tablelands, red earth strewn with scattered rocks, are held in vast estates, areas taken up by men like Treloar, who lived alone hundreds of kilometres from the rail. They survived there without contacts, without news, without doctor, priest or likely help, serviced with rations or stores by wagons that came in once a year. Treloar took up Abminga station in the 1860s and built up a magnificent herd of shorthorn cattle, only to watch them die. Horses, donkeys, mules and camels all died in the blistering droughts round the turn of the century. In 1926 old Treloar was camped alone in the Musgraves, not grieving but convinced at last of the impossiblity of his dream. The annual rainfall for that area averages 75 millimetres, but how were any of the old-timers to know that except by finding out?

In good seasons cattle roam at will, fat and contented, wandering a little but brought back by boundary riders or 'attenders'. In bad seasons when the waters dry up they head for where memory or instinct tell them water will be. Sometimes both fail and the cattle perish. Following the progress of the migrating herds or shifting the dying cattle to water is work for a special kind of stockman, a bush-wise individual who can cross the unmarked lands and find the right destination without erring in his direction. The country affords no latitude for failure. Men and animals must drink and life expectancy is measured not in days but in

Right: My parents, Joseph and Fanny, on their wedding day in 1904.

Below: My sister Effie and me with our parents.

Above: With my sisters Daisy and Effie in 1924.

Below: Bill Wade (not in the picture) bathing the arm of an Aboriginal woman suffering from yaws.

Children of the desert (about 1927).

Above: The water tank I built at Mt Margaret in 1925.

Below: A camel train ready to travel. The very young camel calves have been packed on top of the loads, and the rifle is packed on the lead camel.

hours in that hot climate. The stockmen who live and work through a drought become elements in the mythology of the bush.

At Oodnadatta camels came and went regularly in strings of fifty to a hundred, and they were loaded by the one warehouse-storekeeper, Wallis Fogarty. Camels being my immediate concern after I arrived, I proceeded to make friends with their owners and I discovered that almost all were in debt to one money-lender, named Kabul. Most of them had bought their camels through Kabul, who exerted a considerable influence. He was chief man in the 'Ghan town', a huddle of mainly corrugated-iron buildings, small and clustered, on the western side of town, over towards The Neales, the local creek. The cameleers had built a small mosque, and they had a mullah to lead the frequent observances. Some of them had reverted to the custom of putting together a harem which they controlled rigidly, and I rather fancy they conducted a brisk business in the buying of women from the tribes in the area. Quite a lot of the women who were living with the Afghans were half-caste or quarter-caste, with a few purebreds.

The Aborigines were camped on the outskirts of Oodnadatta, and particularly on the waterholes of The Neales to the westward. Looking at them I found it quite easy to understand how the Afghans were able to recruit their harems. They were living in serious poverty because the area for at least eighty kilometres around was completely arid and had been hunted to the extent at which no local food whatever remained. Therefore the Aborigines, who came in from various tribes in the surrounding country to live in Oodnadatta on whatever pickings they could get, sold their women for the necessities of life.

I am sure that the women traded in this manner did not believe that they had left their tribal relations. I think they undertook their new connections as a task connected with survival, possibly dictated by the elders. However, I do not suppose they ever returned to their original families. Even the low standards of living among the Afghans would have been better than the conditions their blood relations enjoyed.

Yaws was quite common then, and when I saw groups with whole areas of their bodies eroded I believed, in my inexperience, that I was seeing leprosy, and my sympathies were very much with people so terribly afflicted. But yaws, a tropical disease though not necessarily a venereal one, was caused by a spirochete and could quite readily be cured by the injection of the drug Salvarsan, a trade-name for arsphenamine.

The children were in a pitiful condition. They seemed to be constantly afflicted with colds, running noses and eyes suffering from various diseases. This was in direct contrast to the children of the western tribes I had seen at Laverton, people living still in their native condition. Those people were healthy and in good seasons they were fat and looked fit and well.

Generally speaking, Oodnadatta was a law-abiding community. The chief constable, or sergeant of police, whose name was Virgo, had a particularly efficient team of trackers and a patrol of four bullock camels. His chief occupation was not with keeping the peace but rather the catching of Aborigines who were charged with spearing cattle, and also the controlling of tribes out to the west. He controlled the largest police district in Australia, extending from Lake Eyre to the border of Western Australia, and from the Northern Territory border south to William Creek.

His practice was to round up a team of possible offenders and chain them neck to neck, leading them in a column across the desert behind his team of fast-moving camels. This is not hearsay; I have passed these toiling caravans of blacks on the desert pads without so much as a hand lifted in recognition. I do not remember any serious punishment being meted out to them but they were certainly treated in a rough manner. Brought in from hundreds of kilometres away with chains round their necks night and day, they must have suffered great discomfort and great indignity.

I had little time for such methods of control and determined that when I went into the unexplored areas I would try to learn what the Aboriginal people thought about their condition. With little or no contact with whites, they were spread over the huge area, mostly unexplored and untravelled, between Moorilana and Laverton.

For police at Oodnadatta to travel west to capture supposed criminals seemed to me foolish, for the tribes living round the town and as far west as Moorilana were quite different from those living in the Musgraves. It was certain death, as I discovered later, for an Aborigine from Oodnadatta to move into the Musgraves without some special traditional purpose, such as a corroboree.

Buying camels proved more difficult than I had imagined it would be. It was not just a matter of buying a camel; it was a matter of buying a suitable string: bullocks for heavy loads, lighter camels for lighter loads, riding camels for riding. The animals also had to be compatible with one another. I conducted most of my business with Kabul the money-lender and eventually assembled a basic team.

Having done this, the problem was to feed them because the area round the town had been grazed bare by goats and camels for many years. I found it necessary to go out at least thirty kilometres in any direction to find feed, a long walk out and a long walk home. The leader of the expedition had not yet arrived in the north, which left me very much alone; but I was learning something of the country, of the Afghans and, of course, of my main concern, the camels.

There must be still a lot of people alive who remember the great camel teams that used to go out from the rail-points. I used to watch them closely: the method of loading, the method of making the saddles and the way in which individual loads were packed, particularly difficult loads such as three-metre troughing. There are many different kinds of loading, and each follows a different procedure.

Contrary to public opinion the camel can be a lovable animal. It is an intelligent animal and, like the elephant, does not forget. If ill-treated it remembers the person responsible. Many of the old camel-drivers had mutilated arms and shoulders where camels had bitten them.

An old fellow I worked for later specialized in breaking camels to the buggy and I well remember his method. He used to use a sandy corner where large sand-hills existed close to the station. There he would tie the camels down and hitch them to the buggy, and then, although he was a fairly fat man, he would get up on the buggy and ask the boys to let go the ropes on the camels and away would go the team. They were well tied together, and after they had ploughed through the sand-hills for a few kilometres they were fairly quiet. The majority of camels were easier to break and much more docile than horses.

Chapter Three

Bill Wade, who headed our expedition, was an ex-sailor, born within the sound of Bow Bells. He had sinned in every port in the world and led a rough life, but his conversion to religion was total and sincere. Although camels are the ships of the desert, the job was quite foreign to him, so all the handling of the camels and the whole process of obtaining area maps and the direction of activities rested on my shoulders.

Bill's reformation had made him a 'born-again Christian' and he spent much of his time going about and telling people he had been 'saved by Grace'. I found this embarrassing, because the Afghans, whom I respected, had a different type of religion and they did not understand how a man needed 'saving'. Their philosophy was quite different from a Christian's, and I found their routine of praying several times a day, and bowing as they did so in worship of Allah, a much more convincing way of expressing their faith than Wade's habit of telling people he was a saved man.

It seemed to me also that the Afghans had a more stable way of life than many of the Christian people I had met. Time was to change my attitude to Wade, but then I found him difficult to take, particularly as he displayed his leadership by treating me as the inferior. Being young I expected this to some extent, but I did know that I was his superior in some significant matters like bushcraft and the handling of animals.

Our expedition looking into the numbers and conditions of people in the Everard, Musgrave, Petermann, Mann, Tompkinson and Rawlinson Ranges, and all adjacent areas north and south of them, was sponsored by semi-government institutions and was of some importance to the Surveyor-General. It had been proposed that a huge area here be set aside for the Aborigines, Western Australia contributing half and the Northern Territory and South Australia a quarter each. Our programme was also associated with some of the major Aboriginal missions which were sponsored by the various churches. Hence, of course, the appointment of such a man as Wade to head the expedition.

The assembling of food and the many other items necessary was in his hands. The camels were my responsibility and I found it more expedient to live out on one or other of the watercourses where grazing was available, so I did not spend much time in Oodnadatta. This was quite a novelty for a time, though it became lonely. Nevertheless I became interested in the work of the cattle-stations around me and became friends with the people running them. I found such places as Macumba station totally to my liking.

On one of my trips back to Oodnadatta to obtain supplies Wade expressed a wish to give me some relief by taking the camels north to the Alberga River to feed them. I believed it might be a risky thing to do but felt that the experience would be good for him, and as the responsibility was his, it did not greatly concern me that he might lose the animals. And so he headed north and I gratefully stayed in Oodnadatta.

I spent much time there with the Afghans and the Chinese, whom I found entertaining, and I made friends with an old driver who for many years had been taking camel-trains north for the firm of Wallis Fogarty. Bill Gregory had a hut fairly close to town and I chose to camp with him, unrolling my swag on his verandah. Living with him was an old camel-driver named Fox, who had been mutilated by a bull. His custom was to start drinking early in the morning and become progressively drunk towards the day's end. But I liked old Mr Fox, and I also liked the atmosphere of the camp where I was always welcome.

Bill Gregory had married a girl from the hotel many years before, and now had six children who were all living in the south. Every night he would light a kerosene lamp on his table and would encourage those who wanted to gamble to play cards until eleven o'clock, when he would religiously retire. A requirement of the players was that they should put some money into the lamp-box and he told me he had educated his family from its contents. To my knowledge the police never raided this small gambling operation, and I approved, for I didn't think any harm was done.

Not much other entertainment existed in Oodnadatta in 1926 but Chong, the Chinese baker, had an old His Master's Voice gramophone and it gave me a lot of pleasure to hear the tunes of the twenties being played on it. In fact the same tunes make me quite nostalgic now. I had had no previous experience of music outside the chants of school, and I found the records fascinating.

Chong ran a sort of open house. From a long passageway, small rooms opened out on either side. People of many nationalities came to eat there, and for a small amount of money they could sleep there. Like the Afghans, Chong had the knack of picking up any girls who were available and willing to work in his menage. I found this environment most exciting; much better than camping on faraway watercourses with only my camels for company.

As time went by and Wade did not show I became concerned lest he had gotten lost. He was no bushman. He had indicated that he would travel along the old track towards Todmorden station until he reached the Alberga River, about 140 kilometres north of Oodnadatta, where there would be feed for the camels. I had two options. I could walk, or I could borrow an old pushbike and attempt to pedal the distance and find Billy Wade. I decided to bike it. In the exuberance of youth and the belief that I was indestructible I failed to carry water with me, relying on getting water from a well along the way. When I reached this water it proved undrinkable. None had been pulled from its great depth for quite a time, and the water was not only foul but bitter, and so I had to go on without a drink.

This almost cost me my life. The great heat of the track dehydrated me and soon I was crawling. I had just about reached a state in which I was incapable of reason, scrabbling in any small depression, desperately seeking water, when I saw a light ahead and thankfully had the strength to make for it. This saved my life.

The man with the light looked after me, made sure I was rested and gave me enough water to carry on. He was able to assure me that Bill Wade was camped within a few kilometres. I had not previously been glad to meet and talk to Wade, but this time was different. We went back to Oodnadatta where by this time most of the stores for the expedition had been assembled. Bill Gregory had allowed us the use of the verandah of his gambling house as a depot, and from there we loaded our camels and set out to make our way westward. By that time it was May or June of 1926.

Four days' walk brought us to Todmorden, the first cattle-station on the road west, and it was here that a wild camel came into our camp. He had two nose pegs, indicating that he had been previously captured and pegged ready to make him a riding camel. Possibly he had escaped from some Afghan's team. Wade was excited at the prospect of capturing him and getting a fat, useful-looking camel for himself.

He was not hobbled and I could not see how we could capture such an animal wild and free. We decided that the best method would be to put a rope round the neck of our largest bullock and, mounting him, drop a loop over the head of the newcomer. The bullock we used for an anchor was huge, the largest of our camels, and the ruse worked. The loop settled over the other camel's neck and moved up to his throat, and when he pulled back the anchoring bullock choked the big black wild camel to his knees. We then managed to put ropes round his knees and tie him down. We got some excitement out of the incident.

In his ignorance, Wade put a riding saddle on the camel. He thought it would be easy to guide the animal with its two nose pegs and to break it for riding. It was a resolve born of great foolishness or great courage. I suggest it was possibly both. We strapped the saddle to the camel's back, tied the girths tightly, and then when Wade was in the saddle I handed him the reins and undid the knot on the camel's knees. Away they went!

He was gone at least four hours. When he returned his mount was obviously exhausted and so, of course, was Wade. Even more noticeable was that he was raw from his ankles to his crutch. He had lost a great deal of skin. But I give him credit—unstinting credit—for that courageous ride in country without fences. He could have been taken hundreds of kilometres without anyone knowing where he had gone.

I was very glad to see him back, and I am sure it bolstered his confidence to have mastered the situation. Wade never mentioned the incident again, but he wore his blooded trousers like a guerdon and did not wash them for a long time after. I think he saw in them the evidence that he was now a superior camel man. Neither of us rode this camel again, but we loaded him with heavy boxes. This experiment was a failure. After he developed a habit of bucking them off, we were content to let him go.

The Aborigines Wade employed to guide us took no part in this camel operation, and strangely did not at any time assist me in loading and handling the animals.

My boss was a mission man, but very much the boss. He told me to look after the camels and to know my place. He talked a lot about being saved and everyone knows that when you are saved you are a good man, but I sometimes had doubts about whether I preferred the good man type or the drunken kind of comradeship normally available, and I have never really sorted out this difficult problem.

At any rate my boss Bill attacked every old bushman he met with tracts and a fierce attempt to save him. Old bushmen don't need saving; they mostly have had their share of hell and the only thing they crave is a loyal mate. But this I still had to learn. My crusading mate had a special relationship with God. They talked together for hours, sometimes into the night. My concern was making sure Bill found his way back to camp after the session. I confess I came to hate Bill with the single-mindedness of one who lives solely in the company of another for too long.

We headed west, leaving a trail of good and bad men wondering if they perhaps might need religion. A hundred kilometres; two hundred; three hundred. I stuck to the camels and watched to see if there were anything big for me to learn. We came to the end of the roads where the last of the 'need-saving' people lived with one or two gins, stocked up with rum, carried guns and used them on blacks who were tricky.

Their life-style appealed to a young adventurer, but then we were past the last of the unsaved and on our own in the big country. There were no roads, no tracks, no maps. It was better not to depend on the maps of the explorers who had sometimes marked the waterholes twenty or thirty kilometres out of position, and those waterholes were small and un-detectable from a few metres distant. We had no instruments other than a small pocket compass. Our way was ever west, and the only help we were liable to get—and in fact did get—was from tribesmen who had not been 'helped' by the tea, sugar and tobacco people.

The last seriously occupied land was Moorilana, a cattle-station subsequently and probably better known as Granite Downs. Mick O'Donohue who owned it in those days ran his establishment on primitive lines; his loo consisted of three greenhides, laced as they came from the beasts on lengths of sapling and partially enclosing a rail that served as seat. Mick was as crude as they come, a true son of the soil. He was quite a philosopher in his way, and yet unsure of himself, carrying a gun. At that time the tribes had no love for such people as Mick O'Donohue.

Further out the landholders lived in scattered camps, running a few sheep, owning a few cattle, living almost under the stars in bough sheds. The most civilized camp, and the furthest west of Oodnadatta at that time, was under the shelter of a great rock and near it was a soakage cut into the earth, a soakage which carried white water. This was the best water we had come across, and I still look back on it with nostalgia. Years later I returned to see if it was still there but it had been neglected and the soak had fallen in.

The Aborigine who was the lone survivor of our team of guides now felt he couldn't go beyond his own tribal territory, and left us just at the stage where we needed him most. White settlers had told us there were no tracks beyond Moorilana and nobody to tell us where water might be found further out. None of them had ventured any further west. So we headed for the nearest high hills, where we hoped there might be water.

Fortunately for us it started to rain the first day after we had left water, and it rained for fourteen days, not heavily, but enough to wet everything we were unable to cover with the few sheets of canvas we had. We travelled with much more confidence, knowing that every pool and rockhole carried water.

About seven days after leaving the white water camp we came across a rockhole with signs that someone had been there before. A camp had been established and we could see where horses had been hobbled nearby. I returned to the spot a year later and found horses here, although their hobbles had worn out and they had bred and become a brumby mob. Pack-saddles which had been hung on a rail were still there, unshifted and rotting in the sun. Quite evidently some traveller had perished near the spot—a lonely death indeed.

The great Musgrave Ranges were visible on the skyline, among their impressive peaks Mount Woodroffe, at around 1500 metres the highest point in South Australia. We headed for the range, and eventually reached it without having seen any traces of Aboriginal occupation. The Ernabella Spring at the range's eastern end was quite easy to find because of the animal tracks, mainly kangaroo and emu, all converging. Ernest Giles, who discovered the Musgraves in 1873 and named them for the Governor of the Colony, Sir Anthony Musgrave, also discovered the Ernabella Spring, but named it the Ferdinand, after Ferdinand von

Mueller. It regained its much more appropriate and beautiful name, meaning 'creek with waterholes', during the First World War's passion for eliminating German names.

'This was really a delightful discovery,' Giles wrote. 'Everything was of the best—timber, water, grass and mountains. In all my wanderings over thousands of miles in Australia I never saw a more delightful and fanciful region than this, and one indeed where a white man might live and be happy.' It was the only large water at this end of the Musgraves— one might say the entrance to the country where the wild tribes roamed free.

Naked tribesmen were at Ernabella with their families. The women were the first I had seen running naked and it was something of a let-down to find so little romance in the female figure unveiled. The young ones had firm round breasts and were graceful, but their older sisters were long in the breast and wrinkled in the belly. The men were mostly splendid athletes. They were friendly and I learned to talk to them, establishing quite quickly the meaning of the more commonly used words. Years later I gave what I could remember to the museum ethnologists.

Now that we had found the big water we were established with a base in the Musgrave Ranges from which we could come and go. However, since it was situated at the eastern end of the range, with the Manns, the Tompkinsons, the Rawlinsons, the Petermanns and the Deering Hills all lying to the west, it could not serve for the major part of our task, and we moved on. An old black tribesman attached himself to our outfit. He showed us water, speared an occasional kangaroo for us, taught me to track. I suspect he was some sort of super-spy for the tribes. He led us to the Erliwanyuwanyu waterhole under the foot of Mount Woodroffe.

Because of the recent rain the camels' feet left deep imprints as they marched single file, south across the muddy plain. This very track was to save my life the following year. We headed on out and in due course found a huge gathering at the waterhole. We counted more than a thousand people, a large aggregation in those ranges where people quickly exhaust the hunter-gatherer supplies of kangaroos, wallabies, seeds, grubs, reptiles and, of course, rabbits. Groups of them had come from Laverton, the top of the Simpson Desert, the Gibson Desert and even from Ooldea in the northern part of the Nullarbor Plain.

It was a great man-making assembly, and all rituals were observed. Marriages were arranged, boys were allocated to their clan relations for training, girls had their vaginas opened and stretched with conical stones, and old men had additional mutilation of the penis, extending the subincision by splitting. Some of the oldies demonstrated the wide flat split penis in proud display. They had suffered and, I suppose, had at last arrived at the happy state in which they could take the young camp-followers without being any nuisance to the breeding programme of the tribe. Nevertheless there must have been some strict regulation about which man took which girl because the hunting teams took only young girls with them.

They were quite willing to lend us the best of their girls, but Wade would have none of this. He was the first and probably the last man of his age that I would say was completely safe with women. God bless him, he was really converted when he left his wicked ways in the merchant navy to join the ranks of the saved. My trouble was that for all his sterling worth I could not put up with his expressed conviction, every time I came back from some difficult episode of exploration safely, that it had to be God's doing. He had prayed me in. Perhaps he was right, but I could have used a little of the credit.

When the tribes offered me the hospitality of their finest young females I was a little aggrieved that Bill was so saved, but of course he was my boss. Still, who knows? He might have saved my life, because in the end a man fights for his rights and I was never as good as the blacks at that game.

The men of the gathering ranged over large areas killing game for the feasts and the women combed the ranges for the rabbits which were in plague numbers then—probably a major reason for the choice of this spot for corroboree. I learned to catch rabbits with my bare hands, spear them where they sat or dig them out with a pointed stick, arts that were to stand me in good stead in the Depression years to come.

So many of their skills were of abiding interest to me. I would watch the way the women made their coolamons, their wooden dishes, and the way the men extracted from the animals the sinews with which to fasten tips and hooks to their spears. I admired the rhythmic skill with which the women collected seed by yandying it with their wooden dishes in the wind. I learned much about the animals, the desert rats and the bilbies, small white animals something like rabbits, but rare.

I accompanied the boys on their hunting expeditions which I found fascinating. They would make a camp at mid-day, having speared some rabbits and gathered other food like lizards and witchety grubs along the way.

To make fire they shredded dry kangaroo dung into a crack in a fairly substantial log of wood, then two of them would rub the hard burnished surface of a spear-thrower across the crack, causing smouldering material from the log to fall into the tinder in the crack. When enough had gathered they tipped it out into a bunch of dry grass, waving this into the air to fan it into flame. Thus they seemed to make fire without much effort; it wasn't quite as easy as striking a match but it took only a few minutes.

Cooking simply consisted of throwing the unskinned but eviscerated animal on to the fire. The result hardly suited my taste, but the boys seemed to tear the flesh from the half-baked rabbits with great relish.

From these young men I learned to track and throw the throwing stick and, in an amateur way, to use the spear. I never did learn to throw the boomerang properly because this is a great skill. It can easily be made to return, but it is quite another matter to have it hit the target and sometimes still return, and I have never seen other than tribespeople able to achieve this. The best of the throwers could make the boomerang travel quite a long distance, hit the ground, rise into the air and return; some could also make it describe two wide circles and return.

An effective ploy against an enemy would be to have a boomerang come at him from the opposite direction, causing him to look around. I never did see any used in actual warfare, but I did see spears used in fighting. Also at that time I saw spears used in punishment. The offending party had to stand and allow the other to put a spear through the leg. It was essential that the spear penetrated the thigh, and I have seen men carrying as many as five spear wounds in the thigh at one time—strangely enough, none of them fatal.

I have also extracted a spear which protruded from an Aborigine's neck. The operation must have been exceedingly painful for, because of the barb, the spear could not be pulled back and had to be thrust through. It left a fearsome hole but the victim was quite stoical about it and survived the operation.

The fighting with spears occurred during a great intertribal settlement of grievances. Some of it seemed quietly, even peacefully, executed; some of it by the noise was done in anger, but the results spoke for themselves. Justice must have been done that day because when it was all over no animosities seemed to remain, despite the casualties. Those seriously injured were grateful to have their wounds dressed. The Aboriginal ointment was a mixture of the ashes of the tchilga bush and kangaroo fat, and it proved effective. The same ointment is used for healing burns. When Wade used other ointments they took much longer to be effective.

These desert people lived in a state of mental contentment. I attributed this to the centuries-old practice of a religion that was not a spiritual seeking but rather a total immersion in the mysticism that provided a pragmatic solution to any problem of survival. Whereas my needs for spiritual satisfaction included a promise of change, a hope for something better, the Aborigines—and in fact most Stone Age people— live and die content in the complete religion that explains an environment they do not want to see altered.

I loved the stories the tribesmen so eloquently told of the stones and the waters along the way. For their part they loved the land that had nurtured their forefathers, with its reminders of battles fought and deeds done. Who could need books to read when every tree and stone had a history that needed telling? There was always subject for conversation when the day's exploits of the hunt were told around the campfire, and sometimes pantomimed to help the telling.

When I looked for the elements in the religion of these dark people of the desert I found not hypothesis or speculation, but a solution to every problem of living. John the Baptist lived a short time in the whispering sands of the desert; these people had lived in the howling sandstorms and withering droughts of centuries and had answers as if from God concerning their every need. I liked them and their philosophies and confess that my whole life since then has been influenced by their acceptance of the implacable hand of Nature as the Hand of God.

Home was a row of bushy leaves torn from the nearest tree. Bed was the scooped-out hollow behind the leaves. Warmth was the small fire laid on the dusty earth between each body. Protection was the bundle of spears standing at the warrior's side. Each morning when he rose naked from the earth and took them in his hand he needed nothing else to make him total man, able to provide for his family through the coming day.

This ability to live and thrive in the wild truly impressed me. I am more than half a century older now, but the aura of self-sufficiency that enclosed them remains as an inspiration. Their influence set a pattern for my life. And I liked it all: the country, the tribes, the adventure, the search for water, the big granite mountains.

Necessarily, such a great congregation had to disband. The kangaroos would be practically exterminated here if the people stayed to hunt them. The men, women and children vanished into the distant vastness and within a week no smokes marked any of our horizons to tell us that people were here or there.

We travelled west along the southern side of the Musgraves. On reaching their western end we turned north and came in contact with a group of Aborigines who took us to a large water they called Oporinina, about 160 kilometres south of Ayers Rock. The big monolith was quite visible from the top of the hills, and we were able to identify it as a place where we might get water. At a later time we did, but for now, with the guidance of Bill's heavenly Help, we headed west.

Crossing this desert we had some temporal help from a small family group of natives. These people had evidently had no previous contact with whites because they had none of our language, but by this time I had collected a smattering of Pitjantjatjara words which made a meagre communication possible. I knew how to ask directions, for example; and I knew how to ask for water, which was the essential. This family was a unit of a Mann Ranges tribe and they took us to their home territory.

Here I had an experience which was to teach me a salutary lesson. I had been camped on a waterhole which they had pointed out to me and I had allowed the camels to graze within hearing range. Foolishly I allowed one night to pass without bringing the animals back to camp, and next morning set out believing they would be within a reasonable distance and I could track them. This proved an almost fatal mistake. They had set out to return to the Musgraves, and in single file and in hobbles they had padded away back east over the desert. I tracked them out, and having gathered them up I tracked myself back to the water. It took me two days and by that time I was in a serious condition. I never made this mistake again. It is the kind of mistake I am sure which, a couple of years later, made the old prospector Harold Lasseter lose his life. He lost his camels.

We were now far away from civilization and we continued north in the Mann Ranges to the South Australian border, the 'corner' where Western Australia, South Australia and the Northern Territory meet. This we could only estimate by the direction in which we had come and by the mountain ranges which Sir John Forrest had marked on the map fifty years previously. Few people had crossed this area before our inspection of the ranges.

Bejah the Afghan passed close to this point when he led his expedition across the deserts from Marree to Hall's Creek; in my opinion one of the great desert expeditions in Australian history. Some of his party lost their lives but Bejah made his crossing successfully and the survivors indicated they had passed somewhere to the west of the Mann Ranges. This would bring them through the Petermann Ranges which were at the time isolated and lonely. The tribes in the area were not friendly like those of the Musgraves, who had not shown us any animosity. They were a friendly people but the Mann Ranges people showed themselves rather hostile and dour in outlook. The old men apparently resented our intrusion.

I was extremely grateful for the heavenly Help accorded Wade when early one morning in this area we faced a howling mob of spear-carrying men all painted for action. My old hunting gun was packed on the front camel and since he had already sprung to his feet it was too high for me to make a quick draw. But nothing like fight entered Wade's head.

In a fast trot he headed out to meet them, arms outstretched. He hailed the leader with a torrent of the only good words he knew in black language and hugged the fierce armed warriors as though they had been long lost brothers.

'Yamargi! Yamargi!' he was crying. 'Friend! Friend!'

But then, of course, these were God's long-lost children, and he had travelled many kilometres to tell them about their great Father. I felt ashamed, humiliated, almost convinced by Bill's great confidence that he was one of the Chosen. Nevertheless the signs were bad, and I insisted that we camp that night far out in the sandy desert, knowing that the warriors would have to go back for the tribe and we would have one day's start.

The country on the border below the Petermann Ranges was and is one of the driest and loneliest places on earth, and we headed into the Gibson Desert moving south towards the Rawlinson Ranges. Peaks showed away to the south, far, far out beyond the flat sands. Wade wanted to see this corner of his appointed parish and with much misgiving and some fear I agreed. We marched south into impossible country for seven days. Without Bill's God we had to die because we had passed the point of no return, and only water in this waterless place could save us.

Wade rode at the back of the camel string and, looking behind me, I could see his jaw set and his eyes closed and I knew that he was doing business with Heaven. Camels have to drink in spite of what some say. I know that they will survive for fourteen days (perhaps with the help of succulent forage like parakeelya or munyeroo) because in a later year I had to prove it; but after seven days in hot country carrying loads through heated sand-hills they are desperate.

We saddled up on the eighth day without a word. I was not in the Club, and had no way of knowing what arrangements Bill had made with his Lord, but the deal had to include water or we would follow the others who had earlier gone to join the long list of the Club's permanent members. We plodded on.

Far out on the top of the Nullarbor Plain, the extensive flat that stretches for hundreds of kilometres without a tree or a break, a flint lay in the sand . . . a broken spear . . . a mound of gathered spinifex grass clumped into a windbreak. It had to be either a wet-time camp of blacks living on quandong fruit or else a native well. The blacks hide their wells from everyone but their own, but it would have to be near a flat rock. . . . We circled the place for signs, found the well and survived.

Bill's sense of duty led him into the desert area of the Gibson sands and down on to the empty north of the Nullarbor. We wandered far away from water, sometimes getting back with nothing to spare, the camels perishing and the water canteens empty. We contacted the isolated people of the deserts, plotted our course by the compass, guessed where we might be, drew maps, estimated the distances travelled. Our guess was that we had been in Western Australia and the Northern Territory. We drew sketches of creeks and ranges. We put cairns of stones on mountains. But we never really knew where we were except that Oodnadatta was four months' travel east.

During a pretty courageous effort by Wade to examine the far southern reaches of the plains below the Musgraves a leak developed in one of the water canteens which had rusted at the joins. These were the standard canteens of the time, but I felt there was great room for improvement in both materials and workmanship, and later in life I acted on the thought. At the time it was instrumental in our running out of water, and we found it necessary to cross the spinifex desert to the Musgraves. The task was formidable, because the sand-hills in that sector run north-east to south-west, and we were obliged to cross them all rather than march down their valleys. We were heading for Erli-wanyuwanyu, a destination readily identifiable because of its location beneath Mount Woodroffe, the highest peak.

A coherent story of that journey back to the Musgraves is beyond me, but the impressions still remain: the sharp metre-high spinifex ... camels staggering down the steep sides of the ridges ... Wade's grim figure perched atop the tail camel ... his stubbly beard ... his grim uncompromising face, still strengthened by belief ... legs bleeding ... feet leaving a trail of blood. We pulled out into the big hole under the great mountain. The hole was dry.... The disbelief in the old man's face ... the pain of betrayal.

We had to go on to Ernabella, but a sandstorm was rolling up to us like a great ball of glazed fire. We had no choice. By afternoon we were staggering. But again a miracle! I stumbled on the deep pad made by our own camels a year before when we had come out of Ernabella in the wet. When the dark of the sandstorm gave place to the dark of the night we were lying in the clear spring water of Heaven.

The best part of the year had gone by. We ran out of flour; the last of our sugar had long since run out of our packs during a soaking; nothing was left except salt and a small bag of rice. We were practically living off the land but little game was available and at one stage we were reduced to eating emu, which I can assure you is not palatable. We decided to go to the Everard Ranges and then, heading still further east, return to the spot where we had begun, Granite Downs.

Crossing the dry spinifex area between the Musgraves and the Everards, a trackless waste, was made possible by the discovery of a saltwater soak along the course of The Officer Creek, which runs between. This water was just potable. The camels didn't like it but they did drink it, and we carried it in our cans. We believed that because we had always been successful at finding water in the ranges we were invincible, but this of course proved to be a mistake. The waters in the Everards had all dried up. Animal tracks indicated that they had not been used for some time, and we proceeded east in desperation because we were now past the point of no return, and once again had to find water or perish.

At the nadir of our misery we cut a kangaroo pad running north and south. In which direction should we follow it? Fortunately we turned north and, following the pad into some low hills, we came upon a huge rock, a large granite monolith. We left our animals at its foot and climbed it to look for waterholes, such as often appear in the surfaces of such large granite outcrops. While inspecting a crevice I saw bees drinking and followed it down, disturbing some pigeons which were sucking water from a small dampness in a hollow. Still further down the crevice the rock was steep, and in my excitement I slid over the surface, bringing up at a small cave.

Its narrow entrance was only large enough for me to crawl into, but the floor was damp and I scrambled in about six metres, not caring, in my desperation, about how I would get out. I estimated that by scratching in the sand I would find water, so I backed out and returned, pushing a bucket and a pannikin ahead of me. With the pannikin I dipped the water out of the hole I scratched and filled the bucket. Slow work—but in this manner I crawled in and backed out, finally filling seventeen buckets with water. I gave some to the camels and put the rest into our canteens. This water was our salvation. Though it tasted earthy it was potable.

We did find another water in a rather deep rockhole before we left the Everards, but it had turned green with decomposing animals and our camels would not drink it.

We headed eastward from the Everards but because of our lack of maps had little idea of where we might be going, but we were lucky enough to recognize the silhouette of hills above the Moorilana camp where we had started out the year before. We reached it in a slight misty rain and were delighted to meet Stan Ferguson there. He took a keen interest in what we could tell him about the Musgraves, questioning me closely on the feed and the possibility of starting a station in the area. On the basis of our description he later made an application to the South Australian Government and received a grant of Ernabella.

Wade's task in the Western Desert had not been to put new places on the map, but to evaluate places already recorded, however sketchily. We were interested especially in the human distribution and therefore we worked from this series of bases without being much concerned to establish new routes. The explorations accomplished by Ernest Giles, Larry Wells, Lindsay Carruthers, William Gosse, John Forrest and, of course, David Carnegie were all known to us and had been recorded on some sketchy maps which were available. The Gibson Desert had been crossed several times and many journeys had been made on the Western Australian side, especially nearer the coast.

But all this information was of no use to us because we had no means of accurately locating their waters, no scientific instruments, and lacked the ability to use them. Many of their observations were not accurate, as can be judged from a reading of Carnegie's book, *Spinifex and Sand*. Several times we checked directions given by explorers and found them

Above: Young men holding rabbits caught on a hunting trip. I went with them, barefoot, and they taught me to hunt.

Below: The cave in the Everard Ranges where Bill Wade and I found water.

Above: Me talking to some of the Musgrave Ranges Aborigines I used to go hunting with.

Below: Some of the wild Aboriginal boys from Days Gully in the Mann Ranges.

Above: A group of Aborigines in the Tomkinson Ranges near the Western Australian border.

Below: My guide and a group of women at Mt Carolina.

Gordon Billings with our camels in the Musgrave Ranges on our 1928 dingo scalping expedition. Harold Lasseter died in this sort of country about this time.

several kilometres out in their location of given waters. With a mistake of a few hundred metres, or even a few metres, it can be very difficult to find the waters because in the Western Desert most are underground, and the only visual evidence is the depression above.

Aborigines often camouflage the waters, not necessarily to keep them hidden, but to keep them away from animals which might foul them. The native camps are usually quite a distance from the waters, often because of the absence of firewood. They will use the waters and then go to a suitable place to camp. As various explorers have written, Aborigines are often loath to show where the wells are. Almost all the explorers had been in a hurry to go from one place to another, and for this reason they sometimes failed to find water, or had great trouble in doing so. Several captured Aborigines, put them under restraint and tortured them with thirst to make them disclose the location. They had great trouble finding water and suffered severe hardship, and not infrequently men and animals died for the lack of it.

Our only way of staying in the ranges on a permanent basis was to find a good water, such as the pool in the Mann Ranges, the water on Latitude Hill and the water in the Petermanns, and the permanent waters like Oporinina and Ernabella, establish a base camp and work out from it. From these we made useful expeditions, especially after a period of rain. At such times if the parakeelya shows itself in any quantity it is possible to travel great distances, because the camels do not need to drink if they are feeding on this succulent which grows on the sand.

We carried over 1000 litres of water on a camel, half in a cannister on each side. Of course the areas where the parakeelya grows are not consistent, and in moving from one to another we might find that the rains have not reached an area within a hundred kilometres of where parakeelya is plentiful, so that moving out from the ranges was always a bit chancy. But this was the way in which we did get a fairly useful knowledge of the section from Oodnadatta through to Laverton and from the top of the Nullarbor to the MacDonnell Ranges.

As a result of Wade's work the area from 350 kilometres west of Oodnadatta to Laverton in the west, and from the top of the Nullarbor to Hall's Creek, an area of roughly two and a half million square kilometres, is now Aboriginal country, most of it legislated and the rest desert and unoccupied. White men may not enter this country without a permit.

Wade had become an experienced camel man, and I had no qualms about leaving him after we moved on to Mick O'Donohue's primitive homestead at Granite Downs. Wade had told me of his intention of returning to the ranges, starting again from Laverton and working east. In Oodnadatta he married a girl with a cast in her eye and took her out to

Laverton, travelling east from there and establishing a mission in the Warburton Ranges, near the Rawlinsons in the Gibson Desert. Here he served his God and his adopted people many years until his death. He was impossible, but truly great.

I never met him again and I fear I was not very tolerant with him but I have the utmost respect for his bravery. Only a man of tremendous faith or utter foolishness would have attempted some of the things he did. Three times he headed into desert country quite unknown to us, without a guide to show us where water might be. On each occasion he passed the point of no return, believing that somehow water would be provided. This laying of one's life on the line seemed a dangerous way of testing the Almighty's willingness to look after one, and I'm afraid my faith didn't run to this kind of exercise.

Life is the raw material that each of us shapes according to our dreams. Change runs headlong through it. Knowing nothing else, my dream was the dream of knowing. Everything was still a mystery. Knowledge is power and power is fortune. What feeble chance set anyone on his path? Some call it luck, or accident, or fortune. Call it what you like, life and change remain in the mysterious hand of God. But no young man ever admitted that.

From this expedition I was able to make my own contribution to general knowledge by sending a consignment of fifteen species of birds to the South Australian Museum. They included a specimen of the Oriental Dotterel, the second recorded for the State. There were eleven more species from the Musgrave Ranges and three—a red-capped robin, a chestnut quail-thrush and a black-faced wood-swallow—from the country between the Musgraves and the Mann. I also sent them photographs of the Kukera tribe in the Tomkinson and the Mann ranges, and the Wilulara, in the Musgraves, as well as some of the children of mixed tribes at Moorilana.

Chapter Four

I stayed with Mick O'Donohue some months, riding his large extent of cattle country, cleaning deep wells and tackling other jobs as the necessity came up. I had noticed that all through the ranges where we had been were great numbers of dingoes. I told Mick that I intended to return and collect scalps, which could be traded from the natives and were saleable to the government at police stations for seven shillings and sixpence each, the buying power of which would now be equivalent to $25. Mick advised me to wait until I could collect a string of camels and a good mate, with enough tea, flour and sugar. I took his advice, and after a few months moved to Oodnadatta.

Earlier, about 1925, the Commonwealth Government had called for tenders to build the long-delayed extension of the railway from Oodnadatta to Alice Springs. Winner of the contract was a man named Simms, who proceeded to gather labour, materials and data. Most work at the time was done by straight manual labour with horsedrawn drays. Pick and shovel men were a breed apart. To handle them, the overseers or gangers had to be rough and brutal and were necessarily feared. Any man caught leaning on his shovel too long or too often was out, and others were waiting to take his place.

The blistering heat of Oodnadatta, together with the evil sulphur-smelling water of Wire Creek Bore, the only available drinking water, created serious discontent. The living quarters were primitive and there was no refrigeration for food. All this, plus the constant, loud-mouthed niggling of the gangers, fomented a revolt among the huddles of toiling navvies, and they went on strike.

The single pub at Oodnadatta was ready for the strike with a train-load of all kinds of liquor, and the resulting mêlées, fights and fatalities were such as cannot be imagined by a law-abiding community. Sergeant Virgo, the only policeman, was totally overwhelmed. He sent for help and the man supplied was a heavyweight boxing champion of the state police force named Francis. His weight was felt, but the whole town was committed to one long drunken brawl.

Food was scarce and drink expensive, so that when the sergeant announced that a train was going south he must have imagined it would be loaded with paying passengers. Not so. The train was packed with struggling men, but few had paid fares. Most were drunk. Sergeant Virgo approached the dilemma like a good tactician.

When the train pulled out of Oodnadatta he and his fighting offsider were riding the engine cabin. Several miles out the driver slowed the train and the two policemen with, I suspect, some enlisted helpers, hurled the drunks off the steps of the carriages as it rumbled on, leaving a long line of shouting, cursing, sometimes inert bodies beside the track. The strike was over. After a long walk home the men went solemnly back to work, thirsty, broke and hungry.

In the meantime I had camped with the trackriders from Todmorden, a cattle-station the homestead of which was 140 kilometres from Oodnadatta. Their land, however, extended to the town limits and included a long waterhole called the 'Anglepole', from a crooked pole on the Overland Telegraph line that ran right by it. The telegraph had been put through to Darwin fifty years before.

The area around Todmorden had been famous for horses for seventy years or more. Old Mr Breaden who took up Todmorden was the same Joe Breaden who had joined David Carnegie in his expedition of 1896. For a time I worked round Breaden's estate. I think a man called Young had it at that time, and I was tempted to stay there because of the fine horses running on the Alberga River. Todmorden then took in Lambinna, which was on the Alberga and which was exactly 100 miles (160 kilometres) from Oodnadatta. The reason I am sure of the distance is because of old Tom O'Donohue's boasting. He used to claim that he could tie a camel up to a prickle-bush and, getting up early in the morning, ride into Oodnadatta, get drunk and have a fight before dark. And I'm sure that Tom made this good many times, because that was his way of life.

I worked around Todmorden, Lambinna and Henbury for Young and then, because I had attended a muster with old Mick O'Donohue, I went back with Mick for a while working on that barren area of ground called Granite Downs. Mick also had some quite good horses, particularly some good coloured horses—he was very fond of the 'paint' horse. He was also capable with camels, because in his old age his favourite means of transport was a camel buggy. Mick was a specialist in breaking camels to the buggy and I have described his method.

Back at the Anglepole I was camped with a mate, Paddy DeConnolly, with whom I had picked up in 1926. We were trackriding Todmorden bullocks, which tended to drift across the north line and wander out into Macumba station, or alternatively across out into the western desert and down the line of The Neales creek. They also wandered if there were any shower of rain, feeding on the parakeelya which came up. The season was fair, and the cattle fat.

During this time Lord Stonehaven, who was then Governor-General of Australia and a conscientious warden of his responsibilities, came up the line to inspect the new work. The telegraph advised the time his train was to arrive at Oodnadatta. The Oodnadatta butcher Ly (for Lycurgus)

Underdown was to supply meat to the train, and he delegated us to bring in fresh beef. Evening came, and from the west the stockboys brought a mob of mixed cattle down the creek and pulled them up facing the camp, where some gidgee trees with twisted branches stood—the only trees in the area.

Paddy and I were waiting for them. He climbed a stunted gidgee, carrying his .32 rifle, which was the best he had for the purpose, and settled himself into the branches while the boys moved the mob slowly towards the tree. It was the custom to shoot 'killers' from the branches of a tree because it is the only safe place to be when cattle rush and also because cattle can be moved close to a tree, whereas they will not move close to a man.

Paddy knew from experience that the old Winchester .32, with its lead bullets and short range, would only kill if the bullet hit exactly in the curve of the forehead. He was taking no chances of having the herd split and gallop off at this time. With the Lord's meat at stake the event was momentous. Humble stockmen as we were, we were greatly honoured by the responsibility of supplying meat to the great man.

Paddy made it with his first shot, and the sleek, short-horned bullock went down. I rushed to cut its throat before the blood stopped circulating, pumping the body with my feet, knife in hand, waiting for the last red drops to spill out on the dusty soil.

The cattle sped away, leaving us with the bullock. Steel and knife, forked stick pointed into the long sinew to keep the beast upright, we laid open the hide, leaving us with a clean skin on which to lay the carcase. There were no trees large enough to hang the bullock on but none were needed for men experienced in killing on the ground. We soon had the legs off, hanging them one by one on the low branches of the gidgee—just high enough to keep them off the soil and away from the ants. We proceeded to carve the rest into useful and manageable portions, keeping the fillet for ourselves. It was a great occasion.

The contractors arrived just as we finished off the kill and, with the cool night coming on and having no lights, we lit a big fire, as is the custom. We had fresh meat, royal meat; and Ly and his mates from the horsedrawn buggy gathered round. They had come to celebrate, and they had brought the wherewithal. We could see the lights of Oodnadatta dimly, eight kilometres away, and the royal train had not yet arrived. The party was progressing splendidly with Paddy singing all the Irish songs he knew, everybody roaring, full voice. It was a party to be remembered. The Lord would soon be with us.

And he was! The train came rattling in to Oodnadatta. We could hear it from sixteen kilometres away and consciousness hit us all at once. Where was the meat? What would we send him? Most important: what could we wrap it in?

Paddy was not so far gone that he could not rise to such an occasion.

We rescued the hide from the dirt, shook it well and wrapped it round the pick of the rumps, trying it with strips of hide.

Time was against us. The buggy men were not fit to travel and we decided that if one of us would gallop the eight kilometres to Oodnadatta he might well be in time to deliver the precious meat. I was selected to make the gallop. It was a great honour. I tightened the girth on the night horse, still saddled from the evening's kill, and, exalted with knowledge of the great honour thrust upon me, I spurred off into the night, hugging the slippery hide and its bloody content of rump steak.

This had taken time, and my horse was not up to a full eight-kilometre gallop, nor could I hold the heavy hide-wrapped parcel at that pace. We settled down to a steady trot. The train was standing in the station and looked deserted, but—praise be!—there was a light in one carriage. I dismounted at its steps and knocked loudly on the window. The Lord himself came to the door and stepped out on the carriage platform! I had one foot on the bottom step and was struck silent by the enquiry in an aristocratic English voice as to what I wanted. No doubt if it happened today I might find the right words, apologizing with all the grace I could muster, but all I could say then was, 'Here's your meat, Mister.' These words have been ringing round my head for fifty years, flushing my older memory with the hot failure of youth. No doubt Lord Stonehaven in his London club told the story with relish.

When I got back the fire had burned low, the buggy was gone and Paddy was out to it in his swag. He never asked me about the meat. Paddy was like that.

At the same Anglepole the dull crack of a rifle brought me up from afternoon sleep. It was 110 degrees F in the shade, and nobody I knew would be shooting for fun. Besides it was the dull 'phut' of an old-fashioned Winchester .32 and Paddy was asleep on the other side of the waterhole. We were minding cattle, and cattle don't roam at noon in that temperature.

A puff of smoke showed from behind Paddy's windbreak, followed by the sharp whip-like crack of a high-powered Savage .22. I dived behind the packs and felt for my only weapon, a small .25 automatic, waiting for something to happen. The crack had come from my side of the waterhole, and I could see the shape of someone crouching behind a log not 200 metres from where I watched.

The only cover Paddy had was his pack-saddles, and I could see him stretched out as flat as he could get into the dust. Time for me to move. But where? And how? One does not tackle a Savage with a pop-gun and my only use would be the creation of a diversion to let Paddy move. But when he heard my first shot the stranger must have seen some risk, for he made off as fast as he could.

We only saw him once subsequently. This was a week later when

Paddy and I were sitting, squatted on our heels, in Ly Underdown's shop in Oodnadatta. The door opened and the same long figure showed in the opening, peered in and jumped. Paddy came off the floor sideways and hit hard as he rose. The stranger had a knife. It was the only knife fight I have ever seen. There was not much of it, but it was fast. A sideways blow to the jaw and a knee in the stranger's gut, and the battle was over. The door clanged and Paddy resumed his squat. He did not speak. The only explanation I ever got from him consisted of three short but significant words: 'Over a gin.'

Apart from the Afghans and their camel transport, Oodnadatta's frontier days were in these late 1920s when the labourers from the rail camps poured into the town, before the line was built to Alice Springs. Men did get killed. There were fights every day, and once I was the only man sober enough to be priest, pall-bearer and gravedigger. Old Scotty the corpse never had a prayer except for my few salt tears and his grave was shallow. Nobody will ever know now who he was or where he lies. There were others like him.

The waterhole on The Neales called the Anglepole was my second home at that time. It was there that I watched Paddy's long-range gun battle. It was there that I learned the weary ways of track-riding. It was from the Anglepole that I had set out with Billy Wade to go west and, earlier, to find him when he was lost with the camels, on which expedition I almost perished. From this camp, later, I went out with Gordon Billings to go into the Musgraves. So I have many reasons to remember the place. Ironically, my daughter Jocelyn spent some years of her life in a fettler's camp at Oodnadatta near the same Anglepole.

Now, fifty years later, Oodnadatta has been relegated to insignificance. The railway line has been shifted west and no roads go by. I have no doubt that the Anglepole has settled back into its pristine loneliness and few, if any, visit it. The beauty and the solitude of these lonely waterholes provide the romance of the Central Australian Outback.

In partnership with a man called Gordon Billings I had got a good string of camels together and we headed out to the Musgraves again to make our fortunes with the collection of dingo scalps. Passing through Moorilana we heard of various troubles with the Aborigines. From 1924 Central Australia had been under the most severe drought in its history. From 1926 its effects were bad enough to drive the people from the desert. Some perished, but a good percentage was forced to beg food from the whites they had hitherto avoided. Some of these moved into the gold-field near Tanami and The Granites, where friction had previously existed, caused by miners taking the women. Others went on to the better watered Lander Creek district, where their arrival in significant numbers seriously embarrassed the cattlemen who were themselves in difficulty with the drought.

An old prospector named Brooks was camped at a soak on Conistan Station, through which the Lander runs. Some of the Wailbri tribe came and camped nearby. He shared food with them when they first arrived, but when he refused them more they clubbed him and rifled his stores. About the same time another group of Wailbri robbed a settler further north on the Lander, wounding him in the process.

A policeman from Alice Springs then called in assistants and led a punitive expedition, surprising natives at several camps on the Lander and shooting all in sight. An official enquiry exonerated the policeman, though he admitted killing seventeen of the natives and described them as 'members of the Walmalla tribe from Western Australia who were on a marauding expedition with the avowed object of wiping out the white settlers and native boys employed on their stations'. The Walmalla form a section of the Wailbri. This could mean some danger for whites travelling among the tribes, but we were now on the limits of civilization and we headed out into the west.

We followed more or less the tracks of the previous expedition, concentrating more on the larger waters where we would find an abundance of dingoes. We had no trouble with natives in any place, though they must have been well aware of the massacre. On several occasions we had evidence of messages being transmitted from tribe to tribe over several hundred kilometres with no period of delay. The swiftest of runners could not have carried such messages in the time. We had seen smoke signals used, and that was a fast means of communication. They had ways of varying the colour and frequency of the smoke and some of the messages were in great detail. They had plenty of reason to resent a white presence, but we did not suffer.

Some of the stories they told me concerned a man named Davis who had an unpleasant habit of cutting out a native girl, running her down on camelback and raping her. Sometimes when a girl was so chased she would squat down and fill her private parts with sand. It was an effective deterrent.

Although we did not cover so wide an area as I had with Wade we made a deep penetration, going on from the Musgraves to the Mann Ranges collecting and buying dingo scalps from the natives. We pressed on after that to the Warburton and Rawlinson Ranges in Western Australia where the bounty on dingo scalps was two dollars. A number of prospectors and miners combed these areas and we were able to sell our scalps to them, at a heavy discount on these prices.

The news of the Conistan massacre had evidently reached all the tribesmen, though they did not talk about it. In the Musgraves they remained friendly and approachable, but the dour men of the Mann Ranges presented a different proposition. Going through their country we went in constant fear of our lives. I saw a spear behind every rock.

Every track in the sand meant that its maker was close and could be waiting. The spear is a precision instrument in the hands of the desert warrior. It comes off his meeroo (spear-thrower) spinning like a top and whips its fearsome way accurately for fifty metres. It is a killer at a much greater distance.

I fortified myself with the knowledge that only the elders of the tribe in that area were capable of initiating an attack, and at every opportunity let them see my powendjka kill game at a distance. They circled me several times, attempted to kill me once, stole my provisions and gear once, and I became the hunter. I was 600 kilometres from the nearest replacements. I found most of the missing items in a cave on a granite mountain. I did not get them all, but enough.

By the time the yen for civilization got strong we had several thousand scalps, and with these we returned to Oodnadatta. They had to be presented to the local constabulary for payment but we found there would be quite a delay before the money arrived, so we discounted them for five shillings each to Jim Mitchell, a trader who had a small store in Ghan Town.

I had another reason for avoiding close contact with the police. After the Conistan massacre Sergeant Virgo had sent his assistant to sieze all the weapons belonging to the people in the west, on the assumption that this would help to prevent more trouble. I did not agree that weapons should be taken from such as myself who needed them to obtain food as well as for defence, travelling alone in that area.

Virgo was in many ways a great old policeman, and quite broad-minded. He turned a blind eye to my old friend Bill Gregory's gambling establishment, and my main criticism of him was the way he brought his tribal captives in from the west with their necks chained together. I used to wonder whether he caught the real culprits, or whether there were culprits. I realize there would be no other way to handle such a number single-handed, but I believe they were being badly treated in general and it became an obsession with me to see that something was done to help these people.

Young fellows on the Todmorden, Lambinna, Macumba and other stations were very interested in the stories we told about the wild blacks, the naked women and the freely available dingo scalps. I suspect they were also interested in the plentiful supply of young wild native girls. Two such men, Paddy DeConnolly and Victor Dumas from Todmorden, set out and travelled through the Musgraves towards Ayers Rock and the Petermann Ranges beyond. Paddy told me a good story later of how Victor had set out one morning to look for their strayed camels. He did not return for several weeks and it says much for Paddy's capacity for patience that he stayed in the camp until Victor showed up.

He had travelled to the east as far as the railway line to catch the camels, and I can imagine him on foot tracking them from day to day, sleeping on the tracks and living off the land, obtaining water where he could find it and eventually coming back with the camels. It was a story of courage and initiative seldom equalled.

Paddy later took up with an Aboriginal woman and had two children that I know of. Her tribe attacked Paddy at one stage, and in defending himself he was obliged to kill at least one of them. Tried for murder at Port Augusta, he was freed on the basis of self-defence, but I rather imagine the tribes had a point.

From these two men I learned many of the bush crafts that later became my way of life. They were fine bushmen. I was able to repay Paddy later by getting him a start on a station called Mount Conner. Victor died a wanderer and I do not know where he is buried.

I had got to know many of the people out on the isolated stations in the north-east of South Australia, and about this time I got a job for my girl Thelma as cook-nursemaid for the McDills on Andado station just above the border in the Territory.

I made one more trip into the Musgraves for dog scalps. I did not believe the rumours that the blacks were staging a 'get rid of the white' campaign, and I still do not think they were. But when I got out to Granite Downs I found Mick O'Donohue carrying his gun night and day, and the whole frontier was ablaze with the rumours. On this occasion I had taken some steel spear-heads with me as presents for the blacks, mistakenly thinking that it would save them from making wooden points every day, and that I could trade the steel points for dog scalps.

It was brought to the notice of Oodnadatta police that I was carrying steel spears and Virgo decided I should be stopped. He delegated a young energetic trooper who wanted to get out west to take the gear off me. With him was a famous tracker called Scoundrel Bob, who must have had a leg in each camp because the smoke signals or whatever telepathy the blacks used reported that these two were headed west and looking for me. Now that was a challenge to any young camel man because Virgo was supposed to have the finest and fastest camels in the territory, big beasts in good nick with well-fitted saddles and feather-light canteens.

I had picked my own camels with great care. They were a fine lot of well-trained animals and I had a 300 kilometre start. I told Mick O'Donohue what I was going to do and he told me he would find out from his gin what the police were doing. This was as good as arranging a telegraph station—a bush telegraph with smoke signal. Water was a modifying factor in choosing a route.

I made it to Ernabella in a bit over six days; then, covering my tracks, I headed down the Glen Ferdinand Gorge and out on the southern side of the Musgraves. I had no blacks with me and so did not know what the police were doing, except that I knew they would not be gaining on me. Two days along the Ranges I knew of a gorge so narrow that only a beast without a pack could squeeze through. I turned north into this narrow chasm and carried my packs through the pinch.

Once out on the north side of the Musgraves I was in something of a quandary because I had no way of knowing which side of the range the police patrol would select, but it was almost certain that Scoundrel Bob would somehow pick up enough of my tracks to know that I had gone from Ernabella down south and that I would then turn west to avoid the desert. It was a fair guess that I would be safe unless he picked up my track through the narrow gorge, and I had been at some pains to cover it by walking the camels over bare rocks. Besides, there was a fair wind blowing to disguise the turned pebbles that even a camel's soft foot will leave. On the north of the gorge was a rock massif known as Mitchell's Knob where there is almost always water, and here I camped. Speed was my only final safety, and so I raced on to Oporinina, the big water south of Ayers Rock.

From there I intended to head due west into the Mann Ranges and across the border. Instead, when my stores were used, I came back through the Everards to Granite Downs. I reached there after dark one night, and hooshed my camels down a few hundred metres from the long, rectangular mud-stone hut where a light was showing. I unsaddled the camels and hobbled them out. When I reached the door my knock surprised a red-headed, bushy-bearded man called Brown who had been giving his full attention to the stove. He turned with a quick response. grabbing a gun that was lying on the table.

'Who are you?' he asked abruptly, and I could see he was one of those against the world. When I declared my name he asked where I had come from, and I am sure than he did not believe me. A bushman of the better. explorer type, he knew that the deserts to the west were very inhospitable. He said rather grudgingly that he had heard of me, and apparently he had something against me, for I do believe that he was half inclined to shoot me there and then. I persuaded him that I could not possibly be the one who had caused whatever troubled him, and he eventually dished me out a share of his meat and onions, which was very acceptable because I had been on hard tucker for some time.

His hobby was plaiting, and when we had finished the meal he showed me some special leatherwork. He was making an intricate watch-pouch worked from a single strand of kangaroo hide. I had seen and admired something of the sort before and was immediately interested in his technique. He showed a lot of patience once he sensed my admiration and showed me the turns and convolutions that comprised the plait. He showed me other knots too, and though I did not master them for many years that evening turned out to be the inspiration of my later life, a starting point of my interest in making bush things.

Brown was afterwards killed on a piece of country he took up about 160 kilometres west of Granite Downs on The Officer creek, which runs south out of the Musgraves. His occupation was probably not legal. He hacked a dugout into the bank and covered it with logs and he and his wife and their small child were living there when one night The Officer came down in flood and engulfed them. According to the story the blacks told, the child was out playing with tribal children, and although this is only rumour I do believe the blacks adopted him. I do not know if he ever surfaced in civilized areas, but it remains a possibility that there is a wild white man living in the Musgraves. If that is so I am sure he will have a head of flaming red hair.

When Mick O'Donohue returned I told him that I wanted to go up across the border of the Northern Territory to Andado Station where my girl was working. Mick talked me into working a short while at Granite Downs and tried to persuade me to stay. He offered a half interest in the property if I would, but I was determined to go.

I went north to Tieyon station, at that time owned by Frank Smith, who warned me that if I wanted to cross directly to Andado I would have to cross some very dry desert country which was part of the Kidman estate. Called Eringa, it was in a bad way and had been abandoned. Even animals which normally manage to survive dry times had perished: camels, donkeys, kangaroos, all were dead around the dried-up water-holes. I did manage to get some very poor water from a deep well at Eringa.

Travelling alone and travelling fast I moved across the deserted plain to the now-established railway line and followed it to the telegraph station at Charlotte Waters, arriving on a Sunday, about noon. I remember quite plainly that we had custard for dinner, something I had not tasted for years. The two linesmen were pleased to see a visitor, a rarity for them, and I asked them which way I should go. They recommended going down the road about 160 kilometres and taking a branch road out. When I suggested it might be quicker crossing the desert they said not even the Aborigines would do that, but having crossed some very dry deserts in my time I felt it was not impossible and started out.

Arriving at Andado I found that the McDills and Thelma had left to go to Oodnadatta, about 500 kilometres south. I had been excited by the prospect of meeting Thelma and this was a bad blow. 'Down to Gehenna or up to the Throne, He travels the fastest who travels alone', so Rudyard Kipling wrote. I felt very much alone on my journey.

When I reached the Overland Telegraph line I followed it down to the road which led out to Tieyon station and camped at the junction.

Fortunately for me an old truck came along and the driver stopped to say 'Good day'. It was Frank Smith. He recognized me and offered to take my packs on to Oodnadatta. This wonderful offer left me free to swing along at any pace and, if I wished, to travel night and day. I did. My hurry almost cost me my life.

I had stopped at dark and hobbled the animals out, meaning to start again at midnight. The camel bells were faint in the distance when I woke on time and, not bothering to pull on boots, I hurried in their direction. The sound of big bells will carry eight kilometres, and these were getting fainter. Without noticing direction I hurried on, and on and on some more, using the bell sound to guide me until I caught up with the grazing camels, which had had little spell or feed on my rush south.

I tied them head to tail and walked in front of the leader, making the foolish mistake of heading out towards what I thought was my camp. I had not stirred the fire when I left, so there was nothing to show where it was. Clouds blotted out the stars and the night became pitch dark. Only a thin small track lay between me and the western emptiness, and my camp was somewhere on that track.

It was cold and starting to drizzle. I knew if it rained I was done, because it would blot out my tracks. I hooshed down the two leaders, huddled between them for warmth and spent the rest of the night there, but in spite of this animal warmth I shivered for hours.

With morning came the first few drops of a light rain. I realized I would have to move fast to follow the camel tracks before they were obliterated or I would never find my camp again. Had I moved in the night I would have been lost. On the east was the fearsome Simpson Desert; to the north the pitiless sandhills; west, a thousand kilometres of empty country.

To my immense relief I found and followed my own tracks, collected the few belongings still with me and was on the road again. Not many men have walked further than I did on that trip to see my girl again. In a few places in Australia even Aborigines can get lost and these featureless plains of Central Australia qualify.

Near Horseshoe Bend on the Finke River I found the sleeve-valved Willys-Knight truck that had belonged to Kurt Johannsen senior, burnt out and left as a wreck. It had been one of the first trucks ever brought into the Northern Territory.

Only 125 kilometres to Oodnadatta! I covered that in little more than a day, reaching it to find that my girl had gone west to a wedding!

Knowing that sooner or later I would have to confront Sergeant Virgo. I walked into his office. He was sitting at the table with his back to me and swung around.

'You!' he said; nothing more. He was always a man of few words, but I knew exactly what he meant. He beckoned his offsider, muttered something to him, and they both questioned me on my armament and about an accusation that I had incited the blacks. My guns were long since cached or sold and of course I had nothing to hide about the blacks, for I had seen enough of black versus white and knew of the enmity between the tribes and the whites who took their gins. The only salve for the white conscience lay in the fact that gins prefer those whites who have some consideration for women. Blacks have little. They operate on the clitoris to stop the female enjoying sex. They give the young gins to the old whistle-cocked men. They leave old worn-out gins to die. Although I knew this latter was necessary in the harsh exigencies of desert life, I have seen old gins so left and have pitied them. So I suppose there is some reason to say that the gins went to whites of their own accord.

When I was through with Sergeant Virgo I met another crisis. Over the past year I had developed a toothache. It was getting painful and I was anxious to have the tooth out. I had tried to pull it myself with pliers but found this impossible as it was a double tooth. I knew I had to do something about it. I sold my camels, packs, rifles, canteens, boxes — everything I possessed — for £20 and caught the train to Adelaide.

Chapter Five

From the railway station in Adelaide I walked up King William Street until I saw a brass plate beside a door advising me that a dentist had his surgery upstairs. I went up and asked him to pull the tooth. He wanted to give me a needle to stop the pain of the extraction but I told him that I had had all the pain I could stand and asked that he pull the tooth immediately.

In my haste and confusion I had stashed my swag at the back of the Cathedral in Wakefield Street. When I returned for it after visiting the dentist I was distressed to find that it had been stolen. With the few things wrapped up in it, the swag was all that I had in the world, so the loss left me destitute and penniless. Without a swag and blankets one is poor indeed.

The only person in Adelaide I could think of who might help me was Sir Sidney Kidman, the 'Cattle King', whom I had met at his Anna Creek station. I walked to his home at Unley Park, which was quite a way, and on reaching it felt overawed by the grandeur of his mansion. Lady Kidman answered my knock at the front door; her husband was away. I explained my predicament and told her that I knew of Sir Sidney because of my association with Anna Creek and its manager, Archie McLean.

She did not even ask my name. Telling me to wait she went indoors and returned with a fresh canvas, two blankets and two straps, constituting a new home. I was back in the world of the living, the owner of a fresh clean swag—a home indeed for those who have no place and nowhere to go. Because I had left my father's home against his wishes I was too proud to go near there, and did not see my parents until several years later.

I set up my camp in the Adelaide Hills, on a property called Teringie which belonged to Norman Cole, who was secretary of a large hospital organization in Adelaide. I had established a good relationship with him and over the years it became an abiding friendship. He was quite happy to have me camp on his property which ran from Norton Summit back across the hills and overlooked Magill, the hillside suburb which contained St George's, the first church to be consecrated in South Australia by the Colony's first Anglican Bishop. It was also the suburb where Dr Christopher Penfold had started his first vineyard.

The Great Depression had not yet begun and I got a job carrying bricks, demeaning work for one who considered himself a horseman, a camelman and a bushman, but it was money: £3 a week. While I was carrying the bricks I watched the builders work and I learned a lot about their trade which was to stand me in good stead in the coming years. I knew how to mix mortar, how to lay out buildings and how to lay bricks. There were no cement mixers in those days and the cement was mixed on the ground with a shovel.

Thelma had returned from Andado station and was living with her mother in a small cottage in the west end of Adelaide. Being now established at my camp in the hills and having a job, however poorly paid it might have been, I felt that I was ready to set up a permanent establishment. I asked her to marry me, and she accepted. We married at the Wakefield Street Registry Office on 25 May 1929, the day after my twenty-first birthday. We called in two people off the street to act as witnesses.

We were very happy in our camp in the hills. It was at least a shelter, and we did not need a mansion to make our marriage a success. My wife had the right outlook for a person like myself, and was quite content to camp in the rough conditions.

Within a few months the bottom fell out of our world as the Depression started with an onrush frightening in its velocity. Nobody seemed to know who or what caused such a world calamity. Like the beetle that is crushed by the boot, we could not guess who wore the boot or why he used it. After half a century of sieving the evidence I think I know the boot and the leg and the man and the motive. If I did not believe that the mills of God grind small I should seek out the monster, and if it proved too big a dragon I should tell the story; but I rest content in the irrevocable justice of the Almighty.

We had been through a series of boom years, a condition that most of the population believed would last forever. There seemed unlimited work, unlimited money, unlimited opportunity. This ended almost overnight, and the first to feel the blow were those in the building trades, the fundamental work of the cities. Many people had no savings, and for those forced to leave their homes because they could not pay the instalments or the rent there was no alternative but to live in tents. Friends of mine were forced to leave their homes and felt it a great indignity. Women who had accepted that their place in life was secure had had to live in lean-tos, tents or tin sheds, and found it difficult even to get food.

I lost my job, of course. I felt that because I was capable and anxious to work I had to find something, but nobody had the means to employ me. So, sending Thelma to stay with her mother, I rolled my swag and set out, starting in the south of South Australia and working my way through New South Wales, Queensland and the Northern Territory. But

Starting to dig a well in the Gammon Ranges.

Above: A swag and packs—my home and house for several years in the twenties and thirties.

Below: My first camp at Ettalowie Gap in the Flinders Ranges (1931).

Dollar Mick, who shared my camp in the Flinders Ranges and taught me a lot about making leather-goods.

Below: The family in 1943, grouped in the driveway of the house built by Governor Gawler on Strangways Terrace. From left: Diane, Thelma (holding John), Ian, Jocelyn, R.M., Dene.

THE BUSHMAN'S HANDCRAFTS

How to make a Saddle

INDEX

Page

How to Make a Sa... 100

Too... 101

105

107

110

114

HOW TO MAKE A SADDLE

SADDLERY

The following articles are a complete but necessarily short story on how to make a saddle beginning with the tools, materials, the use of tools and the details of one style of a saddle.

TOOLS

Let us begin with a list of tools so that we become conversant with the names, and I will devote this article to a description of the various tools used and a short article on the use of each of them.

AWL

The awl (shown here) is the best type for every-day use and consists of a diamond shape blade stuck into a wooden handle.

The awl blade must be sharp and if you are going to do various sizes of stitching you will want a selection of sizes of these blades, and thev range from about 3 in. to about $1\frac{1}{2}$ in. blades.

The awl is held in the hand as shown.

There are awl handles on the market which will take any size blade.

1
FRONT
2
BACK
3
FRONT
4
BACK
5
FRONT
6
BACK
7
FRONT
8
BACK
9
FRONT
10
BACK
THE GAUCHO KNOT
FIG. 1
FIG. 2
FIG. 3
FIG. 4
FIG. 5
FIG 6
FIG. 7
FIG. 8

Pages from *The Bushman's Handcrafts*, which I published in 1943.

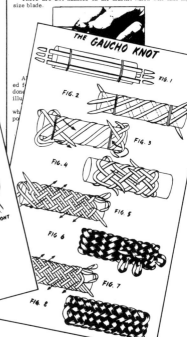

the station owners and others who normally looked to employ workers were in the same position as everyone else. They just didn't have money. Many of them could not even offer food to those of us on the road. I discovered that I was a pariah, an outcast, because people were fearful that I might attempt to take by force what little they had. The police in every town were alterted to pick up vagrants like me, to put us in jail and keep us off the streets. Of course I quickly learned the rules of the game and kept out of sight.

In some towns so many people were camped around the local showgrounds using the facilities that it was not possible for communities to hold the usual events. Authorities could not get rid of these masses of people. Trains were carrying crowds of non-paying passengers who just took every opportunity to shift from place to place.

A penny has a small value, but in those days threepence would buy a loaf of bread. I found people in almost every town who needed such jobs done as the sharpening of knives and axes, or the pruning of roses, anything at all. They were quite prepared to pay a penny or two, and sometimes as much as sixpence, and I concentrated on this source to get from place to place, supplying myself with food. Occasionally I was obliged to beg. After extensive wanderings I returned to Adelaide. Thelma decided we would be better off in our simple camp at Teringie, but soon thereafter we moved north to the Flinders Ranges.

We owned only the blankets and the swag cover, no place, no shelter, but the hopefulness of youth saw that as small worry. My girl was an Outback type who could cope. She was content to sleep on the ground, cook on the open fire, nurse her children in the shade of a bough shelter, eat rabbits, carry water and wash her clothes in a four-gallon tin. That was how we lived in those early years of Depression. The stations could not pay us the thirty shillings weekly we asked for our combined labour, but the cooks gave us the fat from the boiling of the meat and some gave caustic soda to go with it: we were never short of soap. Or cooking fat.

Sometimes when flour and sugar came our way we used the fat to make cake. We always had kangaroo tails for soup and no shortage of wild spinach or yams to bulk it out. Salt was a problem but we had a salt lake less than eighty kilometres away and coarse salt was easily ground. We had kangaroo hides and the bark from many trees for tanning, the fat to soften the leather; and though our tanning was crude it sufficed. Cloth was a problem, but we patched and managed. The blankets were thin but we slept by the fire. Others came and enjoyed our company and our tea, often made from the heart of the tchilga bush. Bush honey we had and got smart getting it. We went barefoot and never noticed it. Boots are a social habit.

We went back to Adelaide when the birth of our first child was imminent. Diane was born on 5 July 1930 in a Salvation Army Hostel. I bless the Army for what they have done for people like me and I have always honoured Kidman the Cattle King for recognizing its worth with gifts of money.

At that time I became friendly with Alfred Edward Gerard, a wealthy industrialist. He had become associated a couple of years before with the United Aborigines Mission, and had long been interested in the welfare of Aboriginal children, giving them city holidays, and employment when that was possible. He discovered that the State Government would allocate land for Aborigines if people like himself would supply the wherewithal to make settlement there a going concern. Such a place was gazetted, sited in the Flinders Rangers east of Copley. Now in the Gammon Ranges National Park, this is extremely rough country, taking in an immense plateau with scenic gorges. Gerard asked me if I would be interested in sinking a well there for him. So again we headed for the Outback. I took with me several lengths of monitor steel of 28-millimetre diameter, a hammer, a cross-cut saw, an adze and an axe. With these tools I set out to make a place on the land so that I could search for water.

I did sink several deep wells on the property and on one occasion reached twenty-two metres to discover a trickle so small there was no sense going on with it. I was working by myself and had to climb out of the well to take out each bucketful of dirt, so the job was slow and painful. I had previously cleaned deep wells under dangerous conditions when I was with Mick O'Donohue at Lambinna and Granite Downs stations. Without that experience I am sure it would not have been possible for me to work alone in deep holes using explosives, which in themselves take some understanding.

My great-grandfather had been a professional well-sinker. I remember him telling my father when I was a young child how necessary it was to take precautions in loose earth when reaching any considerable depths—and how very much more careful one had to be at depth because of the risk of falling stones; also of the skill needed to line a well so that no chinks existed through which small stones could fall to injure the well-sinker. Of course in the excitement of reaching water one is tempted to go too far and too fast before lining the sides, and the well can slip in. This happened to me once and I learned the lesson. When I reached wet slipping shale after coming on a dampness I neglected the precaution of lining the walls and when they slid in I was almost buried alive. Had it not been for Thelma's presence of mind I'm sure I would not have got out of that well. This must have happened to my great-grandfather because I remember him telling my father: 'Never work in a deep well without a cage'. A cage is a construction designed to be lowered with a windlass to accompany and protect the worker.

Another time I sank a shaft down twenty metres and finished up in dry powdery chalk. Although the going was much easier in this one it still took me a long time working by myself.

Well-sinkers have been honoured from time immemorial. The Scriptures describe wells of several kinds, some of them sunk by famous forefathers. The craft has always been important to agricultural or pastoral people, who did not have the means to provide bores, a comparatively recent innovation. The limit to which a well can be sunk is somewhere about thirty metres. Deeper wells than this exist and I have known some of them, but at that depth they become hazardous. Bores can be sent down thousands of metres so modern boring plants have changed the whole picture of supplying water in the Outback.

I sank several holes without obtaining water, and I was almost committed to telling Gerard that it was a lost cause. He had been supplying the explosives, and for a last effort I put a few shots into the bed of a creek and discovered a fair supply of water at a shallow depth, less than four metres. The discovery was about half a kilometre off the road leading east from Copley, and it made possible the establishment of the place called Nepabunna. The Aborigines were encouraged to go and live there, and they began to concentrate in the area. With them came a man named Fred Eaton, allocated by the mission to look after them. Fred was a benevolent type of chap, and although the mission was not able to support him in affluence it did keep him supplied with food.

When I had first gone to Oodnadatta I had met Charlie Way, a man who lived and worked at Todmorden station on the Alberga River. Charlie had been south to Adelaide and married a girl he had met there, and on his way back through Oodnadatta he had told me of his problem. He had not told his new wife of the Aboriginal woman she had replaced, nor of the fact that he had two small sons living at Todmorden. I told him that there was in Oodnadatta a woman called Miss Hyde, who had a small establishment on the eastern side of the line on the town's outskirts. She was gathering and caring for the unwanted half-caste children who were in a similar position to Charlie Way's boys. Charlie accepted the idea eagerly and he sent the two youngsters, Paddy and his brother, down to Miss Hyde on the next mail.

While I was in the Flinders the same Miss Hyde wrote to me, asking if I would take Paddy Way to train in any bush skills he might need before launching out as a stockman. Paddy helped me build a slab hut for us in the hills. We wheeled pine logs down from where we had cut them, sometimes as much as a kilometre away, and then sawed them into slabs with a cross-cut saw. To do this we positioned the logs in the forks of two trees that branched at the right height and sawed them down, working to a chalk mark.

We cut slabs for the table and the chairs. I found an old stove on a station dump and fixed it up, building it into a stone and mud fireplace with a slabbed log for a mantelpiece. It added to our possessions and I took pride in looking at it. Paddy stayed with me at least three years and then kept in touch for many more. He became an excellent horseman and after he had been with me for a while I sent him to Murnpeowie station where he became the horsebreaker because of his love for horses. He would take a known outlaw, a horse which could not be handled, and in a few weeks he would bring it back to the station and lead it through the house. He had a talent for taming the untameable.

I took a number of these boys from Miss Hyde over the years and did my best to fit them in some way for their life amongst white people. It was evident to me that these youngsters with Aboriginal blood all had enough of the call of the wild to make it necessary for them to live in the bush. Station work was much more acceptable to them than any other. They could breathe in their native air. Quite a number of the girls that Miss Hyde rescued after they had been abandoned became nurses and sisters. I often wondered whether they had the same call of the wild as their dark brothers.

Bobby Amos was another half-caste boy sent to me by Miss Hyde. A quiet and lovable boy, he had been rescued from some Aboriginal camp, and I often wonder what eventually happened to him. After the law decreed that whites had to marry their black lubras, many of them broke up long associations rather than do so, and I personally took twenty-five half-caste children and delivered them to Miss Hyde's care. Alfred Gerard was one who heard of this rush to get rid of unwanted kids and decided to establish a place for them further south. Miss Hyde was installed as matron of the Colebrook Home at Quorn, named after T.E. Colebrook who had greatly influenced Gerard's interest in the missions.

Gerard had been very generous in supplying me with provisions and the wherewithal to sink wells, but this work was now done. The government was not in a position to help people like myself. The rations for the unemployed at the time comprised 4.5 kg of flour, 1 kg of sugar and 113 g of tea, which was less than you could live on. I could not go back to the city and take this meagre handout so I stayed on in the camp. My parents sent an occasional 23 kg of flour to me at Copley and I always had the meat which I could catch locally, rabbits, kangaroos and (rarely) a sheep.

I felt it was time to move on and approached various stations in the area, offering to work for as little as thirty shillings ($3) a week, usually with the proviso that they would allow me to keep the fat from the kitchen. This was quite important to me because I had discovered that fat could be made into a useful saddle dressing, and everyone needed dressing for their saddles.

At that time there was a plentiful supply of water at a place called
Ettalowie Gap and I became friendly with Harold Hele, a fellow of my
own age who was managing Balcanoola station in the area for relatives.
He was an elder brother of Ivor Hele who later became a famous artist.
He was not in a position to employ labour but he was friendly and
helped me in many ways. I would talk about my efforts to obtain work at
Wooltana and Pralna stations on the Moolawatana sand-hills. I did get
some work but barely enough to buy the necessities of life.

My thoughts were interrupted one night by the clatter of hooves on
the hard stony surface of the road, and round the small hillock where I
was camped came a man driving with a flourish a pair of beautiful bay
mules. Reins in hand, foot on the brake, he sat proud on the seat of his
old dilapidated buggy.

'Can I pull up here?'

It was more an ultimatum than a question. Of course I had no right to
the place or the camp but I told him he was welcome to share it.

Dollar Mick was a wanderer, a horse-thief, a horseman of admirable
style. He was looking for a place where he could hide from the law and
meet his own kind. One of the first things he asked was whether any
Aboriginal women were about. I told him there probably were. He
immediately felt at home and pulled his mules out of the buggy.

I noticed next morning that two heads were poking out from his swag,
so it didn't take him long to find a companion. She was black and she
was fat but she was everything he needed to persuade him to stay. The
man who came, as I thought, for a few hours finished up staying years,
and in fact he became a lifelong friend. I drove his rig and rode his stolen
horses and he was the most loyal mate a man ever had. He made a habit
of camping or working or talking and spending most of his time at my
fire. We discussed various things, such as pack-saddles that could be
made and sold to the various station owners who used and needed them.

The man's name was Dollar Mick. I didn't know him by any other.
Call him Dollar Mick Smith if you like. He told me he had had
experience in making pack saddles, and although the work that he did
was rough, it was also very good, because it was based on experience.
People who needed pack-bags sent orders to us for such articles as
Dollar Mick made.

Fifty years later I had a letter from Innamincka on the Queensland
border telling me that Dollar's body had been brought from Adelaide
where he had died, aged eighty, and was buried in the bush where I first
met him. We were partners in what must have been the humblest beginning ever of what grew into a multi-million dollar business. The ideas
that we dreamed up round the campfire never changed, and the beliefs
that we shared continued to govern our thinking throughout a lifetime.
The patterns we developed to suit a bushman's needs were still good half

a century later when we had made tens of millions of dollars' worth of the articles. My success began the night Dollar came in his mule buggy and asked to stay.

From the earliest days when I had stood beside the bellows in my father's smithy I had always been interested in making things with my hands. I had shod my own horses, mended my own gear, kept my knives sharp and selected my materials. Every new experience added something to my capacity. It had been a triumph to learn the intricate pattern of the watch-pouch that Brown had taught me at Granite Downs. The association with Paddy DeConnolly and Victor Dumas had us competing to acquire new manual skills. Old Mac, at Olive Downs, had demonstrated the value of a dedicated application when he worked tirelessly to perfect a set of dog boots for use in prickle country where the bindis lame a dog in a matter of hours. They had to fit so that the dog could not tear them off and the prickles could not get in at the sides. Also they had to avoid irritating the dew claw. Mac worked and wasted leather until he had his pattern. I had admired the handiwork of Alec Scobie who lived in a desolate place near Lake Eyre and plaited the best stockwhips in Australia as well as inventing the Scobie hitch, which attaches the keeper to the handle. Good stockmen were always proud to make their own gear.

But it was the experience gained from Dollar Mick which really set me on a course of becoming useful with my hands. We made things that the station people wanted, such as spurs, bridles, pack-bags, water canteens—dozens if not hundreds of their necessaries. Although the orders were few and far between they still enabled us to carry on and to eat.

Our biggest problem was obtaining raw materials which had to come from Adelaide, but we found a few suppliers, in particular an old man who had The Avenues Tannery in Thebarton, a suburb in the west of Adelaide. He produced a special kip which was suitable for most of the things we made. With the few sides of kip we were able to buy from him we made pack-bags and bridles, and people came from far and wide to sit at our camp and watch us work. Dollar and I became very knowledgeable about a wide area because of these people, and it was a very pleasant camp.

About this time Dollar decided that he needed boots because he was practically barefoot and it was very important for a stockman to have suitable boots: they were the mark of professional status. So we decided we would make Dollar a pair of riding boots.

This we found extremely difficult to do because we lacked the knowledge to fashion the parts, particularly the uppers. In several months of experimenting we did not find one person who could help us in our search for that knowledge. I suppose a few people could have taught us but we did not have access to their erudition. We kept up our application until at last we had a pair of boots that met with Dollar's approval. We made them in a simple and unique fashion. We shaped them from one piece of leather, blocked while the hide was wet into the shape of a foot. We lined them with fat and wax, and the nails were hand-driven. We put the heels on by hand and the finished boot was an elementary but sturdy construction. This style later became our standard pattern for a riding boot. In the years to come we were to sell ten million pairs of them.

Dollar had an unusual foot. Like most who spend much of their lives in the saddle he had a high instep. It was the equivalent of a man's who wears a size eight boot, while the rest of his foot was a size five, so we had to produce a boot with a special instep. We achieved this by putting in leather to pack out the instep of a size five last, and in our factory to this day we still call the leather that adjusts for those with a high instep 'Mick's Piece'.

We didn't then do much about making more boots because of the demand for us to make other things we knew such as pack-bags. We were doing some brumby-running also and just enjoying the company of the visitors and making the simple things required.

In August 1932 I had to go with Thelma to Adelaide again for the delivery of our second baby. Our son Ian was also born in the Salvation Army Hostel. Ten days later he and his mother were curled up in a blanket and canvas by the side of the road with sand swirling round them while I helped to fit a spare tyre to a truck in which we had borrowed a ride from Leigh Creek to our hut in the ranges.

We reached this home to find the baby's crib half buried in sand. The wood stove I had salvaged and restored was filled with sand. Sand was piled a metre deep to the windward of the hut—the all-pervading sand of Central Australia. Sandstorms are a hazard to life in some parts. I can remember storms that rolled in like great balls of sun-glazed fire, balls that came rolling over and over and at last rolled over me, my horses, my cattle and my mates . . . stinging blasts of grit projected by a blast furnace and covering everything ... screaming down on us with frightening sound and heat...burying packs and everything we had... blinding the cattle and scattering them, so that we never saw any of them again.

In the Flinders the rolling storms sweep in from the Stony Desert, growing as they roll along the sky from east to west, ominous giant balls of darkening, swirling fearsome horror, their fingers searching out before them until the hand envelops all. They leave behind a changed landscape, dying animals and broken people.

Months later after another of these storms I developed sandy blight, the blinding curse of the sandy country. I had to be led about. My daughter Diane, who was then almost three, put her little hand in mine to lead me so that I could carry water from the well in Chinese coolie fashion, with the two buckets on a yoke that crossed my shoulders. I did not believe that I would ever see again. Thelma fell victim to the curse. Diane escaped it, but baby Ian had pus oozing from his eyes even though we washed them hourly with boracic acid. The treatment was partially effective in my case but Ian's little eyes looked opaque. Something had to be done but I was penniless.

Another ride on a passing truck. A borrowed train fare for Thelma and the kids. But for me it was the road again and the swag. I left everything I possessed in the slab hut, not knowing if I would ever return. I never did.

Coincident with Ian's developing trachoma, the mission people in authority at the reserve decided that I was not a suitable person to be associated with the changing of Aboriginal status at Ettalowie. Dollar Mick was always there, and many other white people came and camped temporarily.

At the time we made goods for sale purely for survival—we needed money. But it is quite evident now that had we been allowed to remain and develop the ideas which later were the foundation of our large industry, that alone could have transformed the lives of the people economically. It should be realized that such a change in the economic conditions of the half-caste and the Aboriginal will ultimately determine their standards.

I know the common belief that it is a person's acceptance of religion which effects a transformation, but my conviction has always been that economic conditions have much to do with changing the whole outlook on life. It is the poverty of peoples, world-wide, that has led to ignorance, and it is the rise to affluence which has brought about a change, making it possible for them to be educated. Such a change in financial status has always led to an increase in education and culture.

It is argued that the spiritual standing of a nation determines its culture, yet I think Karl Marx was probably somewhere near the mark in his materialistic concept of history. I do not agree in total with this theory because I have seen that where people have been changed by their introduction to religion they have naturally tried to raise their living standards. Nevertheless the poverty-stricken people of the world tend to become uneducated, and their standards fall lower and lower.

This is so with the Aborigines, and I believe that had Dollar Mick and I been allowed to continue with our work we would eventually have done a great deal for the people of the Flinders Ranges. But it was not to be, and I do not entirely blame the people in control of the Aborigines, because theirs is a common ignorance.

I did not like the city. We camped for a while with a half-caste friend,

Danny Garnet, in a bug-infested house in Carrington Street, but found it impossible to stay. I went back to Teringie in the hills and reoccupied and rebuilt the one-roomed shack I had put there in 1929, facing the city lights. It had no floor, but I still had the carpet square that had served as a rug in many places, a rug that could be shaken out and its surface cleaned with ammonia. We had a cooking fire inside the hut, and though I cannot say I liked the place it served for the time being.

After much seeking I found employment with a man in Port Adelaide who needed someone to carry bricks. This was at least twenty-five kilometres from where I was living, so it meant a long run down the hill from Norton Summit each morning, and a long ride by train and bus. In those days work started very early and finished later, and I did not get back to my camp at Teringie until late at night. The days were long and the work was hard. I knew I would have to make some attempt to strike out on my own. To make use of my experience in making pack-bags and saddles I decided to approach Sir Sidney Kidman, the Cattle King, to see if I could find a market.

1933 was in the worst of the Depression. Prices were ridiculously low: bullocks were selling for thirty shillings ($3) a head, and droving cost about ten shillings ($1) a head for a thousand miles (1600 km). But it was still possible for a long-term strategist like Sir Sidney to conduct his cattle empire however unprofitable it might be for the period, and I thought the old man might still need pack-saddles and bags.

I went to his office manager, a man named Bird, with my request, and was told I would have to see Sir Sidney himself. I waited until he came to Adelaide and went out to Unley Park to see him at Eringa, the house he had named after one of his stations. I had briefly worked for him at Eringa station, but had met him only as an employee whom practically he did not know.

'Would you be interested in letting me make packs for your stations?' I asked him.

He looked at me sceptically. 'Son,' he said. 'We buy our packs from Harris Scarfes. They are good packs. What makes you think you can make better ones?'

For answer I gave him a quote from his old manager at Anna Downs, Archie McLean: 'Some day a better pack will be built using a higher fork in the steel, a deeper side, and rigged with double girths instead of carrying breast-plates and breeching. And the bags will have special gussets for items that have to be kept upright.'

I had remembered Archie's words as gospel, because like the others on his station, including the blacks, I worshipped Archie McLean. He could ride like a centaur, was fearless with cattle or men, handled the desert as though it were his garden—distance was no problem to him.

I did not tell Sir Sidney that his own man had been my teacher, but he sensed that I had something to offer.

'I will give you an opportunity,' he said, and the words have rung in my ears ever since. He asked me to bring him a sample and said he would talk to his managers.

Over the years I had made contact with several of his managers. Besides McLean at Anna Creek I knew Kemp at Macumba and I had made some contact with the manager, Brooke, at Marree. I had no doubt that these people would agree my samples were the better article.

When I delivered that first order, the old man said: 'Well, son, send me the account.'

'Sir, I am sorry but I cannot deal on that basis,' I said.

'Why not? Everybody gives me a month's credit.'

'It's like this, sir. I haven't any money to buy the materials to make the next pack and bags, and if I have to wait thirty days for you to pay me, I will be out of work for thirty days.'

He went into the office and drew a cheque for £5.

Only a small percentage of that £5 was profit, but at least it was a beginning. I had no doubt that in the following years these packs and bags would become standard equipment in at least the Kidman empire and throughout most of northern Australia among the drovers. And I have had the satisfaction of seeing this happen. I knew what a cattleman needed. Kidman gave me the opportunity to supply it.

Chapter Six

My old father's house of retirement stood at 5 Percy Street, Prospect, an address which later was to become better known throughout the outback than any other in Australia. He had a shed there in which he stored wood for the stove. He agreed to let me use a corner of this shed and it was here, with the cut wood rolling about my feet, that I started to make my pack-bags and saddles.

There being little room beside the wood in the shed I worked mainly in the open, and Dad would sit with me by the hour, seldom speaking. I rather think he liked the stitching and rivetting that went on by his side, but he seldom spoke. He had never said a word needlessly, never spent a penny unnecessarily, never borrowed, never lent. I never heard any philosophy or history from his lips. Having left home early without returning until now I had missed years of contact with him. He was the kind that lived what he had to say, which is probably the best way of teaching.

I was sitting in the sun occupied with my pack-bags one morning when a badly handicapped man, Charlie Ferguson, came by to watch. He stood there a while before he said, 'I reckon I could do that.' It was a statement that carried heavy pathos, the statement of a man who had done nothing but wanted to do something. I looked hard at him with his hunched back, deformed legs, twisted neck, eager smiling face. I hadn't the heart to tell him how desperately poor I and my brood were. Instead I told him of my old companion back in the bush experimenting alongside me until we had made a pair of boots, and of how proud we both were when he could wear something we had made. At that he came at me straight.

'Would you teach me to make a pair of boots?'

Again I had not the heart to tell him that I did not have a place for him to work, or the leather to work with, or even the time to show him how. But I could see that time meant nothing to him. His life was timeless; he had nothing with which to fill it. I realized that boots could be made from the scraps of greasy kip left over from cutting pack-bags. This was a start. But I had no bench on which to work and no tools to work with except the primitive knife and shaping tool we had used in the bush. We needed nails and sole leather; but most of all we needed a customer for anything we might make.

It was then I made the most rewarding experiment of my whole life. I spent sixpence on a small two-line advertisement in the Adelaide *Chronicle*. It read: 'Elastic side boots made to order. Twenty shillings. Cash with order. 5 Percy Street, Prospect.' Within days came a letter with a pound note enclosed and a size for the boots.

We had the money now for the materials. Charlie Ferguson was a constant visitor by now and he shared my high excitement. I went by tram to the Julius Cohn store in Adelaide, off Hindley Street, and bought a small packet of brass nails, some light sole leather, some of the correct elastic material and some thread. We blocked the boots to shape as Dollar Mick and I had learned in the Flinders Ranges, sewed the elastic into place first (as months of experiment had taught), tacked the uppers down on an old steel last that Dad had found in a second-hand shop, hand-nailed the soles into place and carved the heels into delightful symmetry. When that was done we polished the leather by hand and admired our work. We could hardly wait for the response to the parcel that we so carefully wrapped. Would the boots fit? Would they please this trusting bushman who had so confidently sent his money to someone he did not know?

I have forgotten his name, but he lives like a giant in my memory. Sufficient that he came from Hilltaba station, ever afterwards a romantic name.

Charlie's share of the boots was eight shillings, which we carefully reckoned to be the profit. We renewed the advertisement and it continued its magic. I had my pack-bags; Charlie had his boots. With this evidence of the ability of the business to grow I moved my family from the shack at Teringie to a rented house not far from my father's, in Prospect.

We were in business now, and the business was growing. Money was still tight, but the 'cash with order' pattern of selling mail-order boots gave us a little leeway, for we used our credit to the limit. Within a few weeks Charlie was making good money, and I was freed of the wearying task of making boots. Soon I hired a girl named Roma Brisbane to stitch for us on a small machine of ancient vintage. When not engaged on the work in hand she stitched leather shirts, jackets which we called 'drover coats' from my memory of long cold nights on cattle watch.

Our drover coats and elastic-sided boots were immediately adopted by the bushmen looking for something they could relate to their work, something made just for them, handmade things and trustworthy. Our small shed became too small within weeks, and we built another for our stitcher girl to work in. It was built of galvanized iron and was hot in summer and cold in winter, but we were happy making things. We knew little about business and lacked the mental equipment to handle the small things that bothered us, so we hired a girl to write letters by hand to our bush customers.

I judged it time to turn to the making of other types of equipment such as canteens for carrying on camels and pack-horses. I remembered the risk that Bill Wade and I had run when our canteens had leaked on that desperate struggle to return to the Musgraves. Most canteens at that time were made from light tin materials, as ours had been, and I set out to make something that could not be so easily destroyed. I made a twelve-gallon canteen, pear-shaped in front and rear elevation, from rolled steel, similar in quality to the heavy steel used in making water troughs for cattle. This steel, shaped, welded into place and galvanized, formed an almost unbreakable article; and so one thing led to another.

From pack-saddles and canteens I branched out into making other equipment which was new and different in style, and the styles were all evolved from bush experience. At Anna Creek Archie McLean had suggested the higher saddle-tree for packs. I had seen an old man named Pompey Trew making such saddles, and he had also suggested interior gussets for the pack-bags to hold upright such stores as jam. Men of the Birdsville Track suggested patterns for leggings; other people came to us with innovative ideas. Outback people approved of my productions—it was not long before the small sheds we were using became inadequate.

I was still working in the woodshed at my father's home when a long, sleek American car drew up and out stepped a prosperous-looking man puffing on a foot-long Havana cigar. He opened the conversation:

'I am G.N. Raymond. I make lasts. I have heard about you from Julius Cohn, the leather merchant.'

That surprised me, and I let him know. 'Why should you bother to call on a one-man show as small as this? You can see I have no factory, no staff.'

His reply will always live with me. 'My father lived in England, and he once took me to visit a small one-man show like this. I said, "Dad, why did you call on him?" He replied, "The day might come when that man will have a street of factory and become your best customer".' How prophetic that was!

Charlie was teaching a fast-moving young man to make boots, and we had progressed with the packs to the point at which a professional saddler was making them. Also we had developed other wanted bush gear like saddlebags, writing cases and swag covers, and by staying with our lucky find—'cash with order'—we had money in the bank. It was not enough, as I slowly developed one new building after another. They went up in a makeshift manner, the only way I could manage because I needed the money for stock, and spending it on building seemed a poor way to progress. Even like this, the time soon came when I found myself heavily in debt. I had no previous experience in business and did not realize that if one sank money into machinery and buildings it represented a loss of trading capital. These things I had to learn.

Relief came from a station manager, Jim Mortimer, who came along one day, decided it could be a good business and supplied the money, a little more than £1000 for expansion. With this payment he became my partner. Jim was then managing Murnpeowie and Lyndhurst stations and these represented a large area of country for which we supplied the goods.

I was in some measure able to repay his timely help in a later day when his son was looking for a cattle-station and I introduced him to a seller. He bought for £32 000, sold at a profit shortly after, and in the meantime had cleared a small fortune selling the cattle from the place. Later he built up a cattle empire and became wealthy, a multi-millionaire towards the end of his days.

We remained good friends through a long lifetime. He had sold his half-share in the business to other friends of mine who, with no interest in manufacturing, had bought as an investment. I am sorry to say it didn't bring them any profit for a long time, because an expanding business like that doesn't pay dividends, but over the years it became valuable.

We continued to move faster than prudence would have dictated. We added trained saddlers to our staff, still giving an agreed piecework price for everything, and no happier band of workers existed than our small co-operative concern. We played games at lunchtime, held picnics at weekends. Prices were inevitably low as these were the Depression years.

In November 1934 Thelma gave birth to my second son, Reginald Dene.

About this time I had a call from Dr Charles Duguid, a surgeon with a considerable care for the Aborigines. This had intensified when, in 1933, he was horrified by the callous and inhuman treatment by police and administration of Takiar, a native of Caledon Bay who had been sentenced to death in Darwin Court for the death of a policeman. The High Court quashed the conviction and strongly criticized the judge. Released in Darwin to make his own way back across Arnhem Land to the Gulf of Carpentaria, Takiar had failed to make it and sinister rumours circulated as to the manner of his death. Dr Duguid had previously been told of white atrocities in the north by a woman missionary he was treating for leprosy, and in July 1934 he set out for Darwin to see conditions for himself.

An emergency operation halted him in Alice Springs, and during a three-week stay there he was shocked by the white attitudes, particularly as expressed by the padre of the Australian Inland Mission, as he recorded in his book, *Doctor Among the Aborigines*: ' "The best the niggers have any right to expect is a decent funeral." '

Dr Duguid's visit to me followed on his learning that I had been Bill

Wade's companion in the Petermann and Musgrave Ranges. He asked if I would be interested in attending a meeting in the Adelaide Town Hall, the outcome of which he hoped would be the setting up of a medical mission for Aborigines. I was interested, remembering the numbers I had seen suffering from what I had thought to be leprosy but turned out to be yaws.

At the meeting he called on me to make a statement concerning the position of the Aborigines in the Ranges, and among other things I hesitantly offered my opinion that it was unnecessary to hire some expensive explorer to look over the region, because of the work already done by Wade.

On a visit to the Lutheran Mission at Hermannsburg to investigate the high incidence of tuberculosis there, Dr Duguid had met Pastor Albrecht, who advised him to visit the Musgraves to see for himself. This he proposed to do, but a busy schedule delayed him. Early in the New Year he was called to be Moderator of the Presbyterian Church in South Australia, the first lay incumbent of the position. He was also elected president of the Aborigines Protection League, but in June he set off for the Musgraves, seconding me to act as guide and taking also a student named Robbie Robinson to help to drive and look after the car, a new Model A Ford.

We had a pretty arduous trip and the car took something of a battering, even while we were still on the road, especially where the wind had eroded the surfaces or blown the sand over it into high sand-hills. Beyond the road were the rocky creek-beds, the spinifex and more sand-hills. We camped with Stan Ferguson at Ernabella in the unfinished house he was building. From here Dr Duguid went further into the Ranges with a young Aboriginal guide named Gilpin, while Robbie and I did what we could to put the car back in condition.

During this expedition the doctor collected much detailed evidence of the need for a mission and he was determined it should be one in which the natives were left to follow their own way of life. It should be a refuge where they would have time to adjust to the changes that were coming whether they liked them or not, and thus have a chance of survival. The most basic feature was the concept of freedom—no interference with tribal customs, no compulsion and no imposition of a white way of life. Special help would be offered at the outset. Only trained people, doctors, nurses or teachers should be on the mission staff and they should have to learn the language. He also felt that the Aborigines should be given the full bounty on dingo scalps, an effective discouragement to the growing army of adventurers trading handfuls of flour for the scalps.

Perhaps because of the pressure of his work, Dr Duguid asked me to convene a small committee to handle the establishment of the mission. This committee included a young lawyer named Howard Zelling, now a

Justice of the Court in Adelaide; a Miss Alice M. McCaul, a philanthropist well known and well loved in Adelaide, and Mr H. Murray Caire, a city manager of the State Bank. Led and inspired by Dr Duguid, this committee put the money together and purchased Ernabella from Stan Ferguson. Ernabella Mission was to become a big factor in preserving the state of Aborigines in the Musgraves, and it still stands as something of a bastion against white intrusion.

The Stone Age people never disciplined their children. There was no need, for the struggle of life was itself a discipline. Long marches on a hungry belly, fierce laws that demanded death if broken, skill to kill as the essential element for survival, and a surrounding of enemies produced a society of people made honest by necessity.

Perhaps enough will never be written of the work of men like Dr Duguid, men who devoted their lives to working for the good of Aborigines. He celebrated a century of life in 1984. I know that his inspiration would be his religious belief. Religion qualifies as a very potent driving force for the human race. Men will become celibate for life; women will sacrifice the prospect of a home and children for a life of simplicity and prayer; nations have fought for centuries to propagate their faith; such believers as the Huguenots of France died horrible deaths to preserve it, and the Jews have kept their religion and their principles through a millennium of persecution. Death and suffering have followed the march of religion. But the marchers' efforts bear fruit.

If anyone doubts the impact of ideas upon the centuries of time and the generations of men, a clear and open glance over the horizon of history will probably focus on at least four men who have left tracks large and purposeful enough to have formed the roads on which uncounted millions have travelled and lived and died. Jesus and Mahomet, Marx and Mao were among them; their unaccompanied physical figures may have been insignificant but their crowds of followers have dominated great areas of the human sphere.

Fifty years after I left Bill Wade, who suffered so much for his beliefs and his efforts to preach religion to the Aborigines, I watched a television programme about a young man who had come from the Aboriginal camp in the faraway Warburton Ranges, where Bill had lived and died. The young man, an evangelist, was making a marked impact on his people. The seed that Bill Wade sowed is still bearing fruit.

One might have thought Bill's a wasted life when he went off to the Warburtons by himself and set up his lonely mission at the western end of the desert ranges. But I could give no weight to that idea when I saw on the screen this black John the Baptist, born in wilderness and carrying the banner that Bill must have put in his hands.

*   *   *

The house I bought for Thelma.

Above: My stables and polo ponies at Neidpath. In the middle is Jackie Cadell, the stable boy.

Right: Thelma as mistress of the castle.

Jocelyn with her favourite grey, Pastime.

The expansion of the business continued and accelerated in response to the mounting orders we were getting. But as I was putting the money into buildings and machinery I was in effect getting deeper and deeper into debt. I kept on trading to the limit of my credit, and that limit kept expanding with the business we were doing and the expansion of our workshops. My family too was growing. Thelma gave me my second daughter and fourth child in mid July 1937. It was time to get a bigger house, and both Thelma and I preferred to buy one in which our style of living could expand along with the inflow of money.

The house I settled on had played its part in the development of South Australia. Sir George Gawler, second Governor of the colony, found it in a state of stagnation when he arrived, and was able to revitalize it, but he was accused of overspending, his bills were dishonoured and he himself was recalled to England in 1841. In his promotion of government spending he sent a list of urgent public works to the Colonization Commissioners. At its head was 'a Governor's Residence' on which he began work immediately. He spent £10 000 on this twelve-roomed house even though, as with other buildings, he left it incomplete, awaiting the addition of verandahs and screens, for instance; and a good deal of criticism was directed at it. Mrs Gawler's description, though, is on record: 'a pretty looking comfortable house, not at all suited as a Governor's Residence'.

The house, on Strangways Terrace, overlooked the Adelaide Golf Links, and I bought it although I was quite deeply in debt. The business continued to expand. My brother-in-law Mike Cummings had joined us, the staff was much larger, and we still had as many orders as we could handle. I felt I had achieved a measure of success.

With the outbreak of war on 3 September 1939, the Defence Department took over our little outfit and, working under officers of the forces, we produced whatever was needed by the fast-growing armed services: uniforms, overalls, leather parts. Mostly we served the production department of the Royal Australian Air Force.

With four young children and ambitious projects ahead I went reluctantly to the recruiting depot. I believed it was everyone's responsibility because of the fear that the Germans would over-run the world. In the light of what has happened since it is probable that these hard-working people might have done a better job of running the western world than we have. But we were under the pressing fear that our freedom was at stake.

I passed the physical examination and was sent on to the allocation officer. He went over my credentials carefully and, telling me that there was a considerable need for people with my special abilities, drafted me into the production department. The restrictions of officialdom were hard for me to take. Higher-ranking men dictated my every move and I felt some of them had little ability. Nevertheless, I learned a lot, particularly from the Air Force, where the requirements for specialized production were such that I was able to improve my techniques in many ways.

Men all around me were drafted into various other sections of the war machine. Members of our staff, relatives of mine and many of my friends from the bush went to New Guinea, and some never came back. Some of the finest men of my age and younger were killed in that campaign, and Australia was very much the poorer for this loss. The Americans 'invaded' Australia and took over the social scene. We men liked them, but so did our girls. The Yankee soldiers had more money and better manners, and they had seen more of the world than our stay-at-homes. They were also doing a good job on the fierce and bloody Pacific battle-fronts, as later I confirmed on visits to Wake Island and Guadalcanal.

Charlie Ferguson was still with us and continued to make his boots, working almost desperately until, inevitably, his afflictions brought about a collapse of his frail body. When he could no longer carry on, our team of workers decided we should continue his pay, which we did. When the end came and his grieving family buried him his wife wrote me what I considered the most valuable letter I ever received. She thanked me for the friendship that had enabled him to raise that fine family of children now able to look after themselves. Charlie was a great man.

At this time I busied myself writing and publishing *The Bushman's Handbook*, designed to assist young bushmen and others who wanted to make things of real worth and serviceability: saddles, boots, stockwhips, belts—anything that could be made from leather, beginning with the tanning of the hide. The articles were designed to show good workmanship, with intricate plaiting, carved leather and solid foundations for the work. It has been a steady success over the years, and has been the means of putting me in touch with Outback people interested in doing things for themselves. There were chapters on making horse-shoes, spurs, bridles and packs, on shoeing horses and the handling of skins. It has appeared in twelve editions with a swelling of interest in the early 1950s and the early 1970s when the times for people were more difficult, I suppose, and the sales still continue.

In September 1941 I went to the wedding of my sister Effie Helena, in Adelaide. Her groom was Lieutenant William Gay, RAN, and their story was a romantic one. In September 1939, immediately after the outbreak of war, Effie, a double-certificated nursing sister, joined Queen Alexandra's Imperial Nursing Society and was sent to France with the British Expeditionary Force. When that campaign failed she was evacuated from Boulogne by small boat. At the time of the evacuation from Crete, Effie was serving at the Sixth General Hospital at Alexandria, in Egypt. She was discharged medically unfit in 1941 and booked a passage to Sydney on the *Largs Bay*.

Bill Gay was a patient in the ward which Effie was leaving, suffering from a bad fever which the doctors could not diagnose. He had been the navigator of the 19th Destroyer Flotilla, which Lord Haw-Haw of the German radio (William Joyce) referred to frequently as 'the Scrap-Iron Flotilla'. It consisted of the vessels *Stuart*, *Vampire*, *Voyager*, *Waterhen* and *Vendetta*. Bill was to be invalided back to Australia on the same vessel as Effie, the *Largs Bay*.

At the last moment plans were changed and Gay was transferred to the *Queen Mary* for a quicker passage. With the co-operation of the Commodore of the *Queen Mary* and a naval padre he managed to have Effie transferred to the *Queen Mary*. This was quite illegal, as by that time she was a civilian and the *Queen Mary* a war transport which, due to customs regulations, could not carry civilians. So literally Effie was smuggled back to Australia by the Commodore of the *Queen Mary*. Officially she was seconded to the staff of Brigadier Lind, the Senior Army Staff Officer aboard.

When the ship was boarded by customs officers at Fremantle Bill Gay locked Effie in her cabin and kept the key in his pocket until they had left. The same thing happened at Sydney. Effie and her luggage were off-loaded by a naval motor launch which Gay had requested for himself and put ashore at Man-o'-War Steps in the heart of Sydney.

When Bill went to thank the Commodore for his great help the Commodore said he was glad to shake the hand of the only man who had ever beaten his purser.

After their marriage in Adelaide Effie and Bill went to Melbourne. Bill went to hospital at Flinders Naval Depot for a cartilege operation and a final diagnosis of his recurrent fever, which he had picked up in the Middle East. In February 1942 he was still in hospital when a signal came from Naval Board for him to join HMAS *Perth* when she called at Melbourne. The senior medical officer, Captain Scott McKenzie, advised Bill that in his opinion he was still not fit for combat duty and did not have to join the *Perth*. However, Bill decided that he should, and did so.

The *Perth* was heading north to join a mixed force of cruisers and destroyers under the command of Admiral Doorman, a Dutch officer, to then prevent a Japanese landing in Java.

The Allied striking force was badly knocked about in the intensive Battle of the Java Sea which, when it concluded, left only two Allied ships, the American heavy cruiser *Houston* and the Australian light cruiser *Perth* still in any fighting trim. Both were destroyed in the subsequent Battle of Sunda Strait. When the end came Bill, as duty officer of the watch, was on the bridge with Captain Waller. In his book of the engagement, *Proud Echo*, Ronald McKie reports that Gay was last to leave the bridge (since Captain Waller went down with the ship). McKie reports Waller's last words as, 'Get off the bridge, Gay.'

Bill was picked up by a Japanese destroyer and spent the next three and a half years a prisoner of war in Japan. The *Perth* was reported lost with all hands, and two years passed before the existence of survivors was reported, a harrowing time for relatives. Effie became seriously ill and died in February 1944 without ever learning that Bill was alive. He remained unaware of her death until his return. He has since kept in touch with our family, and attended my mother's funeral in January 1984.

Two more sons were born to us during the war: John Mitchell in May 1943, and Christopher Kerry in mid 1945. One evening, when Thelma was pregnant with Christopher, she and I went out for a walk before the dark had blotted out the beauty of the park in front of our house. We loved that house, our symbol of success, with its gardens, its cedar doors, its history. In the same street were the grand and imposing homes of successful citizens, much larger and more elegant than ours. We were passing Neidpath, the imposing MacGregor mansion with its stone pillars, silver tower, three acres of garden with scented trees, and gravelled paths.

'When you have our child I will buy you this mansion,' I said, half jokingly.

Mrs MacGregor, the old lady who had been living alone in the house, died and Neidpath came on the market. I rang the agents and suggested I might be interested in buying it. I was told it would go to auction. The reserve price was high enough to make me forget my foolish intention. At the auction no bidders contended, and the property was passed in. Young MacGregor rang me.

'Were you serious in asking about the family house on the Terrace?' he asked.

I tried to laugh that off and explained humbly that I would not have as many pennies as he wanted pounds.

'What have you got?' he asked.

'I own the house on the corner of your street. Governor Gawler's old house.'

'Then sell that, and you can have the big house interest free for ten years.'

I told him that I could not afford to buy the curtains, the floor coverings or even the light fittings for such a magnificent establishment.

He said, 'If you would like to take the place on my terms you can have the curtains. They were taken from an old French castle. You may have the carpets, which were specially made in Scotland and fitted by men sent out for the purpose. You may have the blinds and the light fittings and everything to do with the place free of charge.'

Of course I could not refuse this extraordinarily generous offer and so, very proudly, we took possession of this luxurious home.

MacGregor had had a big family and he had built a house that would last for generations. The basement had been excavated to keep the house dry, standing on its bluestone pillars. Thick pine floors. Walls of cut stone. Lead-lined roof. Tiles imported from France. A built-in vacuum cleaner that served all rooms. Several bathrooms on each floor. Hand-fitted carpets of beauty and depth custom-made in Scotland to fit each room. Ceilings cast in artistic designs. Walls panelled in mahogany. A vast library in glass-fronted bookcases of polished wood.

The gardener had his own house on the grounds. The lawns were rounded on the edges and cut to perfection. The gardens were cycled for the seasons with roses, wistaria and flowering trees. The stables accommodated enough horses to mount the whole family when we rode to hounds and also housed the groom who kept my polo ponies.

We ceased eating at the kitchen table and DINED. We attended the Governor's soirées, me in long-tailed coat, Thelma in fashion.

My girl who lived by my side loved the place. For whatever reason she was possessed of grace that surmounted her humble birth. Possibly her father or his parents had been born to the purple. She rode the crest. But we were not to the manor born and in the end Neidpath destroyed me and broke her heart. In the years ahead we were to part there, having lost ourselves and all that we had fought for.

My four eldest children used to ride to hounds with me. Ian used to ride a little paint horse, just a pony, but a beautiful jumper—never put a foot on a fence in its life. Diane had a big grey, and Jocelyn and Dene had good ponies too. I used to change my own mount often. In the rodeos which I attended as often as I could some spirited magnificent horses would come in that by rights should never have been used for buck-jumping displays. I used to hand these over to Jackie Cadell, my Chinese–Aboriginal groom who came from Mataranka way. Jackie was one of the best riders I have ever seen, and he worked for me for eighteen years. I made a practice of taking these horses out to the hunting field and breaking them in to hunting, and I got a lot of falls out of them. The munjongs had never been trained to jump. But in the field they'd see the leaders go over the fence and they'd get the idea and mostly go over. I used to ride fresh horses most times, and I got some good ones.

One point-to-point I rode a big wild horse called Avenger. I was behind and took a short cut over the top of a hill that the leaders went round. We all met at a gate just over the top, but I was coming in at an angle while the others, three or four of them, were coming straight. They all took a tumble. I went over the gate and then I had no one in front of me except Johnny Winchester, a man who rode in the Olympic team. We came to the water-jump together, and we came off there into the water. Perhaps he had a bit of a jostle.

Jocelyn was a beautiful girl and I remember her as a horsewoman of great skill and courage. I see her now flying over the hurdles in the hunt field, riding with dash as well as courage. I also think of her as a gentle person whose character and other attributes make her one of the most lovable women I have ever known. She married John Sturm when she was quite young and lived for years in a fettler's hut on the Oodnadatta line, bringing up two fine boys in conditions almost as harsh as her elder sister Diane knew in her early childhood.

Diane, as the eldest, has seen more of poverty than the others. She had her early years in the Flinders Ranges, having to eat stewed rabbit, boiled rabbit, potted rabbit, baked rabbit, rabbit and kangaroo, in fact rabbit in every conceivable guise. She had to help with getting the goats and leading her blind father to the well for water, and all these early impressions must have made a big impact on her later outlook. After that she had to help with household chores and minding the younger children, a basic discipline from which she grew into a helpful young lady with the correct outlook towards raising a family. She shone on the hunting field too. In 1951 she married Cecil Cuthbertson, with whom she has six children.

Wartime also thrust me into a new profession, that of magazine editor, proprietor and publisher of books. It all started in a small way by my becoming spokesman for a representative group of rough riders, buckjumpers, bulldoggers—the stars of the bushmen's carnivals. Before the Second World War the Royal Agricultural Society always used to have displays of horsemanship. In 1938 they brought out a company of Cossacks. Other times they'd have the American Rough Riders, something like that. They acted as though they had exclusive rights for shows of this nature.

In the United States rodeo events had been increasing in incidence and popularity for twenty years before November 1936 when the Cowboys' Turtle Association was formed to raise the standards of rodeo, particularly in the five regular events, buckjumping, bareback riding, bull riding, steer wrestling and calf roping, but also in such special events as fancy roping, trick riding and display features such as mounted quadrilles. The Turtle Association, later renamed the Rodeo Cowboys Association, regulates the conduct of both contestants and shows, provides insurance, inflicts fines and issues blacklists. It established standards of saddles and standards for judges. It was well organized.

In Australia, however, contests tended to go by Rafferty's rules, and when public interest encouraged an increasing number of shows, riders ran a lot of unnecessary risks. When the war was almost over, in 1945, the visiting American boys persuaded us that it would be a good thing to have an organization like the Turtle Association for controlling rodeo. Some of our best contestants agreed to form a Rough Riders' Association and asked me to convene a meeting for the purpose. With the help of the world champion buckjumper and bulldogger Lance Skuthorpe Junior, Basil Gollan, Danny Edwards and others, I formed an association in Adelaide which became a success. I acted as secretary for many years and then took on the job of treasurer, a post I still hold. Rough Riders at this time is a well-heeled organization which, by insurance, guarantees its own riders.

In this organization I made many lifelong friends, fellows who have proved themselves to be champions in every way, and when I hear our politicians abusing each other in Parliament I recall that none of our members would speak in such a manner unless he were prepared to do battle on the grass. It may not have been an organization of 'gentlemen', but its members were men who slept in uncomfortable beds, if any. Men who risked their lives day after day on the wildest of horses, leaping headlong on to wild long-horned cattle and facing up to the fiercest bulls that could be found. Men like these are not to be abused, and one is proud to call any of the breed one's friend.

I have noticed that the fellows who have gone down the road to follow rodeo have had the rough edges knocked off them over the years, and many of them have acquired a polish such as has enabled them to meet all ranks of people on a basis of equality. Many of these rough diamonds have become successful businessmen, and all of them have been the better for having followed rodeo.

In Sydney, Gollan, Edwards and I went to see Tom McFarlane, the councillor of the Royal Agricultural Society who controlled the horse events, and suggested that the Society establish rodeo rules: times set, saddle standards and standards for judges. He was not sympathetic.

'We don't need to be told how to run a rodeo,' he said. 'We're very successful. All that the public wants is to see riders fall off their horses.'

As we were leaving, the Society's registrar, Harold Sarina, called us into his office and warned us against starting anything in the way of a union. We went to a coffee house in George Street and got Lance Skuthorpe to join us. He brought along Virgil Reilly, who was an artist on *Smith's Weekly*. Virgil suggested we print some sort of a news-sheet. With the war still on we could not get any paper until Sir Keith Murdoch, of the Melbourne *Herald*, arranged a supply for us. We printed a news-sheet under a variety of names until it finally developed as *Hoofs and Horns*, 'hoofs' because it set out to record the activities of horsemen and horsemanship in Australia, and 'horns' because it was also devoted to the cattle industry. These activities were becoming my main preoccupations.

The magazine has suffered various vicissitudes through the forty years of its existence, but it has always been published each month, and for much of that time I have written the editorials. This has been an interesting literary exercise for me and I have conducted crusades on many subjects through its pages. We have used the magazine to form the Rough Riders' Association, the Trail Riders of Australia, the Endurance Riders of Australia and the Australian Horsemen's Convention of 1972. All these institutions have become nationally established. The bound volumes of *Hoofs and Horns* occupy a space three metres long on my shelf.

Keith Stevens, a lad who left school at the end of the war, has stayed with *Hoofs and Horns* throughout its history, and has contributed more than anyone else to its success. He must surely have one of the longest unbroken careers with one publication.

I have followed the lives of many who have contributed to the magazine, young people filled with energy when they begin, writing verses, riding buckjumpers and taking part in the varied activities of horsemanship in Australia. I have watched them growing old and I have made many friends, and now in these later years we are a confederation of people who have devoted a lifetime to these interests.

The world becomes a little smaller, and for me a little poorer, as one by one these folk pass on to the land of memories. They are merged in what St Paul tells us is 'a great cloud of witnesses'. I like the idea that somewhere in that beyond they watch our activities and cheer us on, and I wonder sometimes whether they do not convey their messages to us.

Chapter Seven

A good friend of mine was Dr Johannes B. Thiersch, who was the Neale Research Pathologist of the anti-cancer campaign of the University of Adelaide and a pathologist to the Institute of Medical and Veterinary Science under the directorship of Dr Weston Hurst. The Institute was created for research and to conduct the laboratory service for the Royal Adelaide Hospital, where Thiersch was Senior Honorary Pathologist. While he was in Adelaide he made acute and chronic leukemia the object of his research and wrote several papers which created interest in the United States, so that in 1947 he transferred to the Sloan-Kettering Institute of Cancer Research in Manhattan, under the directorship of Dr C.P. Rhoads.

Hannes liked my lifestyle, and encouraged me to join him in the study of the physical preparation of the body for physical combat. I was keen to do this because I had seen men I considered worthy, and for whom I had some affection, savaged by bullies. I recall seeing a good friend of mine hit in the neck by a bully and watching him die immediately. I have seen men beaten to a pulp, watched bullies lord their authority over those under them, and I have wished many times that I was not so weak and defenceless so that I could pay these bullies in their own coin. It is one thing to run in the company of violent men and quite another to be their equal. I have known gangers employed on the building of the railway line from Oodnadatta, some of them brutal types who exercised their authority by sheer physical force, and often I have dodged a cuff from such fellows, vowing that some day I would return their savagery; but I'm afraid I never did. Nevertheless I was determined to equip myself a little better to face the physical battles of life, and when Hannes invited me to join him to train under a professional I jumped at the chance. This man was Hughie Whitman, a catch-as-catch-can expert, a man trained in many martial arts: judo, mat wrestling, counters of every kind to physical violence.

At my first meeting with him he clutched me and saying, 'See how you can stand this,' he twisted my neck in such a way that it took weeks to recover. I realized then that without a solid and well-stiffened neck one would not be able to achieve anything much in the martial arts. I now take a size seventeen collar and find it a bit small, so at least I did achieve a neck that could not be readily mishandled.

The first requirement of physical combat is a body which is able to withstand the violent exercitations of being pushed and pulled and twisted to such degree that without adequate strength it could be permanently damaged. This means a strengthening of the arms, the knees, the neck—every part of the body. It takes months, even years, before one is proficient in the more detailed and scientific arts of offence and defence.

The world-class professionals in the art of mat wrestling are not to be found at the stadiums amongst the men who exercise their skills for the entertainment of the public. The true professionals are those who study the fine details of the manipulations of the body. Many a time when I have watched wrestlers and listened to their grunts and groans I have known full well that the opponents, had they wished it, could have broken limbs or caused permanent damage. This of course is seldom done. I found there were secrets and specialized skills in the science of physical combat, and I trained and studied hard, and felt rewarded in the following years in knowing that I was well able to defend myself in any company.

I enjoyed greatly the friendship of Hannes Thiersch. I enjoyed talking with him about his experiments in research. After he left Australia for New York in 1947 he worked on cancer research in the Sloan-Kettering Institute's Department of Chemotherapy with Drs David Karnowsi and Fred Phillips. He and his colleagues laid the foundations of chemotherapy as it is used today. They developed especially the nitrogen mustards and folic acid antagonist and the purine antagonist. Following Thiersch's observation in 1948 of the effects of a folic acid antimetabolite on the pregnancy of animals, he began investigations supported by the US Federal Government as well as the Planned Parenthood organization located at the Rockefeller Medical Center in Manhattan. He soon discovered that materials of this nature, when given to pregnant animals, might cause malformations in the foetus and thus seriously deformed offspring. This discovery predated by twelve years the exposure in 1962 of the effects of thalidomide.

From 1951 Dr Thiersch transferred to the University of Washington in Seattle in first the Department of Pathology, later the Department of Pharmacology, and also established a small research laboratory of his own. Thiersch and his colleagues investigated many natural and artificial substances, and discovered that many had palliative value in the treatment of cancer. He told me how they tested materials found in the forests of Brazil, how they had studied the secrets of African witch-doctors, and even investigated the materia medica of Australian Aborigines. He said they had discovered many materials and processes which he doubted would ever be released for general use because of their sometimes dramatic effects on the body. They made no real progress in the cure of cancer. He believed that the answer might be found in the body itself. Mystery still surrounds the immune system of the body, but therein, he thinks, may lie the secret of the control of cancer.

In those early years in Australia I was sometimes with him while he dissected a body, and I wondered at my inability to handle the situation. It used to turn my face green!

I had a lesson of a different kind the day I stood cap in hand before the Tax Commissioner. He kept me standing only a moment, but it was long enough to feel like a penance for a crime.

'We have given you a bad time,' he said, speaking softly.

And his minions had indeed. They had suddenly produced a list of all my possessions including some private ones, and I wondered how this list had come into their hands. They had taken me into tiny offices and grilled me long and probed deeply, leaving me naked in guilt, although I did not admit it.

'This we think you owe,' they said, 'and we are empowered under the Taxation Act to assess you for what we think you owe us.'

I was set back on my heels. 'Surely you cannot take just what you think I *might* owe?'

But they could, and I went humbly to my banker with the story. It was at a time when I was feeling the many mental pressures on me and encountering trouble at home.

I paid, but not until the chief himself had stood me there on the mat, waiting for another axe to fall.

'Sit down,' he said softly and, I thought, kindly. 'We have given you a bad time. Now let me give you advice probably worth more than we have taken from you.'

I listened wide-eyed.

'Firstly, if you wish, you may take us to court to recover what we have assessed you, but I suggest that you do not, because we have a case, and you might lose. But listen first to me and then make up your mind.'

I was fascinated by the man. He was treating me as an equal while remaining the aloof head of a department with great power.

'There is going to be inflation. Go now and borrow all you can and purchase the largest amount of real estate that you can afford. It will rise swiftly in value and the profit is not taxable if you hold it twelve months or live in it that long. Invest in gold—the profit is not taxable. The profits you make on share transactions are not taxable unless you make a business of it.'

I remained dumb, not yet appreciating the import of his words.

'Do not try to cheat us again; we shall win in the end. The laws I have quoted concerning non-taxable profit have been made for just such people as you.'

I thanked him and if he is still alive I thank him again, for within a short time I had a large property, was mining gold and trading in my own shares and those of others. The advice the taxation chief gave me there on the mat before him was the best any young man can have. Mistakes can be valuable, but only if we learn the lessons they provide.

On behalf of my younger sister Daisy and her husband, Herbert Victor Leonard, I bought the Kurundi and Frew River cattle-stations in the Northern Territory and remained closely associated with their workings. The stations had a common boundary. I was still going further and faster than caution would have permitted, and I was heavily in debt. But Kurundi was a good proposition, several thousand square kilometres of good cattle country plus semi-desert east of the Stuart Highway. The northern border was the Barkly Highway, the bitumen road running east from Tennant Creek to Queensland. The southern border was at Hatches Creek and the western included the ranges that built up to The Marbles. A desert formed the eastern border. Part of the Simpson Desert, it stretches across to Lake Nash and Georgina Downs.

I had another remarkably lonely experience on the edge of that Simpson Desert, running horses. When I got out into that flat, out into the Frew River country, being alone and on a wide plain which is almost featureless, I was completely lost. On this occasion too, as on the trip from Andado to Oodnadatta, I had to track myself back. Tracking oneself back carried a mental strain: knowing that if one failed there could be no assistance. In those days it was not reasonable to expect people to worry too much about folk who were not able to look after themselves.l Besides, the Aborigines themselves had a great fear of that particular flat out of the Frew.

In that area are remarkable cavern-like pits which are frightening in themselves. They have very straight sides, and if one should happen to fall into one of these immensely deep pits, where the flood-out of the Frew goes into the earth, it would be impossible to call out, crawl out, or get out in any way at all. Those pits are real traps for animals or men, and it is just possible that in that area, or some area like it, Leichhardt might have perished, because I have heard from people who have worked there that remains of old pack-saddles have been found.

From experience I can say that the stockmen who ride alone in these desolate areas take their lives in their hands. If their horse were to trip and they were to fall it would be days before anyone would know that they were lost and look for them; and by that time, in that immense heat, they would be dead.

From 1946 to 1956 I wandered a lot in that desert country on the eastern side of the Frew River, looking at the condition of the country, looking for possible waters, stray cattle and, on occasion, for brumby mobs. It is a dry and desolate area, and has given me some awkward days.

I put in a lot of time over the whole huge area of Kurundi and Frew

River, looking after it and handling the cattle. It had been neglected and I realized that to pull it into shape would take the services of the best stockmen available. The best man I had ever had anything to do with in the handling of station work was then managing Durie station above the Birdsville Track for Sir Sidney Kidman. His name was George Crombie. I offered him £1000 a year to come and manage Kurundi and Frew River. It was then a high wage for a station manager and George accepted.

He was a prince among cattlemen, a rider who could cut out all day with a penny between his bootsole and the stirrup. He weaned calves from scrubber mothers, put together plants of fine working horses and hired excellent coloured men. Association with him was a highlight of my life, for the cattle were out of hand and wild and the area was vast. By adding steel yards and handling the cattle continuously in stock camps he brought those cattle into hand and quietened the whole herd, a great achievement.

The sale of cattle from far-out places like Kurundi and Frew River presented a major problem. Bullocks had to be mustered, carefully selected, then put on the road with drovers who walked them down the dry tracks. The nearest killing works was at Adelaide, and to reach it meant a hard 500 kilometre walk to Alice Springs, and then an equally arduous 1700 kilometre journey by rail. The cattle were severely hacked about. So the price we got for the store bullocks was never very high.

When it was necessary to sell bullocks we would set up the mustering camps and travel from waterhole to waterhole, selecting the animals ready for market and slowly assembling a mob which later would be cut out and put in the hands of drovers. This took several weeks, sometimes months, and the work could be accomplished only when the season was right and the feed and water were available.

Setting up these camps for a fat bullock muster required a lot of organization. At least nine men would be needed: a cook, a horse-tailer and his assistant, and six other men to help with the mob. It took six men to comb the country with reasonable care as the toiling mob passed from water to water.

After he had the stations running smoothly George became nostalgic for the life on the Birdsville Track and left. The head stockman, Tommy Parker, also a good man, took over for a while, but he was not keen to shoulder the general manager's responsibility and the job was taken over by Jim Matthews, a drover from the Broken Hill area. After he came to us he became known as Kurundi Jim, and I think he loved the place. He carried on in the footsteps of George Crombie, and later took up the country on the Queensland border known as Tarlton Downs.

The old Frew River station carried the oldest brand in the Territory — OQT. It was first registered by the Willowrie Pastoral Company when it established Frew River. The company built a stone fort for protection from the Aborigines when they opened up the country. I can still see old George Birchmore standing outside the old stone hut when he made the deal to sell me the station. I loved that old stone hut.

The droving plants of men and horses at Kurundi and Frew River were busy the year round. Mustering and branding seldom ceased, this area being south of the monsoon weather pattern and not subject to the long wet periods of the deeper tropics. When the men were not doing this they were likely to be taking our own cattle to market. So it became my custom to hire regular contractors to travel out to the Kimberleys across the Murrunji Track. With a promise of at least a thousand head to pick up and a distance of at least 1600 kilometres to bring them, the big drovers were content to make this a yearly trip. This, with possibly a short trip in the inside country, filled their calendar. I often joined them somewhere on the road and rode with them a few days or weeks. I really loved the quiet occupation of following the herds.

I was determined that my oldest boy Ian should not become the idle son of a rich man. He had experienced the various shifts we had made from house to house, and our progress from poverty to wealth. In his early teens, therefore, I sent him north to Macumba station, where Ernie Kemp taught him about droving and mustering. He was caught out in some big floods, and he experienced the harshness of the Oodnadatta climate. Soon after I got Kurundi I sent him with Tom Parker to bring cattle from Pine Creek in the far north of the Territory above Katherine. There were 350 steers in the mob. We bought them cheap for fattening at Kurundi. Travelling north with some Aboriginal riders and a string of horses, they discovered that the waters on the telegraph line were too meagre to support the mob. Consequently, Tom being the man he was, they searched for and found an abandoned or seldom used stock-route called the dry river route, and they followed this to come out on the Murrunji Track at Top Springs. On this eventful drove they had to discover water as they went along, so Ian served his apprenticeship in a hard school.

I met them at Top Springs and went along with them towards Newcastle Waters. In the meantime I had made arrangements for Ian to go to school in America because I did not care to have him back in the big house on Strangways Terrace, where I feared he would get the wrong impression of life. So he left from his trip on the Murrunji, one of the toughest of stock-routes, to go to Sydney, then San Francisco and Boston where Robert Dawes met him. Dawes was an industrialist who had supplied us with the elastic for our boots, and I had corresponded with him for some years. He had suggested that Ian might like to attend a school in the United States, and if so he would be glad to host him. He was also on the board of Phillips Academy at Andover, Massachusetts, a school with a high reputation which had been founded in 1780—before the First Fleet reached Australia.

Here Ian applied himself to his studies and also to sports, achieving some prominence in that community of privileged lads. He became track captain, and at the end of his sojourn there he won a scholarship to the Massachusetts Institute of Technology. This had been his aim, and it was a considerable achievement.

'I am not as smart as most,' he wrote early in the Andover period, 'but I work harder.'

The Massachusetts Institute of Technology is one of the most prestigious universities of engineering in the world and has comprehensive facilities. It is Ian's pride that although influence gave him a start at Andover, he secured the rest of his education entirely by his own efforts.

One day I was drawing some plans at my desk in the Percy Street factory—not far from my tools and the making of some object for sale. Customers came and went, talking while I worked, without taking up more than my usual attention. Then in the flow of people I became aware of a solitary presence, an old woman, looking lonely and neglected. I said, 'Good day,' and she edged forward haltingly; long black dress, button-up boots, lace collar, wide straw hat trimmed with faded flowers—even in that far-off time she looked as though she had stepped out of another age.

'My name is Weber,' she said. 'I come from Tennant Creek. My husband was a mining man. Now he is dead.'

I did not interrupt her because it was evident that every phrase was hard to put together. She looked exactly what she was, a woman of the far Outback. The black dress underlined the tragedy her toil-lined face reflected, and it was then I noticed her hands: gnarled, veined, black with the sun. They could have been the hands of any old miner, as of course they were.

'I had a son. He was killed in New Guinea. Since then I have worked the mine myself. Now I cannot go on. I came to see if you would buy it. For £72 000.'

'Tell me about your mine,' I said. 'What have you had from it?'

She told me a story of years of sweating and burning under the Central Australian sun and her looks confirmed her words. The lines of suffering were in her face and her carriage. She was stooped with the burden of her primitive life, the carting of water, the cooking for men and the hauling of stone from an open mine pit. She had to be telling the truth.

'Why £72 000?' I asked.

'Well, that's the money we got from the last lot of stone we crushed,' she said. 'And I think there is another lot or more before the mine is worked out.'

'Why did you come to me?'

I could see she was lost for words and tried to help, but helping was hardly possible. Silence was best. The answer came slowly.

'You know the bush ... you have lived in that country ... I don't know anyone else who might help.'

I got her address. She was booked to go back to Alice Springs the next day. I told her I would do what I could but with troubles of my own I did not really believe I could help.

That day my brother-in-law, H.V. Leonard, came to see me, and in the course of small talk told me that he was at a loose end and asked if I knew of anything that might interest him. Again I thought of that gaunt figure. She had haunted me through that day, and without serious thought I asked Len to look at her mine at Tennant Creek. This was exactly in his alley. Within a week he was back.

'It's an open-cut, straight sides, but worked out. Could be some ore in the hanging wall on the north side. There is some gold left there, but how much nobody can guess,' he told me.

My uncle, Hedley Mitchell, was a mining man who for some years had been manager of the Norseman in Western Australia. I took the problem to him.

'Offer the old girl £72 000,' he advised, 'but make it conditional on our winning gold from the mine. It will be tax-free for her, and in the meantime I will see what I can find in the way of an old mining company with an up-calling power on its shares so that we can finance the digging.'

I found old Mrs Weber at her Tennant Creek camp and made our offer. I explained that I did not have the £72 000, but that I would float a company, start the mine again and pay her from the gold we expected to win. Mrs Weber accepted the offer, but she also consulted a lawyer who was smart enough to make a condition that we start the mine within a year and that the money should be paid from the first gold mined.

My uncle selected an old mining company called Australian Development and had it listed on the Adelaide Stock Exchange where its shares had ceased to be called. The shares at the time were approximately a penny each and I believe there were at least a million of them. At this price friends and I bought enough shares to control the company, and 40 000 shares were allocated to my brother-in-law Len.

I bought more than I could afford and paid the threepenny call that we had made on the shares to give us some working capital. We had by this time kicked out the old board and replaced it, on my uncle's nomination, with an old gentleman called Tucker, a man called McWilliams and another, Jack Dewer. P. Meade-Almond continued as secretary, and my uncle and I also joined the board. With the money from the call we bought a small stamper battery of five stamps and set contractors to work digging near the old Weber find.

Jocelyn riding in a hunt.

Point-to-point my favourite hunter.

Ready for polo.

Diane.

The town of Tennant Creek owed its existence to the Depression of the 1930s. It centred on a gold-field where Depression miners got patchy and erratic returns, and a township developed about 1933 round the Overland Telegraph repeater station established in 1872. Malachi 'Jack' Noble, a tall rangy prospector with one eye, was on the field in 1932 and was so taken with it that he sent for friends from Western Australia. They included the Weber family. In partnership with them Jack Noble went east of the developing town and found four deposits—Rising Sun, Weber's Find, Kimberley Kids and the bluff called Noble's Nob.

Noble sold out of the syndicate and for a while operated an hotel in Tennant Creek, where he soon went broke. It was the toughest town in the Territory, with gun battles in the streets. Noble turned to prospecting again, and the quality of the man can be judged by the story told of his setting out from Tennant Creek to go right across the Territory and through Western Australia to the Kimberleys. Noble had very little money and an old utility. He took a load of empty beer bottles from the dump and filled them with water. Knowing that the old vehicle might not get him there, he buried three bottles of water under his tyre-tracks every ten miles as he travelled, so that if the vehicle broke down he could comfortably walk back and have a drink at each camp.

Before the call-up for the development money we had a slight hitch. My brother-in-law could not afford to pay the three pennies on his 40 000 shares. The board of old-timers decided to auction his shares, as the rules of the Exchange provided. We had a board meeting on the day of the auction, and as the hands of the clock moved slowly to the hour of the sale (three o'clock) I pointed out that if we sold Len's shares at whatever the bidder gave, this amount might not reach share value plus the money of the call. I was the youngest of the team and naturally shy of being heard, but if the bidders were not prepared to pay twopence for the shares, the shareholders were not likely to meet the call. We could not risk losing the threepenny call-up.

Other board members hesitated. They were all old men, undecided and hesitant. The clock crept closer to the deadline and the room was in silence. With three minutes to go I picked up the phone, rang the floor of the Exchange and cancelled the sale. We voted Len his three pennies on his 40 000 shares, and when they were split later and reached £15 a split share that call was worth a million dollars for Len. I mentioned that to Len and his reply was, 'But look at the experience you are getting!'

We abandoned the original site where the lead petered out in country rock and proved useless. We rigged a hoist on a new spot 300 metres to the west on the adjoining lease called Noble's Nob. It showed small values from the start, and when mysterious rumours of this potential reached the Stock Exchange we had no trouble in collecting the three-penny call.

Developing that Number Two shaft was expensive and we had little money. The rock was hard, and those were the days before tungsten drills. We had to sharpen the ordinary steel drills in a forge. We had no mining machinery and only the old five-stamp mill. None of us were experts and we hired a leading mining engineer from Melbourne to erect the plant, remembering that time was running out. Under the terms of the option we had to have the plant running and producing gold by 17 October 1947, and by this time we could not hide the fact that the values were fabulous. Every financial exchange has its spies and these things leak out.

A few weeks before the expiry date the engineer came down to Adelaide from Tennant Creek and told us that no power on earth could finish the erection of the plant and get it in operation by the due date. He could have been representing other interests, and as things turned out it just seems he might have been. Certainly he would have known about the incredible values at sixty metres down in the Number Two shaft.

Again the old heads drooped around the board table and when the engineer had left the meeting there was a wringing of hands. Now it so happened that I had in my employ Reg Willing, an engineer mate who was inventive and resourceful. The board gave me leave to take full control for the intervening period before the expiry date, with directions to get things moving. I gave Reg Willing full authority to go ahead with no holds barred.

Knowing that he was doing well, I did not expect a desperate call on the night before 17 October announcing that he could not have the wheels rolling next day because the bull wheel on the top of the stamp plant was stuck and he had no pole big enough to rig a pulley to release it!

'What to do? Is there no such pole anywhere in Tennant Creek?' I asked.

That produced a long silence. Then: 'There is such a piece of steel down at the Number Two Government Battery,' he said, 'but it would have to be taken down and transported up here.'

'Could this be done?' I asked, again into a long silence.

'The pole would have to be cut off at the base with an oxy plant.'

'Have we such a plant and a truck?'

'Yes, we have, but—this is a criminal proceeding and I would be arrested in the morning.'

'Cut it down,' I said. 'Arrange for the bank manager to sign a paper in the morning stating that the wheels were turning on 17 October. Work all night. I will have a plane waiting for you at the airfield in the morning.'

Early in the morning of 17 October I flew him out with the precious document signed by the banker. A criminal charge was laid that day and an extradition order issued to apprehend the criminal who stole the government part. For the time being I hid Reg Willing in an isolated area near Adelaide and I let him take the blame. This went on for some weeks until I knew that the game could not continue, so I telephoned the powers that were holding the gun and introduced myself.

I told them, 'You don't want my man. You want me. I ordered this operation. Can I meet you tomorrow in Alice Springs?'

The meeting was arranged and I remember stepping out of the plane wondering whether the opposing forces would be for sale. If so, I was prepared to pay well. We settled in short order and the extradition was lifted. Reg had weighed sixty-eight kilograms when he went up to Tennant Creek, forty-seven when he came back.

Meantime in the Number Two shaft we cut oxidized ore that crushed 500 ounces to the ton, which in terms of today's values would have been a quarter-million dollars to the ton, or $250 000 000 a day; but then of course gold was worth only £15 ($30) an ounce. Still we were rich beyond anyone's dreams. The mine quarried a lode thirty metres wide and averaging two ounces to the ton.

In the years to come the managers slowly ate away that rich central pillar which was supporting the overhead plant until one night the whole plant went down the deep mine and it took fifteen years to clean up the mess. But that was well into the future.

The drama of development had just begun. Managers came and went, frustrated by the impossibly hard stone and badgered by shareholders to dig more and more gold. It was not impossible to keep the monitor steel up to the underground men, but a hand-forged bit would dig no more than two metres of hole and we were sharpening bits with an old hand-blown forge and hammer-pointing the drills. We burned the charcoal in forty-gallon drums from whip-stick timber too small to make a good fuel.

Someone suggested using compressed air and a star-shaped die for the drill ends; this was an improvement but still slow. The saving factor was the good gold in the Number Two shaft but we had to leave much of it intact in a supporting pillar. Incidentally, it was soft material, and when it did collapse millions in value went down to a great depth in one of the greatest cave-ins Australia has ever seen.

Chapter Eight

Now I was beginning to taste success beyond my dreams, beyond belief. The mines were turning out a steadily flowing stream of wealth. I was engaged in numberless activities. My business affairs were prospering, with the factory in the good hands of friends whose loyalty and good faith were sterling. The mansion we had coveted but thought we could never own had fallen into our laps in a dramatic exuberance of fortune. It was a year too of social activity pursued in an environment of rich furnishings, sweeping lawns and flower-beds, parties and polo ponies.

And then, with a sweep of the arm of God, my mind collapsed. From taking an interest in many subjects, engaging in a rich variety of activities, overseeing business ventures vigorous with growth and promise, I turned to sit by the hour, uninterested and without words. I rejected friends and all who came to reassure me. I had been a man with total control, unbounded energy, enthusiasm for everything that concerned human life—and now I was nothing. Doctors and psychiatrists were brought to my beautiful rooms and gardens, all rejected by me as intruders. I knew what ailed me, but saw no light in the loss and loneliness of what I felt to be personal failure.

I suppose no amount of luxury can turn the man from the campfire into a social butterfly. My unjustifiable guilt, my shame for pretending to be what I was not, possessed me. Perhaps it made it worse that the girl who lived by my side was possessed of grace that eclipsed her humble birth, so that she could ride the crest while I could not. Whatever the cause I was close to breakdown, and could see no advantage in pulling out of this deep despondency.

A wise friend, Major Alec Billing, bought me a ticket to India and shipped me unwillingly to Calcutta, where he booked me into the Great Eastern Hotel so lately abandoned by the British. Here in the halls of past splendour the newly endowed Indians ran the place in a riot of neglect. It no longer excluded the beggars of sad India. Cockroaches roamed the palatial floors, and where the pride of Empire had lately paraded through the golden corridors the dirt and filth now raised a stench.

One of my first walks through the streets of Calcutta showed me people who were dying without care, people who had no hope, no hospitals, no security, no social services. The horrifying aspect of it all centred in the priests and the Levites who turned away; there were no

Good Samaritans in those unfeeling crowds, or none that I saw anyway. I watched people coming down the Hooghly in their small craft. When they met the great tidal bore that comes up the river twice a day some were washed from their boats into the turmoil. Pilgrims near the bank had gathered to wash clothes, hardly noticing that at this little distance people were drowning without help, and caring not at all that they did.

When I moved on across India I noticed how like the Oodnadatta country were the highlands of Hyderabad, and how the people in that area seemed so much like the desert people of Australia. The Punjab of India must indeed be one of the saddest places on earth. Millions of people exist on its mudflats in villages linked by tiny paths, sleeping and eating only centimetres above the level of the water.

I watched the snake men talking to their cobras, unfolding them from their mysterious baskets. I saw men making trees grow from seeds to a height of a metre while I watched, and I saw men floating in air, rising against the force of gravity. I was not hypnotized and I believe they can actually do these things. I experienced the wonderful hospitality of 'Weesak', which is something like our Christmas. It makes the people generous and I'm sure the spirit of that time is good for India. I also talked with women of the highlands of Sri Lanka into whose living places men are not permitted.

I was caught in an outbreak of plague in Madras and had to stand in line to be inoculated, wondering if I would ever get out of this filthy city. At that time there was no commercial way I could; the boats were booked out for months in advance and the planes for almost a year. But I managed to get a flight with a naval survey in an old Lancaster bomber, as far as Singapore. I sat in a box at the tail, and looked out on a crowd of little coastal craft navigating the Bay of Bengal.

The old Raffles Hotel, surrounded though it was in those days by open sewer canals, was the acme of civilized living with its huge, open, airy rooms and its primitive air-cooling system. Those were the days when the 'Great World', the 'Old World' and the 'New World' operated — semi-brothels, centres of entertainment, and exciting to me in prime middle age. I fought my way out of a lane at the side of the 'New World' with the aid of a .32 hand-gun. Later I heard that an Englishman was killed in exactly the same place within minutes of my having left it, and I must record my considerable fear of the 'knife-men' of Singapore. But Singapore was a civilized and orderly community compared with the wharf areas of Shanghai, which I saw later.

Hong Kong, before and after the Second World War, was a relatively clean place, with some wonderful establishments such as the Peninsula Hotel. Here this bush boy found himself sitting among the plush surroundings with a man cutting his hair, a little Chinese girl manicuring his finger nails and another at his feet trimming his toe-nails. I knew I could not stand this treatment for long, but at least it is something to have experienced in this old world.

One of the fascinations of the city to me lay in wandering through its streets watching the craftsmen work. The hand-carvers cutting out the old traditional patterns in camphorwood boxes worked with a speed and accuracy that could only have been possible for men doing the same thing year after year, and in exactly the same pattern. The workers in Hong Kong in those days, for example the basket-weavers with their nimble fingers, toiled for a pittance; in fact I doubt whether it was for much more than their food. Even in those days people lived on the streets, having no homes. Now in 1984 the slums of Shanghai have descended on Hong Kong. It has inherited all the Shanghai evils that were in existence before the communists kicked out the exploiters.

I made friends with a Chinese man in Victoria Street and he has been sending me papers concerning the 'new' China ever since that time. I can't remember him missing a month in the last thirty-six years. Printed in Peking, when they first began to come they were solid propaganda, but now they contain authoritative articles on the Republic of China.

One day I decided to take a walk along the coast. There seemed to be nobody about, the coast was fairly rugged, the day was warm and the sea looked very inviting, so I decided to have a swim. Taking off all my clothes I dived into the water and swam about, enjoying the South China Sea immensely. When I looked for a place to get out of the water I found that the tide had carried me along and was running too strongly for me to swim against it back to my clothes. Then I found out the hard way that the rocks were encrusted with razor-edged shellfish. Further along a simple Chinese girl was gathering them and I called to her for help. She kindly reached for my hand and helped me across the rocks, and although my hands and feet were badly cut, at least I had been able to get out of the water. I felt somewhat ashamed by my nakedness, but I was very grateful to that girl. Perhaps that was the beginning of my long sympathy with the Chinese people.

Hong Kong may have been a British possession but in the days of the ferries, before the subway, the city was very Chinese and it was rare to find an Englishman or indeed see any white face at all. I wandered into a Chinese restaurant and looked round on a sea of Chinese faces. Then I spied one chap, sitting on a lounge behind the door, who looked as though he might be Australian. I went over and sat by him. We exchanged names and I found that he was the Australian writer, Alan Marshall, in Hong Kong broadening his experience. He told me that he worked for the newspapers and that he used the pseudonym 'Dorothy Dix'. But he had had a novel published and a book of short stories, and another novel was in the hands of his publisher. I asked him how, as the advice-giving Dorothy, he dealt with awkward enquiries from women, and he told me that his old mother always handled these things.

Alan had been a cripple, walking on crutches since polio had struck him down at the age of six. He was a very engaging and lovable personality and we spent a lot of time together. In the interests of his quest for experience I suggested that the whole of the east was open for examination of the way in which other people lived. In particular if he wanted to see their dives and places of entertainment it would be advisable to get a permit from the authorities lest we should get into trouble. I do not know how much this contributed to Alan's success as a writer, but certainly we enjoyed the whole experience together.

From Hong Kong I went to Shanghai, the sink-hole of the world in those days and a disgrace to the occupying nations that had been in possession for nearly a century. The Shanghai of today under the communist government has cleaned up the poverty and the horror which existed there. One might venture into the back streets of Singapore, but life had no value in the back streets of Shanghai. The communists have taken the women and the beggars from the streets, banned gambling, eliminated the night clubs and turned the racecourse into a park.

I learned in Shanghai that the revolution was definitely coming. People of all classes had already taken sides and decided what they were going to do. This was in 1948, and in September of the following year Mao Tse-tung made his move from the caves of Shansi and proclaimed the People's Republic of China.

I have had some sympathy with revolution since I first learned to read, or before that, perhaps, when my mother read me stories from the *Boys' Own Annual.* One such story told of how the people who controlled the land in Russia oppressed the masses of peasants so that they were required to live in very poor circumstances. As I asked questions it became apparent to me that a great many poor people in the world were treated as slaves, not the slaves who were property bought and sold, but slaves to money and the masters who employed them. Taking the wider world into consideration one sees that this has not altered much.

In 1917 the peasants of Russia seized an opportunity to change their status. Following the teachings of Karl Marx and the leadership of Lenin they took over the whole country, destroying their oppressors. The evils associated with such a revolution are hard to justify, though the evils it eradicated were possibly greater. The oppressions instituted by Lenin and the leaders who followed him may have been as onerous as those under the government of the Czars; nevertheless these men felt they were doing good and setting the masses free from slavery. Sometimes I wonder whether they have not been controlled by the fear that the governments of the western world were always scheming to eliminate the communism they represented because of its threat to capitalist systems.

There is no doubt in my mind that free enterprise permits a better way of life than the oppression of socialistic control, but the association of money with free enterprise is to be feared. Free enterprise is a necessity in every way for the human spirit, but the oppression which comes from the domination of money, associated with free enterprise, is to be feared to a far greater degree than the oppression of masters.

The answer lies in each person working for him or her self. The great social thinker Mahatma Gandhi set it out: the salvation of India could be achieved only by the return to small business, the making of goods by hand, a resumption of village life. Other nations of Asia have realized this and I believe that in time to come we will see the slow diminution of the system of capital production which dominates so many lives.

Another great social thinker of Asia, Sun Yat-sen, saw that the evil of China was the domination of village life by its money-lenders. My own observation was that they constituted the real evil. The revolution was an uprising against them. This was associated, of course, with the oppression of the landlords who took large proportions of farm products as rent for the land. This ownership, or absentee ownership, is not as burdensome in places like Australia as it was in China, where peasants were treated like slaves and sometimes had to pay their rents twenty years in advance. That cruelty had to be eliminated by violent means. I think the Chinese will again revert to private enterprise but if they allow money to become a dominant factor in their lives again, they will be foolish indeed.

Money should be the servant of the people and I am ardently in favour of the thinking which motivated King O'Malley in 1911 to set up a Commonwealth Bank which was a people's bank. Money belongs to the people and should be kept in its right perspective. The cost of servicing money should never be in excess of the actual cost of handling, distributing or managing. This could not be justified at higher than three per cent, possibly a bit lower.

At some stages in history it has been a crime to be a money-lender; usury was considered a great evil. Today half the people in the world live in social systems dictated by hatred of the money system, and introduced by the revolutions in Russia, China, Cuba and many small countries. In their enthusiasm to get rid of the money kings they have made many mistakes, and possibly the greatest has been the enslavement of the human spirit by eliminating the right to individual freedom such as the right to produce, the right to manufacture and the right to run one's own affairs. Perhaps it has been forced on them because of the need they feel to expend vast amounts of the proceeds of production on weapons, ever updated, with which they may have to defend their systems against a new enslavement.

In the many systems which history has seen tried, difficulties have always arisen in the period before people adjusted their thinking to a new way of life. The problems of defending the system and the great cost of providing the instruments of war are probably the factors holding back the progress of such revolutions as have occurred in my lifetime. I hope this is so, because I like to believe that these nations have genuinely tried to escape the bondage of slavery.

Karl Marx proposed that money should never be allowed to enslave other people. If a rich man uses his wealth to enslave another person he has done wrong. Great fortunes have been accumulated because of tax avoidance through capital gains, in other words the rise in value caused by the pressure of increasing population and inflation on land, property and the means of production. This money, seldom earned by its owners, is often invested to make slaves of other people. For example, some is loaned to borrowers to buy such things as cars, and the interest rates are often in excess of twenty per cent.

This is not as high as that charged by the money-lenders of China, but it is approaching that stage, and eventually people will rebel against this usury. Men will fight against slavery and men will be free, but someone will always find some means of enslaving another person and I have no doubt that history will repeat itself. So beware of the bondage of money, beware of being bought body and soul by an employer, beware of indulging in needs which are excessive, beware of the tyranny of prejudice. The bondage of civilization's needs is massive. So let rebellion be the guiding star of life and thus escape into freedom.

The war instituted by Russia and then by China against the tyranny of capital thus seems justified. In their uprising against the Orthodox Church with its ikons and its corrupt priesthood the Russian people were contesting something they could neither understand nor tolerate. When, as a child, I suggested this to my mother, her reply was, 'These people cannot succeed, my boy, because they are rebelling against God.'

My feeling now is that the changes which have taken place in my lifetime were more likely to have been instituted by the Hand of God than otherwise. The world was well rid of the corruption for, after all, 'Beauty is truth, truth beauty', as the Grecian urn in its silence told John Keats. My early belief in rebellion against evil has, I suppose, been the governing factor of my life. Rebellion against dogmas which had a big influence on my mother's life, certainly on mine in my turn, was the reason why I was not willing to be married in a church, or to accept the dictatorship of a church in such important things as my private life.

Much blood has been spilt in rebellions in India, Algeria, Ireland,

Central America, Indo-China. Most of Africa has rebelled against the overlordship of another nation during my lifetime. Marx insisted that rebellion was something which never ceased, a continual battle for the freedom of the human spirit. The oppression of the blacks by the whites as we see now in South Africa will not be tolerated for long. This is another rebellion now in progress, with its proliferation inevitable. The bitterness engendered by the battle of the Vietnamese for freedom from first France, then America, has sown the seeds of a hate which will not decay in our lifetime. Wherever is repression there will be explosion. We call Germany's battle for living space the 'Great World War'; what we should have called it was 'Germany's Rebellion'.

Oppression by religious dogma exerts a powerful influence still. Mohammedans and Christians both worship God, but will happily kill each other to worship in their own way. The Russians and the Chinese both kneel at the shrine of Karl Marx, but they also would probably fight to the death in defence of their differing interpretations. If those who believe in Marx were to stay their hands and spend more time looking for truth, if those who believe in Christ and those who believe in Mohammed were to settle differences and seek only truth, and if those who believe in capitalism and those who believe in communism were to do the same, we should be at peace.

But they are not seeking truth; they are asserting dogma. The dogma of the Virgin Birth, Mohammed's ascent to Heaven, belief in the essential evil of communism, the inflexible greed of the capitalist, have all brought men to the battle. Freedom, above all, in all beliefs and matters of choice is man's greatest goal.

I am shackled by the conventions of civilization. I am burdened by the traditions of the past. We are cursed because we believe we have sinned against God. We are condemned because we will not join the procession of those who are disciplined by the dogmas of the world. What utter arrogance this is!—that men should believe that they alone, in their own schism, can promote the Kingdom of God, that they are exclusive and privileged disciples. We spend the nation's wealth alleviating poverty; we have not the courage to cure the cause of poverty. We send an army of men and women out into the world to convert it to our way of thinking. We do not believe that all men are in the Hand of God. How weak is our belief!

I have followed the progress of the party which set out, first, to change the destiny of Russia and then, avowedly, to change the politics of the world. I am convinced that there has been no change in the outlook or the intentions of those who caused the Revolution of 1917. I do not believe that the revolution of 1949 when Mao Tse-tung took over China had the same objectives. I think he felt he had enough to handle in China, enough to keep the Chinese people absorbed for many generations to come.

But the people who set out to change Russia avowedly intended to change the politics of the world and have consistently worked towards this objective. I do not blame them. The objective was realistic, given their conviction that it was a life-and-death struggle between their ideology and the capitalist system controlled by the rule of money. Sooner or later one side must win. Marx predicted that the capitalist system would break down, but this has been averted or delayed by new theories of money in great part deriving from the financial dicta of John Maynard Keynes. The World Bank, the Bank of International Settlement and the International Monetary Fund, set up to handle the new system, have several times rescued countries which would otherwise have been bankrupt. Eventually we may have an international dollar.

The battle still goes on. The communist ideology holds that the people of the western world still enslaved by the money system must be released. But we do not need to be saved by the ideology of another country. What we do need is to abolish the slavery imposed by our present monetary system, replacing it with one that can be used for the people, by the people, through the people's bank. Not a political dream, it has been earlier propounded by statesmen with the necessary courage, but of course they were crucified, being ahead of their time.

My travels in Asia at this time did not result in a crop of such reflections, but they certainly made a rich tilth of the fallow ground of my mind. Countless minor incidents from the trip were to colour my thinking for the rest of my life.

The Lido, a large fashionable restaurant, stands on the shore of a small bay in Hong Kong. I went out there to have a swim, and when I sat down on the covered plaza overlooking the water I was surprised to find myself next to Churchill, the popular hero who had conducted Britain through the hazardous years of the Second World War. I had particularly admired him for the sentiment he expressed when he wrote: 'We must beware of building a state of society where industry has no reward and there is no virtue in being a prudent and saving person.'

I consider that Churchill's writings contain the finest prose which has come to the English language in my time. I have enjoyed his story of the charge of the Twenty-first Lancers at the Battle of Omdurman which closed the Egypt and Sudan campaign—the last great cavalry charge of the war, and one in which he himself took part. I appreciated his graduation from a war correspondent to a participant. I admired the fact that, in moments of great stress, when others were worrying, he could sleep. When the public rejected him his wife commented that this might be a blessing in disguise. What a disguise!

It is great to meet one's hero when he is of this calibre. Something like this cannot happen to many people like myself in a lifetime. The man may have done foolish things throughout his career—who has not? He was a man I am sure who was prepared to lay his life on the line. He may not have been a humble man, nor frugal, but he was brave, with the skill to inspire a nation. His great speeches should be treasured in the hearts of all English-speaking people.

I do not make any obeisance to wealth or power, but without question they are the measures of the game that I have played most of my life; and those who measure giving by the gifts they receive, and those who value their good names more than goodness itself, have failed in their appreciation of the good people of the earth. The standards which I had as a jobless derelict on the street in 1929 have not changed a great deal, **but I do measure a man by the means he uses to climb the ladder of success. Success has to be a journey and not a destination.**

I met a chap who was going to fly to Guadalcanal, to Wake and Midway, and thence to San Francisco through Hawaii. He agreed to let me accompany him, and I was astounded by the devastation of the Pacific battlegrounds. They had been fought over to the point at which whole islands were covered with wreckage, the wreckage of aircraft and guns and landing craft and other machines. It convinced me, if I needed convincing, that the Americans fighting over these islands conducted one of the most extraordinary campaigns with unbelievable pertinacity. The fighting ability of the Americans will never be in question in my mind, for I have seen the evidence of this tremendous struggle. The same, of course, applies to the Japanese. Not even the excellent first-hand descriptions of the battles could do justice to the carnage or destruction or courage that was shown by these battling empires.

Chapter Nine

The cities of the Punjab, the Highlands of Hyderabad, the misery of Madras, the wealth and poverty of desperately overcrowded India, all shook my self-centred conceit and pity and left me wondering why I had forgotten the Prophet who wept for the unhappiness of man. Shaken, I had turned to cities further east: Singapore, Hong Kong, Shanghai; and there in the bustling industry of China I saw the immortal struggle of Man the Survivor, Man the Undefeated. Patient, enduring China. I knew then that I was ready to return and start again. But only briefly back to the house of deep carpets and deeper care.

Am I unique in having believed that things would remain unchanged? We enter marriage with its seeming permanence and beautiful promise. Then the family comes and the woman's natural affections shift almost unnoticeably to the children at the same time as the campaign to achieve a family security is establishing itself as the most important function in life for the man. Woman's desire changes, and not so far along the way the partnership encounters a natural phenomenon in which the woman weaves a cocoon of isolation about herself before emerging as a more beautiful butterfly wanting a wider life.

God help us! How we have failed our women! We don't see it because our lives are full. We are always on the move. Our days are filled with action. But when the years of change come women need stability, love and tenderness, and some surety that these will continue with the man loved. We have watched them shrink into a metamorphose of change and accepted the belief that our life together is over, that we are no longer loved, that marriage is no longer of value. Some slog on in ignorant duty. Some opt out and cut adrift. Some become furtive and take other women though still under the canopy of marriage.

Looking back I know that wisdom never protected me from error. I had fought so hard to provide, to succeed, to get out of the pit of poverty, never believing that anything would change. I was confident that these efforts were all that was required of me, not realizing that my partner was a growing, changing individual subject to tides of influence that I could not know or understand. In other words, I was entrapped in what must be man's most universal error.

My wife came from the same clay-pit of poverty that I did. We had shared the same hungry days of Depression, enjoyed the little that we had and shed tears over the same small gains and losses. How then could

I interpret the symptoms when she tired of raising children, wearied of my company and sighed for a different fate? I had no knowledge of the change except what I read on the surface. Some of her protests were designed to shake me badly, and they did.

In desperation and ignorance I wrote off past gains and left. Sometimes I wonder if in a deep understanding of the incurable ignorance of man the prophet Mohammed made his marriage laws elastic enough to cope with this inevitable situation, binding the husband to loyalty for life by keeping his first wife chief among others. After twenty years of believing I went to live by myself, to unravel the tangle of the mind.

I took some simple things and went to live in a one-roomed cottage at the back of where Jack Cadell, my stable-boy, lived in the bush. It was on a fifty-five hectare property I had acquired at Northfield. It was the beginning of my return to the bush, my escape from respectability. For five years I lived thus, cooking for myself, trying to adjust. Everything was altered—yet I had many immediate concerns. One consisted of the development of this property. Diane and her husband built a house there and were concerned with the running of the Northfield Dairying Company. I planted large rose gardens and an orangery and set up rodeo yards. I took an interest in winemaking, supplying grapes from a vineyard we leased. I had an interest in a variety of concerns.

Once I had squared up my many accounts and made my company financially viable I decided it was time for me to leave the factory to run itself and turn to the things I best liked doing. I began dealing in cattle throughout Australia and made quite a number of trips across the top of the continent from the Kimberleys into Queensland. The operation was a success each time.

There were of course no transports in those days and it was necessary to take horses from Queensland across to the Kimberleys by road, making a three-months journey in preparation for the season's droving. We then had to collect the mobs of cattle which would later be walked to Wave Hill, Victoria River Downs, then on through Top Springs to Newcastle Waters. From there they went across the Barkly Tablelands. After the drovers had delivered the cattle to Queensland they would have a spell before riding back for the next year's mob.

The chief supplier of cattle was Tom Quilty, who then lived at Springvale station. He also owned Bedford and Coolibah stations in that general area, close to Hall's Creek. Tom was a great horseman who, at the age of seventy-five, took the honours in a rodeo open to all comers. He was also great company, a popular bush poet and a leading figure in the district, loved and respected by his fellows. Each year I would make arrangements with Tom to have a mob of cattle organized so that we could get an early start by February. I would then go to Springvale to stay with Tom, and this meant proceeding to the old hotel at Hall's Creek, where we would celebrate the occasion for about a fortnight before getting down to the serious business of rounding up the cattle.

Tom was reasonable and honest to deal with. He would let me select the cattle and cut them out, and would encourage me to stay at Spring-vale or Bedford until I was completely satisfied that every beast in the mob was in first-class condition. But even with these precautions, and after having inoculated them against pleuro-pneumonia, we always lost a percentage on the Murrunji Track.

The drove from Hall's Creek to Queensland usually took the best part of six months. There was no particular hurry although in some years, if the Murrunji waters were busy with other cattle, we needed to complete the sections between waters on a regular schedule so that others might water their cattle after us or before us. Each year between February and May a regular procession came down the Murrunji.

Those who came late, of course, did not get much grass, and would also have to bear with the winter months on the Barkly Tablelands, a cold, windswept plain. I always tried to get our cattle moving by February. After getting the drove on the move I would leave the drovers for some time while I carried on other occupations. Sometimes I would be away for weeks at a time, but I did manage to get some droving in each year. I enjoyed the company and the job of walking quietly behind the bullocks, which by that time would be well road-broken. We never at any time lost many through big rushes because Quilty always supplied well-handled cattle and we made a point of getting them well road-broken before we walked them off the property. We did this by shifting them from water to water for several days, making sure that they were used to being camped at night. It was a wise precaution because cattle that rush are sometimes never recovered, and often many are damaged and hurt by being trampled on after they fall in one of these big stampedes. We had occasions on other operations where mobs rushed and did damage to both horses and men and we lost a number of cattle. One herd that came off Kurundi rushed twice in succession and finally were lost entirely.

On parts of the route into Queensland we struck problems. The heavy growth on some edges of the Murrunji was particularly difficult to negotiate and cattle were easily lost in the lancewood. Between Hall's Creek and Newcastle Waters some of the mob would contract pleuro-pneumonia. The law at that time laid down that a mob carrying this disease had to be pulled up at a nominated location (usually where the feed was poor) and kept in isolation until government inspectors cleared them. This meant cost increases, delays and the loss of condition and cattle because of the inadequate feed. So we developed the ruthless but necessary practice of examining the cattle each morning and shooting any that showed signs of developing pleuro-pneumonia. Though we lost a number of cattle we were able to reach Newcastle Waters without the loss of time.

Meantime the jeweller's box of Noble's Nob was still disgorging its riches. Gold by the pound! Gold by the ton! The richest single reef ever worked in Australia, and the richest too by size. Many people including some on my staff were becoming rich because they had bought those penny shares. Scores of near relations—much nearer since I became the Rainbow Man—became wealthy. That was nearly forty years ago, and although the old mine still crushes ore it is now on the tail-end of the lode and barely pays its way. Noble's Nob! Weber's Find! Australian Development! All the same! The gold-mine Jack Noble found and Mrs Weber worked has brought luxury to many.

During the days of our great prosperity when every path was paved with gold we did not react strongly to rumour that told of a fabulous amount of gold being stolen. It was part of the game. We felt rather comfortably about not killing the goose that lays the golden eggs. But the goose was getting fat. The law of Moses that proclaims 'Thou shalt not muzzle the ox that treadeth out the corn' is all very well, until the thieves start to get more than their share.

The thieves in this instance were working at the mine and getting rich. Millions of pounds worth of gold were being produced at this time and I estimated that two bars a month were being stolen. When you reckon that two bars of gold is more than one man can carry you can appreciate the amount we were losing. As the youngest and most energetic member of a board composed of old men, I decided to do something about it. Subsequent years of fighting the gangs brought a fairly complete knowledge of the many and varied methods of stealing gold. Perhaps it might help those who come after if I get out a kind of Gospel of Gold Theft. A manual for thieves and their adversaries as well.

It began in the early days when we were collecting all our gold on copper plates, over which all the ground stone and mud was washed with water. We prepared the plates by pounding silver, mercury, copper and tin into a paste we rubbed with a careful circular motion into the copper plate. The formula is well known, but since that time I have had a Chinese partner so adept at mixing this paste as to make all the difference between the success and failure of a small mine. The plates are run in series, but seldom more than three. The sludge that runs over these plates must be extremely fine, but no matter how hard one tries to grind the rock to powder a lot of free gold runs over the plates and washes down into the dump. In the early days we lost more than thirty pennyweights a ton, which we recovered years later through the cyanide process.

The amalgam of gold and mercury accumulated on the plates was scraped off with a rubber kitchen plate cleaner. However honest the

The family, about 1953. From left: Diane, Jocelyn, R.M. with John, Dene, Thelma with Kerry, Ian.

Above: Harry Zigenbine
taking delivery of cattle at
Hall's Creek.

Al McDonald, my partner
in mining ventures.

Above: Among the tea plants at Karanka.

Some of the Kuku-kuku people worked on the plantation.

Propagating tea plants under shade on our Karanka plantation in the
Eastern Highlands of New Guinea.

wielder might be, his honourable intentions often weakened to the point at which he put aside just a little of the loot for himself. So much for the plates.

As the fortunes of the mine prospered despite these losses we decided to instal a theft-proof grinding pad consisting of a cast-iron pan, about one and a quarter metres tall and the same width, in which a rotating spindle worked shoes of steel over other shoes of steel, grinding and amalgamating all the time. As we opened the pan only once in a while to take out the amalgamated mercury and gold it was quite theft-proof. Then we learned from the underground that large amounts of Noble's Nob gold were still reaching the gold ring, as the thieves' co-operative was known. But how?

Naturally the man who cleaned out the pans had to wear rubber boots, and by wearing boots two sizes too large for him anyone bending down on this unlovely job could fill the boots with amalgam. In this case a few bars of amalgamized gold would not be missed, the output being so large.

I managed to stop most of this leakage by supervising the cleaning of the pans, but obviously a man as busy as I was not able to see it all. I suspect that supervisors in places of trust were not above taking a share after neglecting to watch the act. The stealing still went on.

The flow of gold increased as we installed tungsten steel drills, replacing the old method. The tungsten steel tips were welded into the tops of the drills by a simple brazing process. We had dug and equipped a major three-tier triple shaft. We were ready for progress. We had the mine electrified, powered it with huge engines and installed a modern extraction plant. More gold for the shareholders; more gold for the thieves. The extraction fluid was the most poisonous substance known; a taste of the deadly cyanide that is the gold solvent meant death. I never heard of any of the thieves dying, but the risks they took qualified them as heroes of their kind in the gold-thieving business.

At first they waited until the gold had been dissolved from the ore cleaned up in the huge revolving moleskin sieve and precipitated in the Merrill Crow, which is a machine sprinkling zinc dust through the deadly cyanide as it filters through the machine. It is precipitated as a black dust containing zinc and gold. This is mixed with a manganese powder on a cement floor, using shovels, and the resulting compound melted in special retorts which separate the manganese, mercury and gold.

This powder was easily stolen, but tracing such thefts did not get to the heart of the problem, for sometimes whole bars turned up in the market, proving that the trustees who supervised the final cleaning process were less than hawk-like in their watch, or had matching keys to the gold room. The latter I think is evident.

If the precipitation plant were overloaded the deadly fluid containing the gold was stored in vats on a hill slope. No one would dare go near it without following the correct procedure. Yet someone did dare to insert a small pipe into the vat and start a siphon that piped the fluid down the long slope into forty-gallon drums, rolling them away in the night. I found their precipitation plant hidden a few kilometres away in an old mine. They certainly won that round. I set up a small experimental extraction plant of my own, using the precipitated zinc and gold as my base material, and established to my own satisfaction just how it was done and how long it took. It required quite a degree of skill and experience.

My son-in-law Cecil Cuthbertson, Diane's husband, was a capable heavyweight boxer and I asked him to go to the mine as an ordinary worker. The plan was for him to join the thieves, but under no provocation was he to fight. In gangs like this, might is right and the grades of power are defined fairly accurately. There are the simple thugs and the sneaks, the bully heavyweights and the dangerous hit men. Overall there is the brain. Cec drifted down to the lowest form of life in the gang hierarchy. He kept his promise not to fight and every one of the rotten lot bullied him when they decided he was yellow. He bided his time.

In the middle 1950s, when I was living in a retreat in central Queensland, he sent a letter to say that he had arranged for me to buy some of the gold. I arrived in Tennant Creek suitably dressed, looking like something between a businessman and a working type, not too down-at-heel but a bit flashy. The meeting was arranged for that night at the Tennant Creek Hotel, which is on the eastern side of the main street. I was sitting at a table in the corner by the window when Cec brought in a shifty character in working clothes, a rather small, ferret-like fox-faced man who sat down and made light conversation for a while. At last it came out.

'You're interested in gold?' he asked.

'Could be. At a price.'

'Price is right,' he said. 'Half the going rate. Two thousand quid for a bar.' Gold was then £15 an ounce.

He produced the bar which I covered with my hands on the table, pretending to get a careful judgment of the weight.

'Seems to be light,' I said. 'Maybe it's a mixed lot.'

I was suggesting the bar might have a lead centre. This made him indignant. He strongly repudiated the thought that he would attempt to cheat in any way; there is honour among thieves, after all. He produced a chisel and cut off a large corner of the gold so that I could see for myself. I pocketed the piece of gold—I still have it—and arranged to meet him in the morning to finalize the deal. During the night he evidently was given information that I was the mine representative and lost his enthusiasm. He decided it would be wiser to leave immediately, and fled to Darwin.

That particular bar of gold was never recovered but we had discovered who the thieves were and later recovered many bars of the stolen gold. That same morning Cec retired from the physical end of the mining game and caught a plane to Adelaide. We caught up with the gang in Darwin and had our own private revenge.

In the Tennant Creek of those days one never took risks with dangerous men. It was easy to buy a fight, easier still to incur the displeasure of the underworld. I have employed professional bruisers to be my drinking partners in the town's two pubs. I was the director of the richest mine and as such the enemy. Men who helped me disappeared. Any worker who became friendly with me was ostracized by his mates. An old fellow I knew as Scotty came to me once with some information about the thefts. We talked in the street in front of the hotel, out of the hearing of anyone else. Next morning his body was found floating face up in the dam.

I became too hot to know. I employed a bodyguard because I was determined not to be scared away from the bar in the pub. But only once did I have to defend myself personally against a deliberate organized bashing. The leader was a sturdy thick-necked ringer miner who held the record of being head man in that company. He was a bruiser and had had no training. It cost me a lot of money when his body slithered the length of the bar counter, sweeping expensive bottles and rounds of drinks to the floor, but it might have done a lot of good. Twice, though, I have had to sneak men out of the Tennant Creek area to save their threatened lives.

In one desperate instance I was offered elimination of the opposing party. The price was £100. But I can honestly say that I have never been tempted to let such a contract. I realize that the Wild West of those days was never as wild as the cities of today where mugging, theft and murder are endemic, but perhaps being so closely associated with that west has been a revelation of some weaknesses of human nature.

The 'Jeweller's Shop' pillar supporting the workings had been decreed out of bounds despite its incredibly lavish content of wealth. The gang decided to tackle this nest-egg next and one or two made it a practice to stay down the mine overnight, coming up by ladders through an old working and carrying what they could in bags. This ore produced such a haul that it kept the gang busy for a while, but such efforts contributed to the eventual collapse of the mine. They made enormous hauls at the peak of their operations; how much no one will ever know. I still have the chiselled-off corner of the stolen bar; but if it were not for this I could believe the memories were a dream.

From the time that Ian had gone to Boston, exchange difficulties had hampered efforts to pay the expenses of his education there, and had certainly made it almost impossible to keep him in the manner to which the other boys were accustomed. We had managed to finance it in part by sending consignments of *The Bushman's Handbook* to a friend in Plant City, Florida. He used to sell them as craft books and sent the proceeds on to Ian. This was perhaps a roundabout way of dodging exchange, but it did make it possible to keep Ian at school. When he left Andover and went on to MIT, he was able to maintain some semblance of financial stability by working at the tables in a large restaurant called Walker. He had to get up early in the mornings and go to arrange the tables and help in the preparation of the food, and he continued to do this most of the time he was in Boston. I was able to supplement his funds by a rewarding association I made on Kurundi station.

During a muster there I was riding about eighty kilometres from the homestead at a place called Kurunelli when I came across an old Chinese man who was working a gold deposit with the help of his Aboriginal wives. He had a stamper battery, a tiny affair with three stamps only as high as a man, and this was producing gold. With an accustomed hospitality the old man asked me to have a drink of tea with him, and going out to his lean-to shed he cut some black beef from the dried meat hanging there, and cooked me a meal of beef and onions.

Cam Foo and I became good friends, and when I was working at the station I made a point of visiting him often. One day we were chewing away at the hastily cooked meal of beef and onions when he broke a silence by lifting his head, cocking an ear towards the muted sound of the tiny stamper and saying reverently, 'Music! Music!' I suggested he could make louder music by putting in a bigger stamper which had served its purpose in Noble's Nob and powering it with a modern diesel.

'Partners,' he said. I nodded. The agreement never reached paper. It did not need that to clinch the deal; each depended on the other's integrity.

From time to time I would call at the small mine and during the steak and onions bout Cam Foo would disappear into the little shed and produce some small bars of gold cast in his own special way. He would break them in half without special care as to the precise division, and each of us would take his share.

Mine I smuggled to America at Christmas or New Year, taking them to the gold dealers in New York and haggling over the price, which was then strictly controlled on the world market. Sometimes I would sell it in the bazaars in Colombo and buy English pounds, which were prohibited exports, but which sailors sold cheaply in the money exchanges of India. I could double my money in England by using English notes to pay for cloth for the factory in Australia. Such practices of course broke a lot of currency laws, but I found them necessary at the time.

These old Chinese like Cam Foo were pioneering citizens who lived in the Outback and carried out a lot of the development in the early days. Many of them had worked their way south from the Palmer River to become miners' cooks. Some finally became shepherds, and they lived and died on the Outback stations of Australia. Their numbers included many unsung heroes of the Outback. Naturally, they married Aboriginal girls and the resulting crossbreed turned out an excellent stamp of man, suited to his environment. The men were good horsemen, cheerful and hard-working, and the girls were good-looking. Many citizens in the Outback can trace their origins to this Chinese–Aboriginal crossbreeding.

The girls who married the Chinamen played their part. Few men who worked in these solitudes could find white girls to share their lives — lives which the men loved, but which they could not accommodate to the needs of a white woman. It was natural that they should mate up with the black women who were so much a part of the scenery, so accustomed to living close to nature, to carrying water and living on the food available. The pattern of their lives did not change until a law passed in the late 1920s stipulated that the men must marry the black girls they lived with. I do not think that the move improved the lot of the black girls. Often, rather than conform, their white mates sent them back to their tribes and turned to marry girls not nearly so suitable.

Contrary to the loose criticisms thrown about I found the black women honest and not licentious. They were as good as their white sisters or better. They may not have been great cooks, but they were observant, and they were part of the environment in which they continued to live. They took great interest in the animals and birds around the camps and in everything that happened in nature. Their pleasures were simple and they were fond of their children. Most were clean in their habits and they were loyal. Sex was a function to them rather than an excitement but they were obedient to the man's demands. This made some white men adjudge them much more comfortable than white women to have around the camp.

Because they did not need sophisticated excitement they were quite content to take mobs of goats away to pasture and remain with them all day long, happily and busily engaged in observing nature, watching the small animals, the insects and the birds. They took pleasure in raising their children and carrying out home chores.

Kurundi had its own Aboriginal tribe, a branch of Wailbri. They centred on that area and lived around the station, roaming, as is their way, as far afield as Lake Nash to the east and Hatches Creek to the south. These people were quite happy in the life they led on the station and I believe that had the government not interfered they would have remained happier and healthier than they are today. The boys learned to ride horses and became excellent stockmen. The old ladies looked after the garden, and even the very old could help by chasing the crows away. Others would mend the stockyards and were useful in that way, learning the use of tools. It was our custom to employ everyone who wanted to work. They may not have been working hard, but they were always doing something.

The Kurundi people knew all about the life on the vast area of the station. They would know where every mob of cattle would be grazing, and where every brumby stallion had his herd. They knew where the wild donkeys lived, and even when wild turkeys were about.

We really liked the people of this tribe and I think it is a shame that they have been encouraged, by giving them food and money, to go and live in settlements where there is no work, no occupation and no encouragement, and where the young people drift into a life of total uselessness. They were far better off learning a trade such as stockwork, which came naturally to their own way of life. Now they are the people in between; they do not have the opportunities to follow the ways of their ancestors, nor have they accustomed themselves to living with white people. I feel that something must be done to help them find the pleasant existence which is their right.

Chapter Ten

People came to me with all sorts of propositions when they knew of my successes. They knew I was associated with the running of the big mine at Tennant Creek, they knew I was shifting big mobs of cattle across the top of Australia, and they knew me through the mazagine *Hoofs and Horns*. So at this particular stage of my life I was running many operations.

A woman named Edna Brewster came to me from Coober Pedy. She and her husband Jack were storekeepers there with ambitions to corner the opal market and she needed someone to distribute the gems throughout the world. Interested, I set up a connection with a group of buyers in India and Sri Lanka who would take the lower grades of opal and with one in New York who wanted the finer opal, particularly the black opal. The operation ran successfully for a time, but the Indians, of course, wanted lower and lower prices, and the New York people wanted higher and higher grades. The biggest problem was getting in the money from all these sharp traders, and I decided to collect the New York money in person.

The little Jew who was my client took me from his office on Fifth Avenue to the jewel market, a pavilion where an enormous assembly of gems, guarded at intervals by gunmen, was displayed for sale as apples and oranges are displayed in a fruit market. The lavish wealth of this jewel operation, so casual and so public, amazed me, and I told my client I thought he must be very rich.

'No,' he replied, 'I am one of the smallest operators in New York.' Yet when he showed me his safe it contained a large and brilliant collection of stones, fit for a king's ransom.

He took me to all the spots in New York which might interest travellers; one night we went from nightclub to nightclub. It must have cost him a great deal, but when he put me on the plane to Boston next morning I still had not got the money for the opals—and I never did. He must have thought me very soft, and I was.

The first time I caught a plane in New York to go to Boston to see Ian we were just about to take off when a woman burst through the door; she was the last in and was slightly tipsy. She slumped into the seat beside me and I could not help but notice one of the largest diamonds I had ever seen on her finger. She was well dressed and she spoke nicely. During the trip from New York to Boston she plied me with questions, seeming intrigued by finding an Australian in America. When we arrived she asked if I had anyone to take me out to find Ian. He was living in a fraternity house which I had not previously seen and I did not know the exact location.

A chauffeur in a large black limousine met her, and they toured Boston with me looking for Ian's lodgings. At last we found the place and with a cheery 'Goodbye' she wished me luck and offered me her card, saying, 'If you get to New York, look me up.'

That journey took me to London and Scotland, on through France and then to Italy, but I was anxious to return to New York to have a look at this woman's mansion, as I was sure she had to be something of the order of a princess. When I did get back I called at the address and my princess met me at the door. I asked her out to dinner and she accepted.

The restaurant was a good one and the occasion quite romantic but I had a feeling that something was wrong, and when I returned to her establishment on Fifth Avenue I expected that she would invite me in for coffee, but she patted me kindly on the arm and said, 'Son, I'm afraid I am far too expensive for you.' She had me puzzled. I had not dreamt that she was a high-class courtesan. I must have been very green and there, too, I was.

This trip included my first visit to Rome and I enjoyed visiting St Peter's Cathedral, one of the world's wonders. I was staying with old Santini, with whom I had been corresponding some years. He wanted to print the 'Caprelli Papers', concerning a style of horsemanship he believed revolutionary. He lived in the Palazzo Borghese, one of Rome's most magnificent buildings. People such as Santini were allowed rooms in this great home, originally belonging to the Borghese family, in recognition of their social standing and their history of service to the Italian nation. It was rather dowdy splendour where the old man lived in nostalgia, his old uniform hanging in the room, musty and carrying dust. But he showed me the sights of Rome and further afield. It was very expensive. He at last had someone he could talk to, and someone that would pay. I must have still been very green, and I was.

My main concern on that particular journey was to make personal contact with Will Ogilvie, a poet whom I consider to be one of the best in Australian literature. Born in Kelso, Scotland, in 1869, he came to Australia at age nineteen and worked for twelve years as a drover and horse-breaker before returning to Scotland. So many of his poems celebrated the life I loved. Unlike Patterson and Lawson and others, he had lived that life himself. His poems were circulated through the bush, they entered into the rhythms of the life, and often the men who quoted them word for word had no knowledge of who wrote them. Bush people worshipped such poems as 'From the Gulf' and 'The Stockyard Liar', and I had been familiar with his lines for years, but unaware of his history until quite late. I became conscious of the man behind the verses when we were printing *Hoofs and Horns* after the war, and when many poems came to us without the author's name.

Sometimes I have found poems published without the author's name and knowing them to be Ogilvie's I have remonstrated. Only lately some old character sent in Ogilvie's poem 'My Hat' to the *Toowoomba Chronicle*, and this was published as being the work of an unknown poet, 'probably Lawson'. I asked the *Chronicle* to issue a correction and accompany it with a large article on the poems of Ogilvie, which they did.

Towards the end of the 1940s I set about getting Ogilvie material together. His book *Fair Girls and Grey Horses* was fairly well known in Australia, but some of his other volumes were not. I met J.A. Allen, of No. 1 Grosvenor Road, in London, the man who had encouraged Ogilvie and published most of his works. He provided me with many out-of-print books, and from these and other poems my wife, Thelma, made a collection. I supplemented them with poems I found by searching many publications such as the *Bulletin* and the *North Queensland Register*, and indeed papers in New York, London and Scotland. Thelma copied them out in her beautiful hand and presented them in the form of a volume which I took to London.

After I finished my business there I called a cab and asked the cabbie to take me to Selkirk, in Scotland. I had heard that Britain was a small place, and little did I realize what a long and difficult trip it would be. Snow covered the Scottish roads, and we had an adventurous time before we reached Selkirk. Ogilvie knew that I was coming and greeted me with enthusiasm. He was a great host and I regard my stay with him as a highlight of my life. We discussed what poems should be included in the book I projected.

Back in Australia I had the book published as a joint venture with Ogilvie. In a rather foolish enthusiasm I had 10 000 copies printed, and I must confess it took more than twenty years to sell them. When they were gone I enlarged the collection. I had asked J.A. Allen to gather for me every book published by Ogilvie in England, in Australia or in America, where he had been for some years a professor of agricultural journalism at Iowa State College. The items constituted a large parcel. I also had some poems he had written for *Hoofs and Horns* which had never been printed elsewhere. In 1982 I issued another edition of *Saddle for a Throne*, many copies of which I had bound in leather for distribution to my friends.

The book has had a good reception, and I hope that if it is published again it will contain a selection from his English poems and also those which he sent in his own handwriting to *Hoofs and Horns*. Sir Ivor Hele has made a fine painting of 'How the Fire Queen Crossed the Swamp' and he and others have also used other themes. Some others of his poems have been put to music. Slim Dusty has made considerable use of 'The Man Who Steadies the Lead'.

I would like to find other collections of his work. I believe one was put together by a famous Australian, but I do not know where it can be found. I have personally seen the menu of a dinner held for Ogilvie the night he left Australia, attended by Will Lawson and Banjo Patterson, but I do not know who has it. I am proud that Ogilvie himself should have allowed me to collect and publish his lifework, and consider it to be one of my more useful achievements.

Although London, New York and Rome were my stamping grounds at this time I never did feel akin to these 'people of the asphalt'. Few of the 'wonders' of the world stirred my imagination. I could look at, but never become totally rapt in, the Pyramids or Pisa's Leaning Tower, but I did appreciate the work in St Peter's in Rome, and also the way in which the people worshipped in that great edifice. I wandered freely there several times and found a great deal of satisfaction that here people had spent their lives—given their lives—devoted themselves entirely in the service of a doctrine which fulfilled them.

The bigotry of many religious people has repulsed me but the magnificent works in the Cathedral demonstrate a spirit which is surely akin to that which exists in the great outdoors, where one can feel a relationship with the Creator of all things. In contrast to this, the Golden Pagoda at Rangoon does not have for me the spirit of worship within its doors. I have looked always but rarely found this spirit shining from personalities. They say 'Men sell their souls for gold'. I would change that. Gold sells men's souls.

I have ranged through the world seeking adventure, seeking something which in the end is sordid and destructive. I have met and lived with people of wealth, hovering over their fleshpots. I have watched people intent on destroying game in their concept of pleasure. I have watched the crowds shrieking around their cockfights, their dogfights, their bullfights. I have watched the action in the exciting brothels of Asia and seen the depravity of India, and perhaps Kipling summed it up when he wrote: 'The things you learn from the Yellow and Black will help you a lot with the White.'

Ian said to me once, 'Dad, you are lucky; everything bad that could be said has been said about you.' I do not intend to record an endless tale of misadventure even though, with Kipling, at the end I sit 'dreaming of hell-fires to be'.

Enough – life had been an adventure! Still is.

My business being based on handcraft, naturally on my travels I visited craftsmen in such places as Ceylon, Bangkok and elsewhere in the Orient. Specialists in various types of handcraft become acclaimed world-wide, and over the years I have come to know those who specialize in leatherwork, particularly the experts in plaiting and knotting, and similar skills which are not commonly used except in special places; the greenhide workers of the Argentine, for instance, and the leatherworkers of Italy.

From time to time I have been honoured by having specialist groups, such as those in universities, ask me to lecture to them and to give them demonstrations of my work. My book on leather-plaiting, first prepared more than fifty years ago, has been circulating in increasing numbers and many enthusiasts have come to me personally to have the knots demonstrated when they have found it difficult to learn from diagrams. I feel guilty that very little of the knowledge accumulated through a lifetime is in print, especially some of the more intricate knots which I find hard to illustrate.

Among the most highly skilled in the plaiting business—and I believe I have met or heard of most of them—would be my son Dene. In our factory we have a department where handcrafted, braided or plaited leather goods are put together. I do not think there is any similar department operating commercially in other places anywhere. Many individuals of course carry on with the craft, but ours is a commercial venture. We teach young people and we sell the products in our stores. Dene introduced the professional group to the factory and built up the skills, and today we find it difficult to produce enough high-grade plaited goods to supply the world market.

In a world that is supposedly over-producing I find that goods of the better class are still in short supply, which simply means that not enough of those interested have devoted time enough to make themselves specialists in any particular field. Superior craftsmen in any trade will never be short of work. In this world of opportunity every youngster today could get employment if he or she learned some specialized trade, some skill, some ability. The western world at least is full of unskilled people. The eastern nations, more than half of the world's population, struggle for food—but we expect privilege. When everyone faces the harsh facts of life and comes to understand that privilege is not a right but a reward, we shall return to full employment because there is more than enough work to keep the whole world busy.

Any manual skill gives its practitioner much personal pleasure, particularly when it is one that admits of constant improvement. In plaiting, one of the most intricate artifacts I know is the watch pouch, made from a single strand of leather, that Dollar Mick taught me in the camp at Ettalowie. Based on a knot of great detail, it is always a prized possession of its owner. Over the years I have made a number of these and given some to my sons as Christmas presents, together with special watches.

Dollar Mick was one of the best bush plaiters I knew, but the most respected of all plaiters who made stockwhips was old Scobie who lived at Oorwillallannie on the Birdsville road. He taught his sons to plait but none made quite comparable whips. He was dead before I set out to discover the secret of his intricate knots. This happens. We believe that people will go on forever. The Scobie hitch was almost lost, but I am proud that we have re-created the technique. We do not use it in our manufacture because it is too slow and thus too expensive to be readily saleable.

Chapter Eleven

A bush lad named Stan Norgren managing a stock camp on Rock-hampton Downs on the Barkly Tableland came to Adelaide on holiday, and there a fresh young girl fell for the romantic horseman. Her father, who managed a Jewish importing firm, had brought her up very delicately. Stan asked my advice about taking this spoilt young thing into the land of bush toilets or, at times, no toilets at all. He thought it might be possible to start some sort of business in Alice Springs. I agreed to this and together we set up a saddlery—he was fairly handy with saddles.

The store did not pay well, and Stan did not know about keeping books. He also felt rather confined in town, so he asked if I could get him some droving work. I had a mob of cattle at Kurundi that had to be brought to Alice Springs so I suggested he go and bring them down.

The business came to a standstill with his absence, and his wife became lonely, so that at every opportunity she would telephone along the road to find his whereabouts, and if he were near she would demand that he be given a message to come to the phone. Stan did not appreciate leaving the camp, sometimes to ride many kilometres to a telephone, so I suggested that he find a place where he was at home all the time and had a steady government job.

The Australian Government was then starting a cattle project at Arona, in the Highlands of New Guinea. Stan got the job and went to New Guinea to set it up. The first road into the Highlands was not built until years later and the shortest access to Arona then was by riding up the Markham Valley and then taking a narrow native track which rose 1200 metres up the escarpment in a short distance. Stan being an adventurous type decided he could walk cattle and horses up this precipitous route. In the process he discovered that cattle negotiated the narrow way better than horses. On his second trip he lost several horses over the side. The cattle had to follow a single leader all the way to Arona, and I still wonder how he managed it.

The natives built huts for him from bamboo and thatch and he established the cattle on the kunai grass plain they had developed over the centuries. His next move was to take his wife into the Highlands on horseback, following the same route, a considerable adventure for a city girl. The people of the area—Kuku-kukus—welcomed the settlers and cheerfully answered the call to domestic service, though they were not really suited to it. A primitive people, they cultivated small plantations and hunted pigs and birds with bows and arrows.

Life in those Highlands where the nights were cold, the days were hot and the rain was incessant soon palled for the young wife and she found the continued presence of the Kuku-kukus oppressive. By this time she and Stan had two children and were doing well financially. Although it was all a great adventure for Stan, she was not happy and they decided she should go back to her people in Adelaide.

About this time Stan discovered a fine stretch of rich alluvial soil about fourteen kilometres from Arona in the bend of a river called the Wanton. The only access was by horseback, travelling steep, slippery trails. With Stan I inspected this area and we decided its fabulously rich soil with an average annual rainfall of five metres would be suitable for many kinds of cultivation. Moreover, plenty of labour was available. We decided to apply for a lease on this area and set up a tea plantation.

Tea plantations on the rolling hills of Sri Lanka were infected by blister blight, a disease which it was feared might wipe out the industry there. Assam, the northern district of India where British planters had established tea as the major industry, was threatened by the war raging in Burma, and China had already burst into revolution and would be disrupted for a long time to come. I knew all this from personal contact. It looked as though there would be a world shortage of tea.

An essential commodity for many western nations, tea is also used as a currency in certain parts of Asia. The tea-drinkers of the world outnumber the coffee-drinkers, so it has a considerable market. I felt that the price, then two shillings a pound, would rise to £1 a pound and tea cultivation would be very profitable indeed. In Canberra I found Eddie Ward, the Minister for Territories, sympathetic to the idea, so I floated the Karanka Tea Company with partners Claude Thompson and Will Michelle.

No tea seed was available in Australia, but there was one tree of seed-bearing age at Aiyura, also in the Eastern Highlands, planted there no doubt by the progressive horticulturalists who ran the technical section of the New Guinea Administration. Their chief, Aub Schindler, advised me that suitable soil beds under shade would propagate leaves set into the soil. A single leaf would quickly develop into a bush. They did—thousands upon thousands of them carried in bags on native backs. Aub helped nobly and the project was under way. We grew the tea plants between crotalaria bushes for shade protection and to supply nitrogen.

I brought a tea-planting expert named McWilliams from Assam and built him a nice assembly of houses, some with sides of plaited bamboo. The McWilliams family needed fur rugs in the night, even though we were so close to the equator. Days were steamy hot and the jungle intensely dense, so dense that although we could hear the Wanton River pouring its huge mass over the edge of the 1200 metre drop into the Markham Valley, we could not approach the waterfall itself. I tried many times, hoping some day to find a way to harness this vast source of energy, but the steaming, rotten, leech-filled jungle of vines and trees beat me every time.

We also employed natives to cut an airstrip, no easy task working with shovel and basket, but in time we had an airstrip. Laurie Crowley, who ran a small airline in Lae, agreed to land there. It was an adventurous proposition, even a dangerous one. Sheer mountains encircled the short strip and a dense mist frequently blanketed the area.

McWilliams established the plantation and left, and Stan Norgren came from the cattle station at Arona to be our manager. We tried for years to get a freehold over the land but without result. Dr Evatt was at the United Nations then, and the Russians were giving Australia a hard time over New Guinea, alleging that Australia was doing nothing to aid development. I was on the eve of a trip to the United States myself to see Ian in Massachusetts. I gathered up all the lengthy correspondence we had had over the matter and went to see the Minister. I told him that I planned to hand all this correspondence to the Russian delegation so they could use it as evidence for their attacks if we made no progress in our negotiations with the government. The title came through straight away. That freehold lease must have been one of the first issued for the Highlands.

We grew and processed the tea, put it in suitable packets and submitted it to the parliamentarians with a request for concessions that would enable us to introduce our Karanka tea to Australia. They refused our requests. Paul Hasluck, the next Minister, listened with apparent sympathy, as also to our request for a road to the Highlands, but it never eventuated, just as the road promised us to Mosquito Creek in the Territory had never eventuated. I asked in vain for help with a tea-processing plant—the tea we had already produced came from a miniature plant complete with tea rollers and drying process.

I could see that the Australian Government was not intending to develop New Guinea. The local administration was demanding impossible wages for the impossible labour of the wild Kuku-kukus in our area. I sold the place to that faithful and incredible flyer Laurie Crowley. It was a dream gone sour. But I had seen the birds of paradise, another world.

I sometimes regret that the plantation did not achieve a commercial success, but looking back I feel that perhaps I was too involved with many other enterprises at this time to take a serious interest in this one. It was a hobby job, never carried to its ultimate development. But during these years I had great enjoyment from my travels through the terrain, inspecting the wonderful rainforests, seeing the birds of paradise, watching the development of our gardens, seeing the tribespeople and noting the way they lived.

Stan Norgren had done well managing the Karanka property. I think he overcame the battle of loneliness by taking up with some of the available company. The talent was available for the cost of a couple of pigs and I sometimes wondered if he made too big an investment because on my visits to Karanka there always seemed to be more help in the kitchen and round the house than was necessary. I did not discuss this matter with him, seeing it as none of my business.

The various Christian missions seemed to cause problems in the country. They did not seem to work in harmony; indeed I got the strong impression that they resented each other's dogmas and attitudes, and I am sure the natives must have sensed this antagonism. I think this aspect of the evangelization of the backward nations is regrettable, and not in accordance, I am sure, with the wishes of the Almighty.

I learned that gold was quite easy to find in the Highlands, but being already occupied with Tennant Creek I did not consider that the effort required would be justified. I did watch people sluicing the gold from the hills with the abundant water, and I believe there are vast fortunes still to be made in the Highlands.

Meanwhile in Tennant Creek Al MacDonald, a big, tough part-Maori, asked me to join him in a venture to mine wolfram at Mosquito Creek, about 130 kilometres south of Tennant Creek and sixty-five east of the highway, actually on Kurundi holdings. Al had joined a ship in New Zealand and deserted it in Darwin. Powerful, and good on his feet, he had then joined John's Boxing Troupe, and stayed with it long enough to have fought on every showground in Australia.

This was the heyday of the troupes. The spruiker would line up four or five boxers of various weights and announce they would fight any challenger, the showman reserving the right to select the opponent. In this hard school Al had learned all the dirty tricks of the game, and when he settled in Tennant Creek as a miner they served him in good stead because he became the uncrowned king of the Northern Territory. Big rough men who thought themselves invincible would pick on him in the bar, only to fall before long to his fierce single jab.

The wolfram at Mosquito Creek was in an isolated area where a bore had been sunk for water years before, and the lode of ore was promising, though it was not deep. The price of wolfram at that time was something like £100 a hundredweight bag, so we decided to float the mine, calling it the Falcon Mining Company. This had an issued capital of half a million shares and Al and I each took a fair parcel for ourselves. We arranged with a partner, the manager of a large crushing company in Adelaide, to build a crushing plant in exchange for 80 000 shares.

The plant was built in a quarry in the Adelaide Hills, then taken apart

The house I built at Northfield on the property taken over by Playford's government.

Ian left me some cut wood before he went to the Persian Gulf in 1952.

Above: The first house Ian and I built at Rockybar. The stone walls are two feet thick and the beams are hand-adzed.

Below: The A-frame schoolhouse we built at Rockybar.

Charlie Chambers in 1954—an excellent artist and a good
companion. He helped me establish Rockybar.

and railed to Alice Springs. Trucked from there to the site, it was put together by Reg Willing, who had built the Noble's Nob plant. Reg slaved honestly under conditions which were very rough indeed, because Al ran this camp as he ran everything else, by the might of the strong arm. He ran it like an army operation in which he was the general. This state of affairs could not last long and when Reg had finished a good job he retired from the scene. Al had gathered a team of rogues around him and they did precisely what he said. They had been selected for this enterprise. Al was essentially a rogue.

We were sitting in the bar at Tennant Creek one night, drinking and talking about our future, when a mob of rough-necks drinking further along approached us. One big giant of a man slouched across and said, 'Al, I cut that wood for you, but I haven't been paid.'

Al quietly got to his feet, walked up to him and with one quick silent punch knocked him flat.

'You're paid,' he said.

Al had a tin hut at the end of the main street in Tennant Creek and the principal furniture in that camp was the kitchen stove, a wood stove. His wife Mary was a large blowsy kind of woman; the town knew her as 'Bloody Mary'. I think she gained the name because whenever we went to have tea with Al she would go to the refrigerator at the back, cut off a slice of meat and throw it on top of the wood stove, whereupon the blood ran down the sides. She would then return to the refrigerator, get out a bottle of beer and plant the beer and the steak down in front of us — we were fed. That was Mary's brand of hospitality. She had a heart of gold.

Al raised his two boys in his own image. He had come down to Adelaide in a new sharkskin suit, complaining about not having a car to get to the mine, and I had given him my Packard. Back at Tennant Creek, I was mending a tyre of this car in front of Al's hut when one of the boys came out. Standing looking at me with his hands on his hips, he said, 'I'm going to throw a rock at you.'

'You wouldn't throw a rock at Dad's car, would you now?' I asked.

'I'm going to throw a rock at you,' he said again.

Next moment: bang! He had thrown the rock all right, and I said, 'I'm going to beat the hell out of you!' And I grabbed him and took him in to Bloody Mary.

'This boy of yours is growing up to be a very rough kid,' I told her.

'What do you expect?' she asked. 'Mac expects him to have a fight every day. Every night when he comes home he asks him what kid he belted up.'

'What are you going to do about it, Mary?' I asked.

She said, 'I wonder what will happen to the boys. Neither of them has been christened. Mac won't let them join the church.'

'Mary,' I said. 'I have a very good friend, Brother Mogg, at the Christian Brothers school in Adelaide. I'm sure if I tell him the story he will let the boys join the school, and I will pay the fees.'

'If you can persuade Mac to let them go, by all means take the children,' she agreed.

So I took the boys to Adelaide to Brother Mogg and asked him to educate them. A few months later Brother Mogg rang me and said, 'I think one of the boys would like to be christened.'

'That's good,' I said. 'But I'm afraid his father is going to be very upset.'

Al was upset. He came to me in great distress. 'I think they're going to make a priest out of one of my boys,' he said.

'Well Al,' I soothed him. 'He could do much worse.'

Ironically enough, someone rang me years later. 'You remember that boy of Al's you reckoned would make a priest?' he asked.

I remembered him well.

'Well, he's a member of our Masonic lodge.'

Mac is dead now, but I'm sure this would please him.

It was then my custom to give a scholarship each year to Christian Brothers College, and during the time that the boys were at school I received regular reports on their progress. This is one of the few things that I will be able to tell St Peter if I do happen to meet him at the Gates.

The wolfram mine was a tremendous success. One night I looked into the shed and found bag upon bag of wolfram ready for the market. On the strength of this great asset Al asked me for a loan of £10 000 with which to take his Maori brother back to New Zealand. His brother, he said, was sick. In view of the wealth lying there in the shed I had no compunction in giving him the money. But the wolfram I had been looking at disappeared, and Al had the perfect alibi—he was in New Zealand.

The company could not stand this loss; it had no prospects other than the sale of the stacked wolfram and the price of the metal was declining. I had no option but to put the company into liquidation. I well remember being the only director present at the winding up of the company in the old Wool Exchange building in Adelaide. Telling the shareholders that their money had gone down the drain was one of the most humiliating experiences of my life.

I never did tell the whole truth of why the company went bankrupt. The reason given was that the price of wolfram had dropped so low that it was no longer possible to mine it; but in fact the disappearance of the ore testified that we were being robbed on a large scale.

Twenty years later I chanced to be going through Tennant Creek and saw Al sitting with his head on his folded arms, asleep in the bar of the Goldfields Hotel. I went across and shook him, and he looked up with his bleary eyes and welcomed me like a long-lost brother. We talked about old times, and he said, 'Come back to Tennant Creek. We'll make it again. We'll make a fortune.' And then, as if to clinch the deal: 'I've got a few bags stacked away. Do you want to be in it?'

I realized then that he had planted the fortune I had seen at Mosquito Creek, a buried treasure, and that he was offering me a half share. I refused the offer because my position in the community was such that I was not able or willing to indulge in an exercise of this sort, but I still wonder if those bags of wolfram lie buried somewhere beneath the ground, close to Mosquito Creek.

The Princess Royal Gold-mining Company was another with which I was associated, and which had a chequered career. It was handling a lease called the Black Angel in which the mine had got down to partly payable ore in a mud-stone which proved difficult to handle. This was about 1949, and we did not have the capital to provide equipment which would have made the operation a success. Other companies later took over the Black Angel mine and worked it successfully.

Another lease we worked with very little success was the White Devil, with two mines, East and West. Neither White Devil nor Black Angel were profitable to the degree that we could have developed them into such as Noble's Nob. Another company we floated to work mines in the Northern Territory, principally round Tennant Creek, was called the Red Terror, and here again it was not a grand success.

It must be remembered that the price of gold around that time was roughly £4 an ounce, rising to £15 or the equivalent of $30. One had to work a mine intensively to achieve any significant results at these prices.

Al MacDonald and I were also associated with the mine called Edna Beryl. I don't think we ever floated this company, but we were associated, between us, with many small mining outfits which were never registered companies.

At Mosquito Creek we separated the wolfram from the rubbish by a shaking process on a 'Wiffley' table. The man who ran it was named Jimmy Prince. On the same night that I saw the stacked wolfram old Jimmy called me to his tent. In a mysterious way the old man, who was slightly crippled, extracted a bag from beneath his camp-bed and proudly and carefully tipped its contents on to his bed.

The ore was gold embedded in quartz, probably the best gold samples I have ever seen. The gold was visible to the naked eye, which meant that the samples were fabulously valuable. I inspected them carefully without speaking and then, looking up at Jim, I asked him, 'Where did these come from?' His reply surprised me.

'From the Petermanns.'

I knew that they had not come from the Tennant Creek district because none of the ore around there had that particular colour or was that type of stone. I didn't think it came from Kalgoorlie because the ore there is in a different kind of quartz. This was something I had not seen before and I was puzzled. He told me that the deposit was on the north side of the Petermanns, and asked if I would be interested in getting a plane and having a look.

'No,' I said. 'I don't think so. I'd rather use some camels I've got at Kurundi, take you out on them.'

'No. My foot is crippled as you can see. If anything went wrong it'd be the same for me as the others who had to walk back. I just couldn't do it. Suppose you get a plane.'

I was excited, because the samples were fabulous. I left immediately for Adelaide, and while I was negotiating for the plane there I discussed this matter with my brother-in-law Len.

'How do you know he's been to the Petermanns or the Musgraves or any of the ranges in that area?' he asked.

'I never really questioned him.'

'Well, you'd better go back and make sure he's told you the truth.'

I went straight back to Mosquito Creek to use the knowledge of the ranges I acquired when I was driving camels for Bill Wade. The old man's description of the ranges proved his intimate knowledge. No living man other than myself could have checked the exact truth of his story, for I knew the waters and the identifying marks he described. He had certainly been in the Petermanns, and of course this is, by hearsay, the place where Harold Lasseter found his gold. Old Bob Buck had buried Lasseter at Winter's Glen, and this was within striking distance of the spot where Jimmy Prince said he got his samples.

When I got back to Adelaide Reg Willing and I tossed a coin to see who would go in the plane with old Jim to the Petermanns. But during this time Jim must have had a few drinks, for he told his story to Kurt Johanssen in Alice Springs, and Kurt flew him out to Lake Amadeus in his Tiger Moth.

The dry lake surface was too soft for a landing. The Tiger tipped on her nose and smashed one end of the airscrew, stranding them on the lake, for of course they hadn't advised too many people of their destination. Kurt is amongst the best of bushmen, and first he built a little still to distil drinking water from the brine which filled holes dug in the lake surface. Then, so the story goes, he spent two days looking for a mulga with a left-hand twist from which he could carve a new airscrew. This failing, he whittled away the good end of the broken one until the whole airscrew would balance on a knife-blade. Then he replaced it and, leaving Jim on the lake with the still, flew back to Alice Springs.

It must have been a chancy journey, because with the shortened air-screw the Gipsy Major engine over-revved at any throttle setting at which he could maintain height. Reportedly Kurt, who, it has been said, drove his Tiger like his truck, came back with the engine running at 800 revs higher than the recommended limit of 2500, regarded as top capacity. With repairs made at Alice Springs he flew back and rescued old Jimmy, who still had a billy-can of fresh water left.

Kurt before this had invented a tow which, in negotiating a bend, would make a trailer follow practically in the wheel-tracks of the one ahead. He thus introduced the road trains to the Territory, and in its open spaces transported many loads, on one occasion bringing a railway engine and three other units of a train from Katherine to Alice Springs in a single haul.

I did not see any more of Jim. He disappeared from the camp and to this day we have no idea what happened. When he disappeared his story died with him.

If ever 'Lasseter's Gold' existed, this had to be it. Old Jim may have found Lasseter's Reef, because the quartz in his samples was similar to quartz found in the Petermanns. When Bill Wade and I were there on that mission for the government in 1926 and 1927 it was at least twelve months before Lasseter went into that country.

Another abortive enterprise I contracted for was occasioned in the first place by the revolution in China. Horse-racing was a very popular sport in Bangkok. The horse supply normally came from Mongolia; not race-horses as we know them, but small tough, pony-type animals called griffins. The importer was Alfred Green of the Salyalak Company and he wanted a shipment of 500. A contract for special types of horses at this late stage in the horse-breeding development in Australia was extremely difficult to fill, because not enough horses were being bred in a quantity that would permit selection of the type required by the Asian buyers. However, I was associated with several people in Western Australia, among them Le Steere, who is quite a prominent citizen these days, and we had a lot of mustering outfits trying to get these horses in Central Australia.

As the date for the fulfilment of the contract approached we realized that we did not have enough horses of the correct type to fill the ship. Not only that, but the only ship that could take them was the *Asia Maru*, which Frank Pascoe discovered was in the South Pacific with no chance of making the date. Because there was a large amount of money involved we decided it would be better to cancel the contract.

Others took it up, but I do not believe that they ever made a success of it. In fact I think that before she was fully loaded the ship was ordered out of Fremantle harbour because she was fouling it with refuse.

During my travels in Central Australia trying to buy these horses I came across Eddie Hackman, who was then head stockman on a place called Mount Dare. Eddie has followed the cattle business for many years since then, but has developed now into perhaps the leading bronze sculptor in Australia. He discovered this skill quite late in life and left the cattle business to become the famous artist in bronze he is today.

In 1952 I leased from Hew O'Halloran Giles a vineyard of about twenty-five hectares, nine kilometres from Adelaide. The lease provided that I look after the property carefully, top-dress it with superphosphate and dispose of the cuttings properly. Our first harvest amounted to 110 tonnes of grapes. I was interested in the marketing of the grapes. The vintners paid by the sweetness of the grape, or what they called the 'Baume'—the sweetness of the grape when it is ready for the pressing to make wine.

As the harvest progressed, Italians would come to order a truckload of grapes for their own private processing, treading out the load in their small vats and presiding over the fermentation. They were always Italians who came, and I supplied them with many truckloads yearly.

One day we received a telephone message for one of the girls working as pickers in the vineyard. She was to go immediately to Adelaide because her grandfather had died. She arrived there barefoot and in her working clothes, and her family was obliged to get her a suitable outfit in which to attend the funeral. When she returned to tell me that she had inherited a considerable fortune, she slipped in racing down the steep slope to the house and broke her ankle. She never lost the sense of values she had acquired as a working girl. In the following years I found her to have become a well balanced person who used her inherited wealth to bring up a family in a practical and sensible way.

I continued in touch with all the other interests I had assumed. About 1955 I had another mob of cattle coming over from Tom Quilty in Western Australia and headed for Queensland. The drover sent me a telegram from Wave Hill. He had struck trouble and was pulling out. So from Adelaide Jackie Cadell and I flew up with a load of pack-saddles and at the same time old Harry Zigenbine, his daughter Edna and her two brothers Andy and Jack drove out from their station at Hidden Valley to the Number Twelve Bore with an old buggy and twelve horses. The whole family including Edna, perhaps especially Edna, were accomplished drovers, and their feats were yarned about over a hundred campfires in every season. The six of us took delivery of the cattle at the bore and brought them to Newcastle Waters, where I left them.

I was pretty busy with one thing and another about this time. I was spending half my life in aircraft then, what with the tea plantation and other interests. So they carried on without me and in due course had to dip the cattle at Rankin River before they hit the Queensland border. There was too much arsenic in the dip and old Harry sent me a wire: 'Burnt cattle in dip. Expect to lose a lot.' I wired him back: 'Don't come. Sending nurse.'

Chapter Twelve

A beautiful child working at the offices of *Hoofs and Horns* concentrated on the production of art material, water-colours, oils, etchings, drawings in pencil or pen and ink or charcoal. Her ability was so exceptional that I had no doubt that she would go to the top. One day she took me to meet her mother and stepfather who lived in a small single-fronted house in a rather poor district close to my factory.

By this time I had almost forgotten the struggles of the poor, alienated by wealth as I was, but I noted that their burden of making a living and keeping up appearances was just too heavy, and there came a time when I suggested a way to build themselves a house where they could expand. This had seemed an impossible dream for them and I knew they were too proud to accept charity. I had a firm respect for the stepfather, Jim, who like many others living in poverty sought avenues for improvement. The mother, Jeanette, had a passion for racehorses and a weakness for gambling coupled with a desire to get ahead. My plan involved her going to the races each Saturday and betting to my instructions.

I'm not a gambling man and never have been. My main interest in racing is to see fine horses gallop, but I had a plan I was interested to implement. I was sure it would be a winner. I would establish a pool of £1000 with which Jim and Jeanette would go to the racecourse. I would look up the published odds on the horses running there, and then estimate which horse in each race would possibly win. The plan was to win £50 each week to go towards building a house. If our horse failed to win the first race the amount bet would be increased (allowing for the odds) to win the £50 in the second, plus the amount lost on the first, and so on through the card. When the £50 was won, the day's betting stopped.

This was not so hard, of course, if the odds were fairly high, but if the odds were low it sometimes became an exciting gamble towards the end.

For twelve months we managed to win at each meeting, almost without exception, and with the winnings we bought a double block of land. Within a month we had a plan drawn up for a house, and from week to week we bought materials from the winnings. Jim and I went to work to cut the foundations, set the concrete and buy the bricks for the house.

I found the experiment of supreme interest in many ways. It was an experiment in gambling, and I enjoyed the comradeship of working out the odds each Friday evening. I also taught Jeanette to plait, and now she had three strings to her bow: she worked through the week (admittedly at a job she did not like), she gambled on Saturdays and in the evenings she experimented with her plaiting until she succeeded in producing a fine, saleable article.

The money kept rolling in and the building slowly increased in size. The walls were built and the system kept on winning. The roof and windows were in place, trees had been planted in the garden and the house was nearly a going concern. It now had to be furnished and the winnings kept on coming. They never failed, though the risks were high, and on several occasions the bid for the set amount of money continued until the seventh or eighth race.

The house was finished and my friends moved in. They were delighted and so was I, because we had had a year of excitement and pleasure. Then came the great drama, an afternoon when they returned from the races with Jeanette in tears. They had failed to win, and the last race had taken the stake. The £1000 had gone, but the house now stood as a monument to the success of the project and I laughed the matter off because, at that time, £1000 meant nothing to me. I assured them of the great pleasure I had had in watching their faces as they had won from week to week. They had no heart to continue. It did not matter because they had attained their objective. Jim and Jeanette still live in the house, and the beautiful child who had inspired the project is now married and a successful artist.

Robert Gordon Menzies came to the Northfield Hall one night in 1949. Frank Pascoe and I were seated in the back row of the hall; we lived just down the road. Menzies introduced the Liberal candidate, heard the many interjectors and asked for some intelligent questions. Frank nudged me and I hesitatingly stood and asked the great man if he would keep value in the pound as his predecessor Ben Chifley had done.

Menzies gave his answer in his condescending way: 'Yes, my boy, I will keep value in the pound.'

A friend of mine on the Adelaide *News* used the statement and headlined it. A year passed, and Menzies came by chance to the same hall, and Frank Pascoe and I were sitting in the same seats.

After the usual Labor heckling I stood up and, waving the headline of the year before, shouted: 'MR MENZIES, YOU LIED TO US!'

With his great head bowed he sat, then slowly rose and slower still walked to the front of the stage. Here he lifted his head, smiled and said sadly, 'Yes, my boy! For various reasons of political expediency I did let the pound go bad!'—and then, with the beautiful smile that characterized the man, he boomed: 'But I gave you a lot more of them!'

His advice had hurt me financially but his excuse made me his slave for life. I have never ceased to love and respect that wonderful man. He was a giant, a child, a leader of men, a patriot and, above all, a statesman.

Under war exigencies John Curtin had set up various committees to exert total control over the production and distribution of goods and also exchange. Soon after the war it had been mooted by John Maynard Keynes that Australia should join in a monetary pact that developed into the International Monetary Fund. Chifley was against this on policy because he believed with the Australian Labor Party that such a commitment would tie the Australian economy to the purse-strings of the major powers. Later he capitulated, and it was then that he drew up the provisions for the 1945 Banking Act, as a balance to give better internal control of money. After the loss of the referendum to change the powers of the Reserve Bank he realized he had failed, and I often wonder if his death was the end of the great fight to rationalize money for the people.

Some are still alive and active who remember the academic studies which took place at the end of the war and even before, when Curtin took pains to be ready for the end of conflict and looked ahead to the problem of rehabilitating those who were still suffering from the long period of unemployment between 1929 and the beginning of war in 1939. Some of these had lived the best part of their lives under great duress, and Curtin wanted to have them not only fully employed but socially satisfied.

The Joseph Fisher Memorial Lecture of 1944 in which he considered the problems associated with financing the full employment of the nation was an example of this thinking. Many people were involved in post-war reconstruction. Even Menzies took time off to provide papers to the Institute of Political Science. Then came the incident when he gave me advice on inflation, which he described as 'political expediency'. But Menzies is dead, and the programme that he had some hand in starting is like a spinifex fire that needs stopping. I have no doubt that it can be stopped. Most of the experienced thinkers of that day are either dead or now in deep retirement, but I keep gleaning indications still, because of the deep hurt I experienced in those days. Future law makers should be fully aware of what has gone before.

Many barriers divide the haves and have-nots, and make the transition almost impossible. Some are natural barriers, some deliberately set up to protect the preserves of privilege. A natural barrier could arise from lack of culture, education and example. The labouring man despises the attitudes of those who have a position to hold in their peer group and the pretences of social climbers. The educated look on the uncultured masses as almost sub-human. These are natural barriers.

The wage-earner seldom learns of the loopholes and ladders available to the world of money whereby capital can be accumulated: capital gains, expenses on company accounts, travel and transport privileges available to executives, and general trading costs which can cover standards of living not available and seldom known to people on the lower levels of education and experience. Then the barrier of taxable income stops the small trader from amassing anything but a meagre amount of money, which almost never amounts to wealth. To find a path from poverty to plenty through the maze of pitfalls can happen to someone on the lowest level of education and experience, but it does not happen often.

On my own progression I noted first that the real wealth was held in land, buildings, production and mostly in the handling of money. Those starting with a small amount could accumulate tax-free money by investing in land or shares which rose in value and thus provided capital gains, by revaluing property for a non-taxable gain, by digging gold which was not taxed, by improving a property with deductible costs and later selling for a non-taxable gain.

These options were not available to me as a young man with a family and no home. I seldom had money for children's shoes, certainly nothing to invest. But by accident I found perhaps the only loophole available. It carried great risks but required only steadfast purpose and complete trust in one's self. I discovered that the world of commerce worked on a system of trust: the supplier gave the buyer of goods credit extending to thirty days and sometimes to six months. If one sold goods on the basis of cash with order and banked the price of the goods ordered one's wealth increased in direct proportion to the quantity of goods sold. After sixty days' trading one had the bank balance of sixty days' orders standing at credit, and by delaying payments to the supplier a few more days the credit at bank increased still more.

I traded to the limit of my credit, dug gold where I could find it, bought the largest house my banker would allow, sold when the price went higher, traded in shares when I knew of the opportunity (mostly in my own mining enterprises), revalued my assets when it was legal to do so, and thus slowly climbed from the lowest level of unemployed humanity to a position of financial strength.

When I had done this, my conscience bothered me. 'What shall it profit a man if he gain the whole world and lose his own soul?' 'How hard it is for them that trust in riches to enter into the Kingdom of God!'

Some inquisitive reporter once asked, 'Why should a man who has achieved wealth live as you do in so humble a place and way of life?' There you have the answer. I am no saint—far from it—but some day I know that to support my need to protest the great wrongs of the world in which I live, I will have to be standing firm on the facts of my own life. Although I can never claim to have standing with either rich or poor, still I believe that the Man who flogged the money-changers from the temple still calls all men to the heights of moral courage and spiritual peace. I should like to feel that there lies my allegiance.

The building of wealth creates antagonism in those who have not, jealousy in the less well off. Dispersing in the form of gifts amounts to charity, which is demeaning to the receiver. The accumulating of wealth involves a some-time slavery of those who create it. Living from the proceeds of wealth demands that others toil to serve that wealth, providing food, shelter, luxuries, roads, buildings, services and all that money can buy. This is a great evil.

Possessions require security from thieves and care for maintenance. They invite taxes from the authorities and jealousy amongst the inheritors. Great possessions are a burden of responsibility, except for those who hold wealth as a trust to be administered with dedication. If then, the gathering of possessions is not a desirable or a happy end, what does constitute a worthy effort leading to peace and happiness? The answer has long been tossed around by crusaders and the ethical but seldom put into practice as a rule of life: 'Render unto Caesar the things that are Caesar's, and unto God the things that are God's.' A humble recipe for life, perhaps, but one that offers something better than a scramble for wealth. I cannot claim to render in either category willingly, nor do I feel satisfied that I have been a good steward.

At Northfield I had built a house which I shared for a time with Reg Willing. I had planted a garden, a beautiful garden with a total of 1250 roses in plots surrounded by lawns, a garden that promised to be better than that at Neidpath. Diane and her husband and my daughter Jo both had houses on the estate. We built two dams and planted the property down to wheat and paspalum grass. The vineyard I had leased was adjoining. The property contained three quarry sites which had been in use and which I looked forward to developing. We had built the necessary yards and other amenities for a polo ground and rodeo site. I made arrangements with Greater Union Theatres for a drive-in cinema, and my son Dene was building its terraces and retaining walls. The suburbs of Adelaide were moving up to us, and I expected a considerable increase in property values, but the main attraction was the creation of an integrated centre for my principal interests. I had set out to create another small world, and it was taking good shape, but I was not to enjoy it.

The Premier, Thomas Playford, wanted to acquire the property for the State, maintaining that it was obstructing the northward spread of the city. I walked with him to the top of the hill, a vantage from which we could see the whole estate, and I was quite resistant to his offers.

'Every man has his price, you know,' he said, an absurd and obtuse cynicism to address to a man who sees his dream developing.

'That's as big a mistake as you ever made,' I told him.

But he had his way. He passed legislation to resume the land, claiming the greater needs of the State. I fought it in court with the best counsel but he won and left me with a pile of unwanted money—very much larger than the original compensation offered. I told him that I would not live in South Australia while he was alive and I kept my word. I will not return though Playford is dead and his house burned to the ground.

Resentment was not my only reason for this. I cannot claim a vision or a revelation, but from about 1949 I had become increasingly aware of impending doom and developed an urge to prepare my people for whatever might be in store. Common sense dictated that calamity loomed for the human race but I could have no clear picture of how or when or why. Still, I prepared to search for a place and a way that could mean survival for those I loved. It was just an instinct.

I had been increasingly neglectful of the factory, but there I had the great good fortune to have friends and connections who were loyal and competent, and had long proved themselves capable of carrying it on. We had modernized the boot factory and could claim it to be the most up-to-date plant for making elastic-sided boots in Australia. It would have been the largest riding-boot factory in the world, because it concentrated exclusively on riding-boots, and supplied the bulk of them to this country, basically a cattle country. Despite the conglomeration of buildings it occupied, it had become something of a tourist attraction and was on the visiting list for leisure travellers.

I was forty-nine, but I had lived what I felt to be a lifetime. I had built a successful business and run a successful mine, established a tea plantation and shifted thousands of cattle across the top of Australia with droving teams. I had written a book and edited a paper. I thought it was time to retire and promptly decided I would vanish from the social scene and all the other activities connected with my life.

I packed all the horses that I valued and had learned to love into railway trucks and headed them north to Queensland. I had seven of them, and I took two saddles and four sets of packs. Son Ian had completed his engineering course in America and was due to arrive home. I decided to untruck the horses on the border of New South Wales and Queensland and, taking Ian with me, show him Australia from horseback. Ian and I set out from the border town of Casino at midnight looking for somewhere to camp. We walked on till daylight. By then it was starting to rain, but we decided to carry on and walked all that day, and camped that night wet through. It rained for fourteen days continuously, but Ian did not complain.

Nor did I. From the moment we had the open country before us I had a consciousness of freedom. Sometimes there comes a realization that of all the needs of prehistoric man only lately turned civil, the most important, and to the inner mind the most enduring, is freedom. The man at the bench has not got it, nor has the slave to any clock or constriction of life tied to the wheel of progress. The academic in his academy is bound by the ethics of his discipline and his place in the halls of culture. The farmer is needed at the plough and by the animals dependent on his care. The housewife cries out for salvation from her binding chores. High office demands behaviour that is burdensome beyond the understanding of those who suffer the thralldom of poverty restricting their bounty, if not their behaviour.

Shall we ever know freedom who wear the mantle of success? Can the poor find peace of mind in want? I do not say that freedom from all these brings happiness, but that freedom is a beginning of change, an unfinished beginning. It does not lead to any oasis of safety; it is a bird on the wing, but going at least somewhere.

The essential difference between man and the animals is that man has a God-like quality of being able to change his environment. When he plants a seed he does so with the knowledge that some day it will become a tree, and that the tree will provide shade or sustenance. He plants a garden with the knowledge that some day it will give him pleasure. He preconceives the outcome of his activities. To carry this argument to its logical conclusion we must arrive at the decision that we are responsible for the environment in which we live.

As to the mental environment, I think of my father, sitting with his hands on the reins, his jaw set in a stubborn line as he waited for my mother while she made her vows in a little church. And my mother's silent resignation, not hatred but bitterness, to that which divided her and her husband. I did not know it then, but I know now that nothing whatever can justify the bitterness which exists between the various religions. My father probably came from a Calvinistic group; my mother used to show us pictures of the Virgin Mary. The gaping cleft between the two must be bridged, because its presence contributes to an environment in which man cannot be happy, since religious belief goes to the roots of the human soul and substantially influences human reactions throughout life.

Of the physical environment we can make a choice. I took a young horse out for exercise this morning; he had just been broken and this was one of his first trips away from the stable. He picked his way daintily through the long grass, nibbling here and there, and into a lane we call Lantana Lane, filled with bushes and trees and flowering wild plants. Here we smelled a wonderful scent, as beautiful as any that I have ever smelled on earth. The flower that produced it was barely visible amongst the tall grass, and I had to search to find it. Tiny, no more than a centimetre across, it put forth a perfume that filled the vicinity. Further along were buttercups and bluebells and a scattering of other wild flowers.

Surely there are wonderful places on earth, and when you look a happy environment has been provided. You just have to leave the smoky city and concentrate the senses. The smell of animals grazing is itself a perfume; a horse grazing in the mallee smells of eucalyptus.

Occasionally you will find a man or a woman living alone by a waterhole in the arid, semi-desert country which constitutes most of Australia. What they seek is the peace of the morning sunrise when the quiet whispering breeze brings in the day; the quiet when everything becomes still at sunset and the beautiful colours reach out from the horizon. The wonderful peace that attends this evening manifestation is adrenalin to the spirit.

Uninhabited rainforests in eastern Australia are rich with birds and flowers, ferns and wonderful trees. Thousands of kilometres of lonely rivers, even if they do not always run, have waterholes where wildfowl crowd the solitudes. In the north are beaches seldom visited by man. The desert ranges of the Centre present thousands of square kilometres of high peaks and granite monoliths all practically unvisited and peaceful in their somnolent grandeur.

It is not true that it takes money to visit these places or to live in them, for that man is richest whose wants are fewest. To establish my credibility I can cite twenty years of living in a forest in a house I built from sand, granite and local timber; other years in a wooden hut I built in the Flinders Ranges; the spell in New Guinea growing tea; a year in the Gibson Desert and three years in the desert ranges in South Australia. But freedom to choose the environment should not be negated by enslavement to a daily chore. And lonely places can be crowded if others who are there are not congenial. Their very presence may constitute an annoyance.

A past and present evil is the ownership of many of the most beautiful places by absentee landlords who do not experience the beauty of what they own, and sometimes do not even visit it. The Outback lands should be opened to the ownership and possession of those prepared to live there. Then young people could truly make an alternative way of life for themselves.

In most places it is possible to grow basic foods, like pumpkin and tomatoes, and supplement them with game of one sort or another. In barren ground, even in desert areas, one can rake up the leaves under trees or the mulga to form a mulch and, with an occasional watering, grow excellent tomatoes. There are almost infinite possibilities for those who have a piece of ground from which they may not be shifted.

Every young person looking to the future should be concerned with finding a place to live where the environment is suitable. Too many of us grow up with the belief that we have to have a job, something where regular money is always coming in. This, of course, confines us to areas in which we have been put to work by other people. Other such factors needlessly enchain us.

Freedom is one of the essentials of living. This concept contributes to the healthy outlook of the average individual. The protection and the company of urban society is attractive to those who do not have the ability to abandon a regulated way of life; therefore my remarks must essentially be directed to the minority who have a longing 'to get away from it all' and reject the humdrum rhythms of civilization.

This brings us to politics. If it be true that money is government and government is money we must accept the oppression of money as inevitable. Most people believe it necessary to have as much money as possible, to make their lives comfortable, and because of this world politics centre round the idea that the people being governed find it necessary to have a government that handles their every requirement.

It was very much in the spirit of a search for freedom that Ian and I walked our horses hopefully and cheerfully through two weeks of Queensland rain. We travelled to Roma at the eastern edge of the central west, and from Roma we explored the country in every direction, looking for land with the potential to make a family home. What we wanted was lots of water, an abundance of trees and an area large enough to serve several generations.

Ian had done well at MIT. He had obtained his degree and earned some accolades in sporting activities, eventually becoming captain 'on track'. He had a job to go to with an oil company at Bahrain on the Persian Gulf, but first he wanted to spend some months with me. We covered a lot of country and got into the Carnarvon Ranges before he left.

These are wildly picturesque sandstone mountains that could become a show-spot in Australia. Well watered and timbered, they have an abundant fauna and flora and many galleries of rock-paintings left by the once-numerous Aborigines. Consuelo was a big run situated here in the Ranges, and after I had looked it over I made the Queensland trustee company an offer matching the price asked. But the owners would not agree to the division of value I placed against the value of their cattle. They had 8000 bullocks on their books at thirty shillings a head, which I believed would cause a tax problem if I sold them, so I travelled on alone.

From time to time I would leave my horses and packs in some private care and go off with agents to look at other properties. Money was no object because of the settlement by the South Australian Government for the property they took forcibly from me—and for which they had not found a use thirty years later. But often I found myself alone on deserted roads, and very much aware of that solitude after years of living fast, living high and, if you like, living it up. World travel. Polo. Hunting.

Station life seemed as if it would be the only way of keeping sane.

For diversion I took on the breaking of a string of horses for people at Injune. The horses were really too old to be broken in; they were fine animals but wild and intractable. I was able to break them and present them as horses that could be ridden, but I'm afraid they would never have been much use to the owners. Such horses need a great deal of work to make them safe for the average rider.

I continued searching over a wide area of Queensland for a place with reasonable rainfall, plenty of water and trees, and taking up a large area. The idea was to provide a family home for future generations and to this end I was prepared to devote the rest of my life. I did not mind how wild or rough the country was, or how out of hand or neglected. In fact I was seeking a challenge—one of bringing to order country that had been neglected and was more or less virgin.

I found the place, Rockybar, a 22 000 hectare holding on the upper Auburn River, out from Eidsvold. At this location the river is a rocky small creek, and Rockybar has its name because of the huge granite bar that crosses the river where the house is built, and from which a large waterhole runs back for several kilometres. The fences were down and the cattle were wild. The old hut was still habitable and the waterhole was long and deep. Here I could set up a place where there would always be work to do, a place to live in with something to hope for.

A philosopher in a lonely place has always Nature to commune with. If he wants to work he can clear and till the ground; if he is hungry there is fresh meat. If he is ambitious he can buy land from others not so diligent and so enlarge his world. The jurisdiction of money may be universal, but money's filthy hand gets no sure grasp on the man who lives alone on the land, unless he is foolish enough to go to a money-lender.

All around me in this lonely place, so far from civilization, I could see the hand of the man who had lived his life trying to make something of his holding. The fences he had built so well were now in dire repair; the wire was rusty and the posts rotten, but enough was left to form a tribute to the spirit of the man. Slabs split from giant trees had been cut with enormous effort; gates were made with timber—no nails. Axes were so worn nothing was left of consequence beyond the eye for the handle, and shovels that had been thirty centimetres long were worn back to the butts. Such tools told their tales of calamitous poverty and hand-blistering toil. The body of this old battler was buried not far from his hut. If a man has a spirit to live after him, his will always remain at that place and I was proud to follow in his footsteps and try to re-create his dream.

Close by, within six kilometres of the homestead, is a barren area too rough to be of any use for cattle or anything else. Bare rock and patchy

Above: Erica, with our children, Michael, Mary and Peter.

Below: John—we called him Mr Fixit.

Charlie, a natural artist, made this sketch of Ray Crawford, who was
then President of the Roughriders Association.

Kerry with the swag and packs of his trade, about the time he brought the herd from Hall's Creek to Alice Springs.

Saddling up for a wild horse race at Warwick in 1970. I am behind the head of the dark horse in the middle.

spinifex fill deep valleys between its eroded sandstone cliffs, in which the weathering of centuries has cut deep caves. Aborigines have decorated the cave walls with their drawings of spear-throwers and their hand-prints, and in one place the settler who pioneered the place had cut his initials alongside. The music of the wind in the barren crags had a powerful effect on me. Is it possible that our whole developing civilization is fundamentally irreconcilable with the instincts and feelings we have inherited from our Stone Age forebears? We are very much responsive to our instincts and in part we walk the corridors of memory.

When it rains, for example, I have a great urge to get out and plant things, to stir up the land. I have made various forays into the world of agriculture. Growing tea in New Guinea necessitated my learning the propagation and cultivation of tea bushes. I had an adventure into growing oranges and lemons in Adelaide, and I have made several huge rose gardens which I have loved very much. Later I was to set up an irrigation plant at the Rockybar waterhole to grow hay, and later still I propagated eucalypts, camphor laurels, grevilleas and melaleucas here at my home near Toowoomba, and still do.

Seed gathering is itself an adventure towards which young people should be encouraged. Understanding of propagation and cultivation could well be taught in schools since trees and plants are so much a part of the world in which we live. Most people would like to live in a garden but too few learn to produce an area of trees and bushes which would please their senses and give them a feeling of peace. Knowledge of agriculture and botany should run parallel with a knowledge of history, for a person who has never learned history cannot understand either the present or the future. The person who does not know geography cannot understand the topics of the day. It is impossible to expand the curriculum of learning to include everything concerning the world in which we live; nevertheless an individual should have the ambition to know the subjects which concern our environment.

I loved the sandstone caves at Rockybar, the hidden springs, the thick scrubs and the tall timber. Wordsworth wrote: 'Enough, if something from our hands have power To live, and act, and serve the future hour.' I felt I had to do something to serve the future, the future of my people. My translation to Queensland was not an end; it was a beginning.

I had the seven horses that had been for so long on the road with me, the constant companions of my travels. Each morning I saddled up and looked around my domain. The place was big enough to ensure that no one person could truly understand every part of it in a lifetime. Wild cattle had bred up in sheltered valleys without ever knowing the hand of man, and were shyer and wilder than most wild animals. The only way to get near them was to sight them and then chase them at full gallop till they were exhausted.

To bring such cattle to hand one must subject them one by one. Yards can be built round water in such a manner that when the cattle enter them they cannot escape, the openings being set close together and lined with angled spear-points, but this is unworkable in well-watered country. Sometimes they can be coaxed into herds of quiet cattle. But even when such wild cattle are captured and placed in the confinement of small paddocks, they tend to break down the fences and escape. Even if they do not, they take a long time to become accustomed to the proximity of men.

I had an Aboriginal boy about eighteen years old with me. He had been one of those who had mustered the property before I came to see it, and I selected him because of his quiet but strong manner. An exceptional character who seldom spoke, he had a quaint slow smile. If he noticed wild cattle ahead when we were riding together he would never turn to speak to me, but indicate what he wanted me to understand by moving his hand behind his back in the Aboriginal sign language, and I would range up alongside so we could plan our campaign. Sometimes it would be to capture a wild scrub bull. Sometimes it would be to take an old mother cow with her calf, which we would do by knocking her over, tying her up, taking off her horns and then bringing a mob of quiet cattle round her.

This was slow hard work, mostly taking one beast at a time. I had bought a small nucleus of quiet cows, and to this we slowly added the numbers of our captures. We would blindfold some of these wild cattle, others we would peg through their noses, we knee-hobbled some, and we had some dragging chains. We seldom had to kill a beast, but we would kill the incorrigibles for meat.

We would ride out fifteen to twenty-five kilometres in the morning looking for tracks, knowing that most when we found them would have been made by small mobs of cleanskins. When conditions made it possible we would drive as many as we could of these unbranded cattle to a fence and then, by one staying at the tail and the other on the wing, we would race the mob down the fence until they were pretty well exhausted and then, with some luck, get them through a gate into a paddock.

At one stage I had 417 cows and calves of this type stacked up in a small paddock. I rang a dealer named Geoff Curaton and asked him if he wanted to buy some cheap cows. He agreed to buy them and pay £17 for a cow and calf, and sent his drovers to pick them up. I'm ashamed to say that I did not tell him how we had captured these cows or what problems he might encounter driving them away.

The men he sent were good drovers but the job was almost impossible. They set out on the eighty kilometres to the railhead and I don't know how many they lost on the way, but I do know that some of the boys came back trying to recoup their losses, because I found their tracks among my herd. I did not mind too much because I reckoned that if they had as much trouble replacing them as I had had capturing them they had earned their money.

At Christmas time Curaton rang and offered me several hundred quiet cows. I felt a bit dubious, thinking perhaps he wanted to pay me back in some way. I inspected the cattle about 160 kilometres away up in the ranges and found they were a fine line of Poll Herefords, so I bought them, borrowed the agent's branding iron and branded them on the off-side ribs. But that night it rained. For six months we had the wettest season on record, and the Dawson River rose in full flood, making it quite impossible to swim the cattle across.

By June I decided something had to be done and took a team into the ranges to get them. The country was in a deep boggy condition, the fences down and the cattle scattered over a wide area. We could not find them all, but the vendor generously offered to make up the numbers. Looking for the cattle in that rough country I came across large caves in the deep sandstone erosions. They contained Aboriginal paintings and burials. Birds crowded the frequent lakes. Native animals were everywhere.

Eventually we brought our full complement of cattle to the Dawson River, which was still in fair flood about the end of June. We held our horses at the banks and wondered whether it would be feasible to launch the herd into the fast current. The high banks below the crossing place meant that if the cattle swirled downstream they would not be able to emerge for a considerable distance and would possibly drown. We took the risk and followed them in on horseback.

The river was about 150 to 200 metres wide. Some of the cattle turned in midstream and swam back, then circled, creating a dangerous situation of course in the swift current, but we managed to push the majority to a negotiable bank and lost only a few downstream.

I must confess I am desperately afraid of cattle milling round in midstream, especially with horses not totally experienced in river work. Like people, horses panic. I have known them lose their heads and scream and set out to pursue anything that floats. At one stage of this exercise I lost my grip on my horse's tail and was obliged to dive under water to escape the threshing hooves.

These reasonably quiet bought cows formed the nucleus of a herd for future breeding. One by one we whittled down the scrub cattle and settled the place down. Odd stray mobs still have not been brought to hand, but we treat these as fun cattle and if anyone wants a mad dash through the scrub it is an adventure to ride after these cleanskins.

In 1955 I married again. Erica Marjorie Nunn was a fine young horsewoman whose help I had enlisted. The relationship developed and we tied the knot in a civil ceremony at Gayndah. Two years later, on 7 April 1957, I returned home from building a stockyard several kilometres from the homestead to find a great state of disorder. Little David, our baby, had been struck down by that affliction of childhood in which the limbs go rigid and the breathing becomes difficult. The nearest doctor was at Eidsvold far to the east, but our telephone line didn't go there. Slung from trees, the line ran almost 160 kilometres to Theodore on the Dawson River. From there the message had to go to Rockhampton, and from Rockhampton south through Gladstone, then back inland. The long circuit produced a shallow imitation of a voice that was difficult to hear. I pleaded with the Eidsvold doctor to come quickly, a drive of eighty kilometres. But he refused, and as the baby's condition worsened I became more and more desperate and rang constantly. He still refused, and the child died in my arms. We were heart-broken and wept out our sorrow to the wailing wind, for there was no one to share our grief. All I have of baby David is his tiny footprint which I had planted in cement on a wall a few days before his death.

Only recently I have learned that a pioneer family lost five children in this same place. In 1861 a family had left Sydney by bullock wagon and after months of travel had selected this same waterhole to build their home by. The five children died, and the family abandoned the selection. These women of the Outback who pioneered and loved and lost are the country's great heroines.

Chapter Thirteen

Ian came and joined me on Rockybar in 1958. After working in Bahrain for some years he had taken a job with a Scottish company building a railroad for the French in Nigeria. It ran from the port of Lagos to some oil installations they had in the desert north of Lake Chad. Ian was based mainly at Maiduguri, a town in the highlands, and at this time the country was in a ferment of trouble between the tribes. The approach of independence hotted up ancient enmities, and it became evident to him that the Ibos, the tribe with which his sympathies lay, could be overwhelmed.

As the project pushed steadily on towards Lake Chad it traversed deep valleys of rainforest, and in these forests malaria, typhoid and blackwater fever were endemic. Ian developed typhoid and amoebic dysentery and he became very ill. At crisis point, when it seemed that he might die, he was sent to Kano where he was well looked after, as I can record with everlasting gratitude. He went to Beirut later, on convalescent leave.

Beirut, the capital of Lebanon, was then one of the most active religious, financial and cultural centres of the Middle East. It had three universities and was also the seat of several archbishops and bishops of differing Christian communities. It was also the sin capital of the world. Ian was in no condition to do any sinning himself, but he can tell tales of the debaucheries of that city which were many and varied. For a small price a woman would copulate with a donkey, and such exhibitions were commonplace.

I doubt that such centres as Beirut ever descended to the utter depravity of ancient Rome where men were killed for the pleasure of the populace. It interests me that some of the more depraved cities of the world of fifty years ago are now utterly changed. Beirut, of course, has been reduced to almost total ruin, and Shanghai has been cleaned up by the communists. Singapore is another city purged of its licentiousness. I am wondering if and when such cities as Hamburg will suffer the fate of Sodom and Gomorrah. The greatest theme of history still is, and perhaps always will be, the unending story of men's efforts to reconcile order with liberty—the two essential ingredients of a truly great civilization—and we should take comfort from the fact that every reversion from error exerts a mighty formative effect on man.

Looking at the way in which some of the communist nations have cleaned up their bad spots I hope that in some degree they have recognized the dignity of the individual, or they might have to reckon with an aftermath which a seventeenth century epigrammatist, Friedrich von Logau, put succinctly: 'Though the mills of God grind slowly, yet they grind exceeding small.'

Ian returned from Beirut still a sick man but on his way to health. I had already allocated him a share in the property on the Auburn, and he immediately came to me and worked hard, throwing himself into the tasks of quietening the cattle and rebuilding the fences. By this time he was in his late twenties, and despite his international experiences he was mentally prepared to start a new life, saying, with Tennyson's Ulysses,''Tis not too late to seek a newer world.'

On one of our first rides into the bush together we came across a pair of young, active cleanskin bulls, two to three years of age, with sharp horns. They were fighting, and so preoccupied with their battle they did not run away. I explained the procedures we used. After we chased them till they were in position we would leap from our horses, grabbing them by their tails, and throw them to the ground. Normally this was well within Ian's ability and in the belief that he had regained enough speed and strength to handle the situation he leapt from the saddle and grabbed one of the bulls by the tail.

He found himself unable to pull it down. They circled round and round, the bull trying to get at Ian, Ian trying to keep his place on the tail. Obviously something had to give.

'What do I do now, Dad?' he yelled.

I had always carried a heavy Colt .45 revolver for such contingencies, which did occur at times, and I set to work pumping lead into the animal, but the bullets, though fired at close range into his head, seemed to have no effect. Grim and dangerous, the situation was escalating to crisis by the moment and I had no option but to jump from my horse, place the barrel of the .45 in the bull's ear and fire. It was the last bullet left in the chamber and the bull dropped dead. There are times when one gets hurt at this game, but it's a small price to pay for the entertainment of dangerous living.

Since I had already allocated Ian his share of the property, we set to work, when he told me he was getting married, to build a house on a sandy flat facing the Auburn River. We carted stone, sand and timber and had the stone walls built within a few weeks. We put in the big beams, cemented the walls, put in the plumbing, plastered the interior and capped the house with a tile roof. It was entirely a home-made effort, even to the electric wiring. We won the sand painfully, spadeful by spadeful from the local creeks, and the granite from the nearby hills. It took us two months to build, and the thick granite walls would withstand any onslaught of storm or time.

I watched with interest Ian's adventure into marriage with Daphne. Love is always a lottery; you buy your ticket and wait on the draw. But Ian, I think, was blessed by fortune. Trees were planted about the same time as the house was built and now surround it to make a fine windbreak; and when the family gathers or the local people come to a party there, the lights illuminate the trees and the lawns and gardens Daphne keeps so beautifully. With its little stone A-frame school and the row of stone cottages which contain the bedrooms it is a lovely place, and I sometimes wish that old Mr Hamilton, the man who pioneered the area, could come back and see that his work has not been in vain, that the place is now settled and that his spirit lives on. He pioneered this country and had little contact with civilization. He set the example for generations to come—a true pioneer.

It was not possible to spend much time on just building, as station work was constant. The timber ranged from tall—very tall—spotted gum to dense wattle, and getting cattle out of that thicket was a job for more days and months and years than I had reckoned on, but one by one they were brought into the fold and the incorrigible old scrubbers sold to make a place for quiet bought cattle. Every day in the saddle, and I loved it. Chasing headlong through the timber, throwing and tying the wild ones, leading them by blindfold and nose-peg back to the station yards. Within five years the worst of it was over. But drought was still forcing the shifting of cattle, and there were fences to build and mend, ticks on the cattle to be killed by constant dipping and chemicals, and the deep swim-through dips to be kept clean—a constant boring task.

But I found joy in the days in the saddle, lapping up the peace of just riding through leafy jungles of eucalypts and wattles picking up stray mobs, and chasing after bulls that the musters had missed. These had to be chased and brought to the ground, held and castrated, and I would mark their ears with a sharp knife, using the earth as carving board. Repairing neglected fences was the worst duty, an almost endless one, as for 160 kilometres the wires were old and the posts rotten with age. But we slowly brought the boundaries into useful condition, cleared the best of the neglected acres and picked them clean of timber.

Our son Peter Murray was born the year that Ian came back to join us; Mary Ann was born eighteen months later, and Michael Andrew little more than a year after that.

We had experienced some wet years, and in one of them, when the fences were washed away, we wished for dry times—but then came the drought. Our rain usually falls between November and February, and in this summer season the grass grows which will provide our winter feed. When this rain failed we had to look for agistment. One such drove took us south into New South Wales and involved dipping the herd several times. When at last we arrived at the border with a large herd of mixed cattle we waited our turn to go through the dip at Stanthorpe.

The night before we went through the dip the cattle rushed. We were camped in a narrow lane just near the gate, and the herd was spread out along this lane for a couple of kilometres to the west. About two o'clock in the morning we heard them thundering towards us and we raced for our horses, getting there just in time before the lead cattle hit the camp, which of course they wrecked completely. They spread over a large area.

Ian, riding a big chestnut, crossed a barbed-wire fence in the dark, hit the wire and cut his horse's throat right round. It required many stitches and continuing care to save its life, but fortunately the wire had not cut the windpipe.

It took several weeks to gather the cattle from among the isolated farms and old tin-mining camps in this part of the Granite Belt, but eventually we took them through the border and into New South Wales and on to Boonaboonoo, where I had discovered ground freely available for agistment. It was a wild rocky complex of granite cliffs, very rough indeed, but it did have some feed and the agistment was cheap.

Sheer mountain faces and dense undergrowth made getting cattle out of Boonaboonoo difficult, but when they had put on some condition we did get them out and took them on through to southern New South Wales. We sold some to a chap at Bourke and others at Singleton. We had sales at various places until we had sold them all, and eventually got out of those cattle quite well.

Because of this heavy withdrawal we had to build the Rockybar herd up again to an adequate strength. In mustering the cattle to take them south we had deliberately missed several hundred young heifers, and these formed the nucleus of our breeding herd again.

In 1965 as the drought persisted we walked our cattle north towards Moura on the Dawson River, then west towards Springsure. This proved to be one of our most difficult trips because we found that the Queensland Government had foolishly allowed the reserves and their waters to be let to the local people, and when we arrived at each camp we had much difficulty convincing these people that we had the right to water our cattle, or to yard them in the reserves put there originally for just that purpose. This is a great wrong, and should be corrected.

The stock-routes of Australia should always be available for cattlemen to shift their herds in time of drought; the bores should be maintained and the reserves looked after. In Queensland this has not been done and over the years many bores and reserves have got into bad repair. By comparison, in New South Wales the various reserves have been maintained carefully and kept fenced and the waters looked after and policed. The stock-routes in Queensland are in vast disarray and I cannot speak too strongly about this evil which should concern all citizens.

The same could be said about the Murrunji Track in the Northern Territory where the bores have been allowed to get into disrepair. Until they are maintained it would not be possible for cattlemen to walk their herds through from the Kimberleys.

The drought continued for many years and in February 1969, when no rain had fallen that summer, I could see nothing growing that would keep the beasts alive over the winter, not even bushes suitable for browsing. I made a scouting trip over the whole area of southern Queensland and northern New South Wales, and in my travels came across a section of country that had not been used for many years, a forest area called Wongongora, roughly sixty kilometres long by sixty wide and badly fenced. It still remained, of course, under the jurisdiction of the Queensland Forestry Department, but had been leased to a man in Chinchilla who had kept the lease going but had not paid the rates. Consequently he was not difficult to approach, and when I asked him if I might use Wongongora he gave me a sly sort of smile and said yes, I might. On enquiring from others as to what this sly smile might mean, I learned that he had put cattle into the forest many times but had never taken any out. On one occasion he had turned nearly a thousand head of young cattle in and my informants doubted that he had ever got a hundred of them out because they were so difficult to find or drive in the intensely thick scrub.

We were desperate and anything was better than nothing, so I went back to the boys and told them it was possible to use this forest area, and that there was feed there. The difficulties seemed enormous and to other people perhaps insuperable. We gathered our cattle together as carefully as we could, because they were very weak. Wongongora was 160 kilometres from Rockybar, and we walked the herd there by slow stages through the various stations along the stock-route.

Before we set out I asked my company in Adelaide to provide me with 400 large Condamine bells. Such brass bells have a special ring, and can be heard over long distances. The company also made straps from specially thick hide. We passed the cattle through a race and at various intervals strapped a bell round the neck of a cow which seemed strong enough to carry it. When we released them into the forest the clanging of the bells was overpowering. Distance gradually tempered the clangour as the beasts spread out deeper and deeper in among the trees, and we wondered whether we would ever see the bulk of them again.

The job was now to fix the fences. This meant riding long distances every day, carrying the wire to fix the posts that were down, and we at last managed to get some semblance of order into them.

The large area of forest alive with unbranded cattle had been the unofficial precinct of locals who were jealous of their self-claimed rights. When they wanted meat they went into the forest with a rifle. Others who were capable stockmen had trained dogs to take cattle out of the forest, when they could get them. When I discovered they were taking small mobs of my own cattle regularly because they were quiet and easy to handle I began to carry a rifle and advised the powers that be that I intended to protect my interests.

Riding the boundary of this big area was more than a day's work. Some days I discovered that I was more than a day behind the thieves and had to track them to their destinations but I do believe that I recovered most of the stolen cattle. I then decided to take the war to the enemy and advised my boys that we would ride the whole area surrounding the forest so that others would see we were looking for our own cattle. We left as many tracks as we could, usually leading into other areas of dense forest and difficult to follow.

We heard rumours in the district that somewhere in the depths of the forest stood a huge set of stockyards which these people had used for generations. We searched diligently for these yards without success, and we were there for at least nine months before we stumbled on the huge enclosed area. By the look of the ground it had been trampled and used for many years, and some of the tracks were recent.

In the meantime we had been living in the forest. Erica at one time brought the children to us and taught them under the trees. Our camps in Wongongora were pleasant ones; there were some large waterholes and the trees were dense and shady.

On our travels we discovered there were cattle everywhere. Bullocks that had grown up in the forest had got to know the various areas of good feed and were grown into huge beasts, five and six years old and older; some were enormous cattle. The bullocks, of course, were branded but the cattle which had been bred in the forest were not. Mothers had two generations of calves with them and they would run like hunted deer when they heard us come. But they were gradually getting used to the sound of the bells on our own herd, and after a few months we found it possible to drive even some of the wilder ones towards the yards. This we began to do, in expectation of getting our cattle away.

We set to work to cut a road into this hidden stockyard, expecting that we would eventually muster our cattle into it, and this is what happened. In due course the rain fell and we arranged with a young fellow who was starting up a carrying business to take a few cattle out every day. We would yard some cattle, release those that were belled, and truck away the young beasts that were unbranded and those of our own that were unbelled. The forest gradually became easier to muster because the belled cattle were easy to find and the others would be herded up with them.

It became obvious that we would not get all the cattle so we put salt licks in places where it was easier to muster them and the wilder cattle came in to the salt, as cattle do. There came a time when we found that most of the wilder cattle were congregating at the salt licks, and among them were our own cattle with bells.

When there were no new tracks left in the area we decided that we had got all our own cattle and most of the wild ones too. The exercise was profitable because the unbranded cattle we had taken more than paid our way with the agistment. But this was an exercise I would not care to repeat. Riding through the scrub was difficult and sometimes dangerous at the pace required.

A young tall athletic Indian chap we had with us at that time loved the game of chasing wild cattle. He thought it fun to leap from a galloping horse to even a well-grown bull and throw it either by the front leg or by the tail, an exercise requiring great skill and ability. I doubt if many people have ever seen this done. Of course in the days when cattle were handled more intensively many great old stockmen practised this custom on the big holdings. I do not think the matadors of Spain faced wild bulls so utterly dangerous, yet this was done here in lonely places and amongst thick timber. There were no cheering crowds to watch.

Towards the end of those drought years the Department of Primary Industry had discovered that cattle given licks of a mixture of molasses and urea and phosphoric acid maintained health and condition even though the available grazing was extremely poor, and they would ingest materials they would normally ignore, such as wattle and whitewood leaves, and prickly pear. We eventually had several score of such lickers and we have used them many times since. Placed at the waterholes where cattle congregate, they consist of drums installed in such a way that the cattle learn to rotate them with their tongues. The mixture of phosphoric acid and the waste products of the sugar cane and urea is compounded in a mechanical drum at the homestead, then taken out to the lickers. The cattle like it and its ingestion enables the production of protein in the cow's rumen. We would never need to shift cattle away from our stations again. The discovery has revolutionized the drought position; even though it is expensive it is cheaper than shifting the cattle.

Ian used to get up early in the morning to let water into the mixing tank which was mounted on a truck; then having tipped a bag of urea and nine kilos of phosphoric acid in, he would turn on the molasses and leave it to run while he went home for breakfast, because molasses is a slow, viscous material that takes a long time to run through a pipe. On one occasion he forgot about it and came back to a truck standing in a molasses bog. We had that bog for a long time. Even though we heaped dirt over the top of it, it remained a sticky mess, a reminder not to leave the tap running.

In times of drought water brings us a major problem despite its essentiality, and this especially so where dams are the chief watering points, because as the waters recede the cattle have to tread over ground that is ever wetter and boggier and more difficult to cross. In their weakened condition cattle go down in this deep mud. Every day it is necessary to ride out and check these boggy dams and try to pull the cattle out.

Unfortunately few of these beasts can be saved, for cattle come to lose their will. Occasionally you will pull one out that gets to its feet and walks away but this is rare. More often they lie back and die, especially if they have been in the mud for long. Towards the end of the drought we had managed to get every dam provided with small pumps and tanks, and fenced off in such a way that the cattle had to water at troughs on hard ground nearby. In this way most of the cattle can be saved during a drought. Bogging is without doubt one of the greatest hazards in such seasons.

1970 came in just as dry and short of feed as its predecessor. We had had enough of the dense forest and did not care to repeat this experiment so we took our cattle on the road and went north. It was a painful journey for many of the cattle were weak. When we came to the boggy edge of a dam or a river some would sink up to their shoulders, and many of these had to be destroyed. Some horses will pull cattle from the bog by means of a rope attached to their tails, so we developed a knot which held tight, and often we saved individual cattle by pulling them from the bogs with one or two horses. That year we went into central Queensland and eventually left the mob on agistment with a landholder who had feed.

Long before this, the two youngest sons of my first marriage had joined the little community on Rockybar. Both were born at Strangways Terrace, and John, the elder of the two, lived there long enough to develop an appreciation of the rich surroundings and the beautiful gardens. At school he showed potential as an engineer. We called him 'Fixit John'. He could fix anything, and this skill combined with his lovable nature and generous spirit made him a special person. He was never a keen horseman though he showed ability to ride and muster when he went back to the station to help his brothers. He has more than a touch of wanderlust; he wants to explore the whole country and indeed has covered a lot of Australia, getting to know his land and acquiring a much wider experience of it than most other Australians. He is also widely read. He has an interest in the classics and a familiarity with the literary world which surprises me.

His brother Kerry was too young when he left Strangways Terrace to have retained many memories of the mansion there. Thelma encouraged him to become a man of books, or in other words an accountant, but he showed no aptitude for this work and within a short time of his leaving school I was able to place him with a friend of mine who was bringing cattle across to Alice Springs from the Kimberleys. This was a great adventure for a young man, or for any man, because it turned out to be one of those very difficult droves and it set the pattern for his life. It was a rather drastic initiation into the cattle business because the waters were so far apart, sometimes as much as sixty to eighty kilometres. Once he had survived this long overland cattle drive, with all its adventures and hardships, things would never be the same for him again, and he was quite happy to settle down and work at Rockybar.

Kerry was not particularly good at his school work, and in the years after he left school he didn't read much, but like most young men he became interested in the 'girlie' magazines. This improved him out of sight. Eventually he graduated and arrived as a reader and something of a scholar, He has never looked back, and though he has lived for many years in lonely places he is now an educated man.

He developed a love for cattle and for horses before he came to help Ian as a cattleman, and later to take some small part in ownership. As the years went by he became an expert in many branches of cattle husbandry which marked him as something different from the ordinary cattleman. For instance he became skilled in artificial insemination and in spaying cows, specialties of considerable worth.

His next ambition was to run his own establishment. Ian helped him to develop a partnership which became profitable and he was able to buy a place called Dingaroo, a rather small property in comparison with some cattle-stations, being only about 8000 hectares, but probably having more fattening potential and carrying more cattle than many places two or three times its size. He has a special affection for this place and has developed it well. He and his brother John put up a fine set of steel yards. They have developed waters all over the property. They have cleared it; and with it he has the makings of a successful cattleman.

The fifteen-year drought broke in September 1970 and by that time I had had enough of fencing and fires and drought and bog, and with Adam Lindsay Gordon's 'Sick Stockrider' I was saying it: 'I've had my share of pastime and I've done my share of toil.' The three children, Peter, Mary and Mike, were of an age at which they needed higher schooling. Erica had patiently taught them and brought them to a standard from which they could carry on at public schools, a fine achievement because it meant instilling the capacity to adapt to the new ways of teaching and the new mathematics. None of the three appeared to be scholastically brilliant, but I was comforted by the thought that when I had left school I had not been really literate, and that I had had some success without the aid of higher mathematics. I intended to leave the station to Ian and Kerry, and for the second time I set out to inspect Queensland, this time with the idea of buying a small place close to a high school.

I purchased a run-down farm on the Darling Downs. Evidence of poverty was everywhere: old sheds built from secondhand iron, pigsties which had become dilapidated, stockyards which had fallen down, fences that had slowly become washed into the ground. Rusty barbed wire was lying everywhere, together with piles of accumulated rubbish. I brought in a bulldozer to accomplish the clearing up and trucks to haul away the rubbish. I cleared the place bare and started afresh.

I grieve for people who have lived out their long lives on such properties, being unable to make a decent living and finding no hope because of their poverty. As Thomas Gray mused in his country church-yard:

> But knowledge to their eyes her ample page
> Rich with the spoils of time did ne'er unroll;
> Chill penury repressed their noble rage,
> And froze the genial current of the soul.

But as the 'Elegy' also tells us:

> Let not ambition mock their useful toil,
> Their homely joys, and destiny obscure;
> Nor grandeur hear with a disdainful smile,
> The short and simple annals of the poor.

Many of the sons of pioneers in their poverty went unschooled into life, lived in ignorance of the world around them and died believing that they had had it good. All this has changed, for of course few men would grow up in this modern age of communication without knowing something of the great world around them.

Old Bill, who had sold us the place, kept coming to see what we were doing with the plot of soil he had loved and lived on for so long, the place where he had tried to match the endless task against time that was never enough. He was old and gaunt, a tall old eagle of a man with a spirit that looked out of his eyes and seldom got as far as his tongue. He knew that he should never have sold the place. He kept coming to me with offers for old pieces of iron which I was sending to the dump. He watched the stables being built and knew that soon horses would be back on his old farm, and I think he wanted to live the old days again, even if it meant cleaning up the stables, which is exactly what he did. He came and camped with us and shared the resurrection of old times.

One morning we missed him at the usual breakfast table. He was not at his camp or anywhere about. He had taken off early to visit somebody close by and, driving his old utility something like he had driven his old buggies, he had met a fast-moving vehicle head-on, and that was the end of Bill. We missed him very much. He was the last of a generation, one who had walked behind the old single-furrow plough driving one horse; one of the generation that had dug post-holes deeper than they needed to be.

The Darling Downs, like other great black-soil plains of the world, are almost devoid of trees, and the previous owners had cut for fencing posts the few they had found on the property. I set about planting trees, hundreds of them. Some grew and some didn't; I chose some that would withstand frost and some that wouldn't. It took a long time but at last I have the varieties that will grow and have planted them in great numbers. I may not see them in their full growth but they will be there for my children to enjoy.

I accomplished this by using large amounts of mulch, straw mulch when I could, after an initial deep ripping to allow water into the soil. This changes the ecology dramatically. The black soils are alkaline and the acidity of the rotting straw changes it to neutral, or the acid that trees seem to prefer. I made a potting mix of granite sand and red laterite soil with well-rotted stable manure, a mixture that brought the plants up well when the pots were stood in a centimetre of water. Native trees were transplanted into fairly deep pots when they were quite small, a couple of centimetres high, and then planted out as soon as they were advanced enough for an outdoor life.

About 1972 Erica bought a property close by and went to live her own life. I must admit that ambitions have kept me constantly straining at the leash. I have always been up and going, always anxious to enter into new enterprises, new adventures, seldom allotting enough time to the noble art of staying married. So it was chiefly my own fault that two marriages had been failures. But with it all I would have preferred to live a stable life, a routine life, a settled life.

I could never claim to have been a glamorous type. I am not tall, and my face has been bashed about in the vicissitudes of the years. My nose has been broken many times and my front teeth have been screwed back into the butts now and then. This usually came about through being associated with violent men, men of spirit, men who cannot be bullied and will defend themselves when necessary.

Ian's comment that I am a lucky man, that everything that could be said about me has been said, was true. Such a dishonourable reputation takes some living up to and it was in periods while I was unattached that I established this elevated standard of dishonour. Though at other times I have been the model of upright citizen I seemed then to have no such standard to preserve, and the world was wide.

Long ago a good mate of mine whose life was exemplary received a letter from one he trusted—his girl. Jim did not hesitate. He walked into the bush with his open cut-throat razor and justified its name, cutting his throat from ear to ear. I then made a solemn decision that when something such happened to me I would walk over the hill and keep walking. No razor solution for me. It happened, and I walked over the hill—many hills!

Some take consolation in liquor, some in drugs, some in seclusion. Being free, I looked out on the world at large and realized that there was much to see, many lives to live, secrets to investigate. I do not want to pose as a Lothario, but with freedom one wonders if perhaps there has been something one has missed. I can lay it on the line that within given rules there *is* much to see, and many eager ones to share the adventure.

Deep in every experience is a new world, and one needs to get close to others in an intimate way to know what lives are being lived. Kipling devoted one of his best known poems to his women. His last lines were:

> But the end of it's sitting and thinking
> And dreaming of Hell-fire to be.

True for Kipling perhaps, but that is not how it affected me. My own nature required a permanent relationship, and although I must confess to having seen it all, I do not care to discuss the many special ones, the many curious ones, or the worthless ones; but for future generations who might wonder and never have the chance to find out I would like to put it on record that what most, if not all, women need is to be loved and for their loved ones to be faithful. This is probably the one good thing that a scoundrel can pass on to those who come after him. It is the punch-line of this book.

So much for confession. Not so long ago a famous author wrote to ask if he could write my biography. I was at a loss for a reply until I remembered Adam Lindsay Gordon and the excellent answer incorporated in his 'Confiteor':

> Go to! Shall I lay my black soul bare
>   To a vain self-righteous man?
> In my sin, in my sorrow, you may not share,
> And yet, could I meet with one who must bear
>   The load of an equal ban,
> With him I might strive to blend one prayer,
>   The wail of the publican.

The author did not reply.

I have often wondered what brief advice I would like to suggest to those who come after. Having considered this well over a number of years I can say now with confidence, 'All that needs to be said has been

Above: My great horse, Shiekie.

Below: Reaching the top of Bonner Pass in the High Sierras, USA, during a 100-mile race in 1968. I finished 19th out of 220.

Above: Erica beating me by half a second in a Hundred-Mile Gold Cup ride.

Below: Getting our breath back after the race.

Right: Kerry in 1980.

Below: My eldest son Ian.

Above: Mary as Toowoomba's Carnival Queen.

Right: Mary, Miss Rodeo Australia.

said, and anyone willing to know the truth on any matter can find it through simply seeking.' This is not dodging the issue. I could turn to ethics and say, 'Know thyself!' or to religion and say, 'God is Love!' or to cynicism and quote 'Religion is the opiate of the people', but I do now have a strong conviction that *God is no man's debtor.*

I have not taught my children religion, but I would like to believe that they are trustworthy. This will be sufficient. God does not live in temples made by hands. God is everywhere. It's a pity that it takes a lifetime to come to any conclusions.

Thinking of religion I cannot help recalling that saint among sinners, Billy Wade, pleading there under the stars with his God, wrestling with the Almighty for an answer to his immediate problems and then heading out into what cannot be described other than as an unknown waterless wilderness. That is faith. I like to think I might have been the horrible type sent to rescue him from time to time. At least that is another slender thread in the argument I am preparing for St Peter. Time is marching on.

Chapter Fourteen

Home in Queensland in my new way of life there, I was now alone, but never lonely, for the passing parade interested me immensely. I was bitterly conscious of having failed in two marriages and sadly disappointed, but I was determined to salvage something of my life by taking a greater interest in my children. Also I had learned that the veil which hides the face of the future is woven by the hand of Mercy, and that many times the road from disappointment leads to new and unexpected satisfactions in a freshly ordered existence. I realized that I was richest when my wants were fewest.

So I settled down to grow a garden and create a simple place of peace and beauty, believing sincerely that 'one is nearer to God in a garden than anywhere else on earth'.

The study of botany is unending. It would take many lifetimes to understand the plants which grow on earth; even families which are so common to Australians, the eucalypts, the melaleucas, the acacias, the grevilleas and the eriomophelas, each of which includes many hundreds of varieties. Not all the eucalypts will withstand frost, some are easier to grow than others, some need an acid soil. Success can be achieved only through experimentation, and the same applies to each of the other families.

The garden of trees and shrubs which I am slowly producing will eventually be a place of beauty. The birds are beginning to gather in the trees, and I have hopes of contributing something to knowledge of the area.

With peace and contentment my attitude to life underwent a sea-change. I had left the busy industrial world in 1952 with an overcrowded mind which almost persuaded me to shut off the whole hectic scene. Living in the bush where no telephones rang and no perplexities worried me, I slowly recovered my interest in life in general, and with the reading of many books gradually became a more settled person.

With my past behind me and nothing particularly demanding in the future I discovered that my interest in the whole wide world became more intelligent and more intense, and I developed an increased ability to handle situations. At the age I then was, statistics would have relegated me to retirement, no longer useful as a contributing member of society. But I believe that many an oldster would probably prove very useful if he had time and space in which to recover from the fiercer battles of life, and in still more advanced years would be a wiser and more competent executive.

I started to take a deeper interest in the affairs of my company, which was still trading profitably in Adelaide. I had been fortunate in the loyal friends and relations who had carried it on, knowing my state of mind and suspecting that I would never recover. I have not reassumed a total control because I believe that those who so successfully developed it into a prominent company deserve to hold that pride of place. They were my son Dene, my good friend and brother-in-law Mike Cummings (who was also a son of the rebel leader of the 1891 shearers' strike), Eric Dragon, another rebel who escaped from Europe and has been better than a son to me, and Keith Stevens, who came to me as a boy looking for a lost cause and developed into a brilliant organizer, editor and dedicated publisher. Those friends still sit on the board of what has become one of the most successful of private companies. They deserve the credit. I have been largely a figurehead.

For thirty years I had enjoyed the security of having a top man as chairman of my companies. John Swain was the son of an old friend who had made a lot of money with me in the mining days. The father had called me one day in the late forties to organize a luncheon at the Botanic Hotel on North Terrace, in Adelaide. At the luncheon he told me, 'I will not be with you very much longer, and when I go I want you to promise that you will make my son John here take my place as chairman of the companies.' In exchange he turned to John and extracted a promise that he would at all times respect my wishes in the control of the companies.

This deal made over the table stood for thirty years, and John was a remarkably efficient chairman, bringing the company through difficult times to considerable success. But all this was over. John had been trading in many ways and had gathered a considerable fortune. In his travels round the world American friends had advised him that there was a considerable likelihood of the dollar collapsing, and they had suggested that Australia, being in a vulnerable position and tied to the American dollar, might not be a good investment for his money. They suggested that there were places in Europe which might be safer for him if there was to be a crash of western currencies. This vulnerability of the western currencies was obvious to anybody who had considered the the financial statements issued by the great banking institutes of the world. I had no doubt that he could be right, and did not take serious exception to him trying to protect himself in this way.

On his leaving Australia the position of chairman became open, and although I had wished that my son Dene might have taken the chair, he didn't feel that the time was yet ripe for him. Conscious that I had neglected the business for thirty years, and feeling able and willing to go back to do some work to make up for those wonderful years that I had been almost on holiday, I took over the day-to-day running of the company, not from the comfort of a managing director's chair at a table, but using my communication facilities. I continued living at the farm place in Toowoomba and, more or less from the seat of a saddle (as it was my custom to ride almost every day) I conducted the affairs of the company. I used telephone, telegram, telex and various communications such as regular messenger services. This system worked well because with the clear thinking possible on rides in lonely places I was able to give a considered opinion on many matters which may not have been so well thought out if I had been in the cluttered circumstances of an office where many people had access to me.

It was an exciting juncture, because the nation's economy itself was subject to the heavy winds of change. Two governments had continued to lower tariffs, and cheap goods were coming in from Asia. It was up to us to improve our techniques in the production of goods and also to make sure that our standard of quality was so high that the Asians could not copy us.

But it is not enough to produce a good article. The article has still to be sold, still to be marketed, still to be placed before the public. To this end we opened first a retail store in Adelaide. It was quite an adventure, because the rates in the Adelaide Mall were high. Nevertheless the project was a success and we moved on immediately to Collins Street in Melbourne, and this business, though small, continued to be a success. We then took over expensive premises in Castlereagh Street in Sydney and from this beginning we realized that the captive market of our own stores was probably the answer to our problem.

We continued expanding into the Mall in Brisbane, and from Brisbane went on to set up another business in Parramatta on the Sydney outskirts. The Parramatta store was not a success so we closed it within a few months having experienced our mistake, for as the philosopher has said, 'Every return from error has a great formative effect upon the human race,' and certainly this was a lesson to me. The next move was into the Mall in Perth, and this looked as though it might have some success, although slowly. We failed to be established in Alice Springs, but kept that as an objective.

Our business with the American Tandy Leather Company was expanding, for we had bought a half share in their Southern Pacific activities, and this had been a standby giving us considerable turnover. Although the profit margin was low we continued to trade profitably.

We had used trade fairs to gain access to the American market, and although we discovered that it was not wide open to us we did manage to gain a footing with some of our lines, particularly our saddle dressing, and later our clothing which became fashionable in the United States.

Most of our competitors amongst the Australian manufacturers who were producing boots similar to ours, although not of the same high standards, had found Asian competition too great and had for the most part collapsed, leaving us, not exactly with a monopoly, but with a considerable part of the Australian market. The Australian Standard Boot Company, owned by Johnson of Sydney, had ceased to exist when the old man died. Our chief opposition, Dixon's, had gone into receivership. Baxters of Victoria had been propped up by the New South Wales Government. Friths of Adelaide had tried to match our product but had not had great success. Another competitor who had watched with interest our venture into retail stores had set up similar establishments in various cities, but through lack of facilities of production similar to ours, and possibly because they had not maintained the high standard of quality, were soon in receivership.

This did not leave us with a monopoly on the Australian market because of competition from cheap Asian and Brazilian imports. I am convinced, and would like to see the politicians of Australia similarly convinced, that if the Australian working people are to be kept in employment at the high rates of pay which they enjoy, it will be necessary to have some protection against imports from countries where people are prepared to work for ten cents an hour.

My son Dene had been a strong force in keeping the business on the rails. His mastery of the many facets of business life surprised me. He became considerably wiser than I had been in the handling of money, and he learned the intricacies of the manufacturing trade to a degree that I had never mastered.

Dene was raised in the elegance of the big house. I believed at the time that this would not make him the working man I hoped he would be, and I set him to work as an apprentice to Harry Groves, an old friend in the building trade, a first-class bricklayer and stonemason. Dene became a master bricklayer and certainly a most efficient stonemason, proving it in later years by building a magnificent stone house to live in.

Dene married Alda Boccafuoco, a cultured and ambitious Italian girl who, I am sure, helped to promote Dene's ideas about achievements within his grasp before that marriage broke up. When he came over to R.M. Williams Pty Ltd Dene became the expert in many things, and for a start a much more skilled plaiter, braider and tradesman than I had ever been.

Eric Dragon joined me in the company just before the Second World War. He came to Australia from Hitler's Germany, determined to make a place for himself in the sun. Shortly after he arrived here the outbreak of war isolated him and forced him to spend much of his time under the supervision of the authorities. He came to me as a willing young man eager to learn the English language and the Australian way of life. His spirit was something quite exceptional, and he mastered many aspects of our business, becoming an expert in the manufacture of clothing, boots and steel products. His wide-ranging curiosity led him to master mysteries of making things that remained mysteries to most others; his executive ability was outstanding and he produced new products; and finally he had the satisfaction of sitting on the board, governing the company in which he had started working as a boy. We owe him much of our success.

Hitler's Germany had long gone when he decided to contact his family. He had one brother in Germany and one in Poland. They came to meet him when he landed in Germany, and the one who lived in Poland, accustomed to a frugal way of life, suggested that they catch a bus. Eric demurred; instead, he said, he would buy a Mercedes. This story pleased me immensely, because I'm sure the incident marked the zenith of his career. Soon it will be time for him to retire, but he has achieved much, mastered many difficult problems. I hope he has made a happy life in this country.

Until comparatively recently the complex of buildings that constituted the factory was quite flimsy. Additions had been made *ad hoc* for each expansion of our work. But as its reputation grew, the factory had been listed in the overseas journals of the P. & O. liners and such as a place to see. The Dunstan Government offered to finance the construction of more modern premises and gave us fifteen years to pay. Our acceptance of this offer has been of great assistance in the company's progress. It was a big step when we took it because we were not sure we could ever repay such a large amount of money, but of course inflation has helped. The process of developing the factories over the last half century has been a story of slow and painful expansion.

Nobody really likes change. Man has an assurance of safety in seeing the same processes go on smoothly in the same way from day to day and from year to year. But I live on change. My function in the organization is to provide change. I don't think they like to see me coming down to Adelaide.

For example, we have this new line in buckled boots. I wanted us to produce buckled boots because at my age I'm having a bit of trouble getting down to my elastic-sides. So I got Eric Dragon to cut out the patterns. But there's much more than that in starting a new line of boots. When you start you have to have a new line of lasts, and the set of lasts will cost maybe about $20 000. Then there's the cutting. You need to cut 290 pairs in one cutting; this is to feed the racks and the machines and the sequence patterns. There's the knives for the press, and the machines for stitching the boots in position. It takes maybe $100 000 to express a new idea.

But my function is to make different styles and different commodities. Take the watch-fob pouch, for instance, which is unique. It sells world-wide. And the plaited belt. For that I started a plaiting department. I taught Dene, and he may be the finest plaiter in the world. That plaiting department in Adelaide makes fine whips and belts that people all over the world take pride in possessing. Now I'm on to this new style in trousers . . .

My acceptance of the Calvinistic heritage of poverty for its own sake had many modifications. 'Whom the gods love dies young,' Menander told us, and that may be, but I would suggest a corollary, that whom the gods wish to destroy they first make wealthy. Although for sure the gods or the devil have many more wiles than money. Shut a healthy man away from the good life and if he is too proud or too heavily weighted with the traditions of the past he will break out somewhere.

The power of hatred born in the years of want burned slowly, damped down by success, but smouldering. It only needed release from the blanket of success to come alive again, and it still burns: a hatred of the hopeless slavery of the people I had helped to enslave.

Almost everyone who is successful rides to riches on the backs of some workers. Even the mines which poured out their streams of gold were served by grim-faced toilers who sweated as all miners sweat deep in the heart of the earth, facing unexploded death after every firing. Toilers on the nerve-jarring machines that turn at mind-shattering speed become robots tortured by the needs to service the speeding wheels. Slow death begins at the morning bell and temporarily releases its victims when the day is called at evening.

Do not tell me how the workers fare, or the restless story of their rebellion. I have shovelled coal in 44 degrees Celsius, bogged out the drive at 300 metres, burned my eyes at sewing machines, stooped hours over the ledgers, agonized over the unpaid debt. I made myself free — but for what? The regulated man never drifts; but I found my freedom in working cattle, riding horses as a way of peace.

Nothing pleases the old dog more than an ear eager to listen to stories of injustices to the toiling masses, so that by the time the Great Depression reached me when I was twenty-one I was ploughed ground for the seeds of anti-establishment. 'Workers of the world unite. You have nothing to lose but your chains.' Marx's theory of surplus profit and the materialistic conception of history took equal place with my gentle mother's gospel: 'Render unto Caesar the things that are Caesar's and to God the things that are God's.'

I found that among the lowest paid labourers the law of 'might is right' prevailed, and the higher up the scale they rose the more they sought the protection of the law. To learn both sides has been a lifetime ambition, for without the one you cannot understand the bowed back, and without the other, the fear of losing privilege.

Yet I was confronted outside our Adelaide office some years ago by a union official who was demanding better conditions for workers in our staff quarters. I pointed out that we always provided the best possible for both factory workers and office staff, making the proviso that sometimes money could be the governing factor. It was not always possible to give luxury when the building itself was less than the ideal the union envisaged. The answer from the union official was a snarl.

'What would the likes of you know about work? I don't suppose you have ever done a day's work in your life!'

It's a classic example of what the average worker thinks of his boss. But at that particular time I had just finished fencing Rockybar, and the boundary fence, which I built only with bar and shovel and the help of my own boys, was more than 160 kilometres long. As a boy I cut limestone and burned lime, then cut mulga, the hardest timber in the Outback, for a larger lime-burning project. I then had some years of light work, if riding and cattle work can be called light, then a year of mixing mortar for builders and carrying their bricks up the scaffold in the old-fashioned hod—a task now barred by the unions as being inhuman toil. For ten years I slaved at the telephone and the desk, not hard work, but a killer, nevertheless. Next, year after year of riding after range cattle and fencing and building in stone for my boys and others. Only those conditioned by a lifetime of heavy labour can handle large stones without injuring their backs.

Some workers find writing books to be the occupation they are most suited to. Others think that because they can swing an axe with expertise they are the elite of labouring people. Solomon, or his co-author in Proverbs 14: 23, affirms that in all labour there is profit, and that about sums it up. Everybody should contribute something to the society in which he or she lives. Only that society in which work is considered necessary and honourable can endure, and the prosperity of the people will ultimately be measured by their individual and collective production and industry.

At a time when I was still embroiled in early struggles I stood at a street corner one night talking with a man who had dedicated his whole life to promoting the world revolution.

'The toiling masses cannot wait much longer; we must work for the coming revolution,' he declared.

I said, 'I may be a traitor to my class, but I cannot be a traitor to my family. I cannot wait.'

Half a century has rolled by, and although China has thrown off the people's thralldom to the money-lending class, still her masses toil on, perhaps without the incubus of heavy-interest debts, but still servants to the inevitable law of survival: that men must work.

I have learned that one is alone in this world, and although the bowed shoulders shrug off the load when the burden of debt becomes too great, the universal law will still hold, and Dame Fortune will lay her treasures at the feet of those who try.

I have at times climbed out of the pit where muddy boots are the mark of a man, but inevitably the long arm of Conscience reaches out and claims me as a working man. I am a son of Martha. Perhaps it is the remorse of having failed a cause, but this I know: I shall never accept the accusation of being other than what I am, a working man.

To be a worker, even a successful worker, does not mean that a man is the master of his environment, and this is another desirable resource. To become such a master involves a lifetime of study—and individual study, because no other human being can really help you find out about your own world. Not everyone is disposed to work for a living and at the same time study everything that constitutes his physical and spiritual surroundings because it involves a lifetime of application, reading the pages of history, learning the many crafts that are necessary to support the modern man, and finding time to ponder the mysteries of the world we live in.

Perhaps one of the great adventures is that which concerns the human spirit. I have seen men of India defy gravity, defy natural laws and make living plants grow immediately. I have seen men transmit messages across vast spaces with no known medium. Perhaps the courage and dedication needed to explore these avenues are as great as those we have seen in men crossing oceans, climbing great mountains and exploring the skies.

Being master of one's environment surely encompasses much more than exploring the physical earth, and certainly it demands application and study and endeavour. Even the simple exercise of understanding one's house takes a complexity of knowledge of the plumbing, the electric wiring, the materials of which it is made and the way in which it was built. This exercise is nothing compared to that of understanding the world. For that, one needs a study of the physical sciences—and botany or entomology alone would require a lifetime. It is good to understand the principles which rule the stars, the details of civil engineering that permit us to cross a river by a bridge. So much of life: the known facts fill a world of books. Study, and attempts to understand, give us an appreciation of the wonderful world we live in. They are not essential to existence, but they add a great deal of depth to our lives.

Our consciousness and understanding are as yet underdeveloped faculties because lack of a wider knowledge has so inhibited our ancestry over millions of years. The development of the Aborigine along specialized channels of survival certainly narrowed his abilities to cope with immediate change. A drastic change has developed and enclosed him in the course of just a few generations but his inborn reaction to the wild still governs him.

The perfect adaptation of the Aborigine to his environment, channelling his development between circumscribed lines, placed him in an ironclad mould from which he is finding it hard to get free. In the history of life are many illustrations of the danger latent in perfect adaptation. Again and again the physically biggest and strongest and most numerous creatures, the most perfectly adapted to their time, lords of whole ages, disappeared, leaving the torch of life to be carried on by smaller, more modest and often previously unnoticed forms. These in their turn adapted to the environment they found or helped to create, and in their turn fell into the trap. Museum showcases are full of the fossilized remains of highly adapted creatures that could not cope with change. This poses a question of whether the human being will be another candidate for the museum.

I am comforted by the belief that no sheer chance but a non-materialistic force guides us. In nature I have noticed that the greater the struggle for survival, the less time remains for the cultivation of the beautiful. There seems a more highly cultivated sense of beauty among the birds than among the more lowly animals. Perhaps the Aborigines, no longer restricted by tribal custom, will break free, and among them will arise individuals who will reach for glories still beyond our grasp. Already there are promising artists and poets whose activities in the tribal days would have been restricted by the harsh necessities of survival.

The first time I saw Agnes she was drunk by the side of a dusty gutter at the Camboon races. Very drunk. Her dress was blown carelessly above a decent level. It didn't matter; this was her day out.

Over the years I discovered that Agnes had a keen mind. The second of her two boys was about eight years old at that time, and although Agnes was illiterate herself, she did not want this child to grow up unable to read or write. But she could not teach him herself, she could not afford a teacher, and she lived in an isolated place. But Agnes had heard that the government did provide schools if the district had enough children to justify the appointment of a teacher. She canvassed the local people and found that there were at least ten children who possibly could go to school and who were being taught by their mothers. Through other neighbours she made application for a school, and after much petitioning one was shifted to Auburn from another area.

The teacher appointed was in the unenviable position of being shared around among the parents, boarding with one family and then another. None of these lived closer than several kilometres from the school, some as many as twenty-five; which meant a long drive for mother or father before and after the day's work, a demanding chore.

But Agnes took this on willingly because she wanted her boy to learn. And learn he did. We provided the vehicle and the petrol, and Agnes took this child of hers regularly to school throughout the years until he had worked through the grades.

After that, Agnes retired to the local township and took on permanently her most wanted occupation, that of being perpetually drunk. She could live there almost alone, for she had poor relations with her husband. But I think of her as a great person apart from her drinking habits, for she did her work and educated that boy, and I think this is a classic example of the spirit of the Aborigines.

I met my first black man on the woodheap at my father's house at Belalie when I was just old enough to walk. I have kept contact with Aborigines ever since, mostly the tribes living in the Tennant Creek district where I was associated with both the land and the mines. It was here that the remnants of the Wailbri tribe lived, and they worked for me. There were some fine people among them and a few—a very few—rogues. I have had Aborigines work and live with me whom I would have been proud to have called my sons, loyal, steadfast, brave, honourable.

I have mentioned Charlie Chambers, the young man of mixed race, mainly Aboriginal, who became my helper when I took up Rockybar. Our relationship was good but it did not extend to long conversations. After several years of working with him I discovered that he had a keen ambition to paint. He had had no lessons whatever, either in drawing or the use of colour, and had had no contact with visual art or artists. But he painted and some of his work was good. On inspiration I gave him Henry Kendall's poem, 'The Last of His Tribe', to read and asked if he would base a painting on it for me.

> He crouches and buries his face on his knees,
> And hides in the dark of his hair;
> For he cannot look up to the storm-smitten trees,
> Or think of the loneliness there—
> Of the loss and the loneliness there.

I do not think it is likely that he will ever attain great recognition, but at least his work points to the solid talent that lies unperceived in Aborigines.

About 1980 Dame Mary Durack-Miller kindly invited me to the reopening of her father's historic homestead at Argyle. It had been pulled down to make way for the Ord River development scheme and had been rebuilt on higher ground. Noticeable among the many distinguished guests was a group of Aborigines who had worked for the

Durack family when Mary had been a girl. By this time they were old people, but Mary gave them pride of place, seating them at the ceremony in the front of the gathering. She introduced me to one of the oldest members of the surviving tribespeople of that area. When she called his name and told the old man who I was he turned his sightless eyes (for he was blind) towards my face and said, 'Everybody want to shake my hand.' It was evidently a great day for the old man, but I thought then there probably had not been a great number of such days in the latter part of his life.

It is obvious that the Aborigines do not want to go back to tribal living exclusively. Few would survive, since most have already lost their skills and their tribal ethics. Few Aboriginal women would like to have the clitoris mutilated to comply with tribal habit. Few men would consent to be 'whistle-cocked' — to have the penis split open from head to butt, as I saw constantly in the old days. Few old women would go back to a community which would leave them alone to die. Few young Aboriginal girls would appreciate having been married at birth to an old man of the tribe, or would accept the status of slave that women held in a male-oriented society.

All fair-minded people should assess the Aborigine as he is and try to define what is ultimately possible. He must become assimilated to some extent in the multiracial society of Australia today. To isolate his people would perpetuate the mistakes of the past and simply destroy them by giving them supplies which include money and liquor. They should have the opportunity to go bush on their own country and to establish their own tribal grounds, but not as a totally kept people.

They are natural prospectors and should be able to enjoy the proceeds of their findings. They are natural hunters. Many tribal people in Mongolia, South America, Africa, Indonesia and New Guinea live off their land, and I believe that given the time and some help they can develop a tribal life associated with our civilization. Perhaps it is to these rights that their current protests are directed.

Aborigines today are remaining aloof from us, and tend to revert as far as possible to a tribal relationship which is inherent in their feelings, but of which the form is not yet crystallized. They have a spiritual connection with their historical past and a strong tendency to assuage their inherited needs, so this resistance to assimilation is only to be expected, especially when seen alongside a white reluctance to accept them. But I wonder if the Aborigines could not eventually make a con- tribution towards the stabilization of the sanity of the rest of the community.

Their fierce struggle for survival channelled their development into certain restricted ways. The environment moulded their lifestyle and developed them into hunters with keen instincts, sharp eyesight, highly elaborated perception. But the desperate struggle left them little time or opportunity for other cultural activities. Karl Marx might thus have been right in his materialistic concept of history, the belief that people are what their environment makes them. But when the severe restrictions of this struggle were removed, the people blossomed out into new activities.

Without being thoroughly, understandingly conscious of it we each try to create circumstances in which we can be happy. I do not suppose a few generations have made a real difference to our fundamental instincts. We still have the souls of Stone Age people which is probably why we like to get out under the trees, why we still have an instinct for caves, why we like the glow of the campfire. Countless generations of our forefathers live in our souls to provide us with instincts we can neither deny nor shed.

Modern man does not feel in harmony with his own civilization and this is one of the reasons why Aborigines choose to live in shacks where they seem to be free. One reason for their wanting land rights is to establish a place where Aborigines can wander and feel in harmony with the call of their past. Laws are a product of a mass of people living together. A family living in the bush alone would have no need of laws other than for governing themselves. The Ten Commandments, extraordinarily similar in the big religions, were devised primarily for the use of the family or, say, an extended family just becoming a tribe. They are excellent for this purpose.

In escaping the city we are escaping the many many restrictions which seem unnecessary for our happiness. Every time I come in contact with the city's pitfalls I feel the need for that harmony with nature that is only to be found where there are trees and rocks and space, where the birds fly and animals still roam about. This is the native air we have inherited. The smell of woodsmoke is one of nature's most potent scents. A gentle breeze against the face is a blessing of Nature herself, almost a caress from the Creator.

Patience and the art of waiting are lessons which primitive people had to learn for survival; they waited for game and they waited for the change of seasons—they waited, constantly waited. Our life by contrast is a sequence of constantly going, doing, achieving, quite foreign to our inherited instincts, to our souls. The fatal price we pay is heart disease and the prostration of every good instinct.

Most mornings Nature gives us a visual beauty of the sun rising in the east, with a concomitant sensual joy of a small, quiet breeze. At night we stop to watch the sun go down in wonderful colours. No painting done with a brush can match these.

An inherited instinct that leads us astray today is the longing to be with our group. A group of people to hunt and to fight off the environment's hostile elements meant survival to our forefathers. This led, in due course, to the building of the town, the walled city and eventually the metropolis. But another primitive urge, the instinct to be at peace with Nature, is difficult to achieve in a city. The parks and gardens we create to serve it are poor substitutes for the primeval beauty which our forefathers learned to love, which was their native air.

If and when the Aborigines recognize and express this primitive instinct they will do far better, because their argument will be irresistible. What today they call 'land rights' is really the need for open space in which to live and roam. Their primitive instinct cannot be denied.

We cannot use these powerful forces from the past which dominate our present; we cannot touch them or handle them; we can barely describe them. Many factors directing our actions come within this category. As materialists we have a tendency to believe only what we can see, yet we have much evidence of powers invisible. We use electricity every day, but we cannot see it. Even the powerful force of the wind is invisible though we feel it. Even the images on our screens that steal into our living-rooms, although so visible in place, come secretly through our walls.

It seems inescapable that all around us is another invisible force, all powerful and all governing, that shapes everything of the environment our physical senses detect. Anyone who denies the existence of this force is a fool. When we conquer time and distance we will inherit the universe, but we are not qualified yet.

When I looked at the struggling masses of India and China towards the end of the 1940s, I saw life in the raw, lightened perhaps by some kindness, but of no value in itself. China did succeed that very year in throwing off the shackles of the money-lenders. She rebelled in suffering and will reap the benefits of self-help inspired by the greatest pair of liberators this world has ever seen, Mao Tse-tung and Chou En-lai. The gates of mercy have certainly been shut in India. She groans under the great weight of religion and any rebel who liberates her people will be on God's side.

We can wonder at the inexplicable; we wonder why fine brave valuable lives are wiped out, sometimes by the hands of evil people; we wonder why there is so much hunger, so much misery, so much pain. Each of us seeks a private explanation. But the longer we live the more we see a pattern of progress emerging, for out of this seemingly senseless slaughter, and the seemingly inexplicable hunger of the masses, appear some symptoms of a better world to come.

The thrust and probe of relentless ideology is supposed to lead men to God, but the only miracle that will come out of it all is the hope and experience and kindness born of suffering. It is a long time since the Jews had a Moses, a Joshua or a David. They need one now.

Chapter Fifteen

I stocked the Darling Downs property with about fifty young horses I brought over from Rockybar, where I had started an Arab stud a few years before, and for that reason I called the place 'Rockybar Arabians'. We break quite a number of young horses here; almost every day young horses are run in for one purpose or another. Each year we break them to riding and then, of course, make useful horses of them and dispose of them according to their qualities. Some we send to the station for stockhorses, some go to the endurance riders, and we select the best of them for ourselves.

It is not so long ago since I gave my old friend Dr Johannes Thiersch a horse to ride when he came from America. The horse itself was quiet. It is a horse that I have used many times and have had literally thousands of kilometres of success with in endurance rides. The horse is perfectly trustworthy but because Dr Thiersch is not an experienced rider and probably put his legs into the wrong position, it galloped off and he fell, breaking three or four ribs. These unfortunate happenings are not predictable, and they are part of the price one pays for having a number of horses, endeavouring to quieten them.

I am interested in looking back on the accidents which I have had myself. I have in fact been very fortunate to have remained in reasonably good health, because in one period, I remember, I had three Christmases on crutches.

One of these Christmas casualties was occasioned by a horse kicking me seriously on the leg when I was taking Jackie Cadell off a bucking horse in a rodeo in South Australia. As he passed me on the buckjumper I could see that his foot was hard up into the stirrup iron. I got my arm under his thigh and brought him off backwards, as we had done many times, but I got this bad kick on the shin.

Another time I had taken a horse from a chap who had sold it to me cheap because it had a few bad manners. Foolishly, I put this horse into rather a sharp gallop trying to take the sting out of it, as I thought, but it managed to pitch me over a fence. I hit my knee on a strip of concrete and have been fairly lame ever since. My leg is well out of shape and one of the bones is sticking out. I have considered putting in a steel knee, but the doctor tells me that these things wear out, and he advised me to stay with my knee as long as possible.

Another time I was asked to ride a horse of which I didn't know the history, and this horse reared over backwards, breaking his back on my leg. The horse died, of course, with a broken back and I was in hospital for a considerable time, having injured my spine. This injury caused a crack in my pelvis and it took a long time to mend.

Another time I was bucked off on a sharp stone. The stone punctured my lower lumbar area and completely paralysed me. This took several weeks to repair in any way, and caused me to be incapacitated for several months, without assurance that I would ever be completely recovered.

On another occasion a horse crushed sideways with me, causing me to be severely concussed, and I was unconscious for quite a few days. This same fall also caused my shoulder to become dislocated. It has not completely recovered, and disables me to the extent that I always saddle my horse now on the off-side, using the left hand, as I have never since been able to lift my right hand much above my shoulder.

Although I am not a top rider, I have still managed to sit on all the horses that have come my way over the years, and I suppose that in that time I have had many, many spills from horses that have dropped me — most often through some saddle being insufficiently girthed.

I have discovered that a crupper on a saddle is not necessarily an assurance that the saddle will stay on, because occasionally a horse can slip his crupper. So I have developed a different system of saddling horses. I now saddle a bad horse always with two girths, one in the usual place and the other one coming from the back of the seat. This makes it almost impossible for a horse to buck you over his head along with the saddle. The saddles coming over the head have caused me many, many falls.

I have broken many horses which have given me spills regularly, but I cannot remember any that I have given up without finally mastering them. I have an almost permanent injury in the neck for a twisted fall from which I landed on my head, but this has improved over the years and is better now than it has been for a long time.

I am still riding the young and difficult horses on the place here, but I take great precautions in mounting them, because if a horse bucks away when one is mounting, it is very difficult to keep one's balance. I was rather unfortunate a few weeks ago in that one of the horses which I considered to be fairly quiet reared over backwards, and almost caught me in the awkward position of being squashed underneath her. Fortunately I fell slightly sideways and was able to avoid her kick as she got up. I cannot say how many horses I have broken in my lifetime, but it must run into hundreds.

The shoeing and breaking and handling of horses is an everyday work. For me, of course, this comes in between other tasks I have to perform, but the bulk of my days is taken up with the handling of young horses and it is a job I enjoy very much. Some days we might have a stable full

Above: The first building on the Hall of Fame site takes shape.

Below: Taking a break from building with Bob Sadler.

Above: John Sawrey, who helped with the building work.

Below: After several months' work the roof goes on.

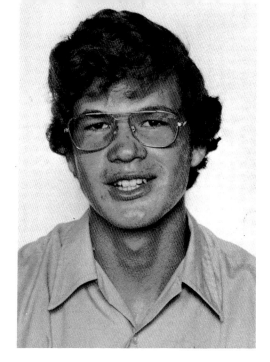

Above: My son
Peter

The stone I have chosen
to be a grave marker.

of horses aged between four and five years and tied to various posts, or tied in stalls. Then one by one they have their feet picked up to have the hooves trimmed; some are quite difficult, but we have methods by which the most difficult of horses can be handled.

We restrain those that are impossible to handle on the front feet by picking up one of the hind feet with a soft leather strap, which is attached with a patent buckle to a strap around the horse's neck. With this the hind foot can be picked up from any reasonable distance, and a stout hobble-strap is placed round the pastern of the front foot. It has a strong ring attached. Another strap is fastened round the horse's chest and withers and buckled tight; it has a ring at the bottom of the girth. The front leg is then pulled up to this ring at the girth and the foot is then quite easy to handle, because the hind leg is restrained, though not pulled up tight.

Using the collar rope to pick the hind foot up for treatment has two major disadvantages: it makes the heel or the pastern sore, and the horse has to be shod with the foot more or less upside down. It is more practical to put a padded hobblestrap on the hind foot and pull it up to the tail, using a special knot on the tail. The horse soon becomes docile and you can nail the shoe on with the hoof upright, which is a great advantage.

Having grown up to the sound of the anvil and watched my father shoe horses of all kinds, I have naturally tended to believe that I should shoe my own. In the early years of this century a blacksmith's shop stood on the corner of every street. There were as many smithies as there were hotels. Boys learned their trade as carpenters do: through an apprenticeship, first holding the horses and working as a doorman, then perhaps at the forge to shape the shoes, and finally graduating to the actual placement of the shoes. The bush horseman of course has to make the shoes, dress the feet and place the shoes, so that he has to become an all-round farrier. As with everything else I have done I have always wanted to become first-class in the art, and I have found through the years that there is a great deal to learn.

Beginners often ask how far one should trim the foot and how low the heels should be cut. In a broad sense the sole of the foot will be a guide to the depth to which the front of the foot should be trimmed, usually so that half the shoe will project above the frog. It is wise to pritch all the holes in the shoe to fit exactly the size of the nails to be used, otherwise the shoe will work loose.

Every young horseman should learn to trim a foot, shape a shoe and fit one, so that he can always do his own shoeing. I still find that I am able to shoe my own horses and do so, particularly for endurance riding. I find it of advantage there because I am able to trim the foot and adjust the shoes to suit the particular horse I am riding. A horse's feet, like a human's, may be conditioned to travel over rough ground without any extra support of pads. A horse trained over rough, gravelly ground, becomes accustomed to this and develops a hard sole on the foot in much the same way as a human being will.

My advice to young men is, if you are going to be a horseman, be a good one. To be an all-round horseman means learning all there is to know about a horse. It is wise to pick up a foal's feet when it is young. I pick up the feet almost from the time the foal is born, and thereafter do it regularly, trimming each hoof right through the growing years, which lightens the task of shoeing it for the first time. Before it is weanable at six months old, I teach a foal to lead, to be tied up and to be placed in a stall, so that it is accustomed to confinement. Before twelve months, the colt is castrated. After this, and before they are two years old, they are regularly handled and their feet trimmed. By three years they should be ridden a little and worked quietly. In the next year they should be shod and worked regularly, and at five they are ready to go into regular, serious work.

The reason that we do not allow horses to enter endurance races before they are five is that they are not mature until this age. Every horseman should learn to tell the horse's age by its mouth. At four a horse will usually have a full mouth of mature teeth, but with mares this is not always so; some do not get a full mouth of major teeth in wear until the age of six, though most have them shortly after five. Some mature earlier than this, and colts' mouths mature earlier than fillies'.

For healthy, prosperous horses that do well and stay in good condition it is necessary to treat them for red worms at least three or four times a year. The red worm circulates through the organs of a horse's body and causes great damage, ultimately death with a bad infestation. Death occurs in many ways, most often from the infestation of a small section of the bowel. The veins are blocked and the small part of the valve becomes gangrenous. This is termed 'twisted bowel', but the cause can usually be traced to red worms. When a horse's bowel becomes slightly gangrenous, even over a small section, little can be done. Few can be saved by operating.

The education of a horse should be approached very much in the manner of educating a child, bringing it from grade one to maturity. Always there is something for a horse to learn, just as there is for a human. After it goes through junior grades it can go on to high school, which means learning many and varied subjects: jumping, dressage, the playing of games. It is wise to allow a horse bred for racing to be fairly mature before it is raced. Horses generally are raced much too young, and often suffer permanent damage as a result.

If one wants to learn about horses, one should go, as in other fields of learning, to the oldest, wisest and most experienced person connected with any branch of horsemanship. It's a wide field and not every horseman will make himself conversant with it all. There is the racing field, the hunting field, droving with its night horses and its camp horses. There are horses to race as trotters, ponies for children, show horses and horses suitable for dressage. If you intend to become a horseman, become a good one and master the whole science of shoeing, breaking, riding, feeding and caring for the animal.

Mahomet is reported to have said that a man who owns a great horse is blessed. Towards that happy state I can claim that I have owned at least one great horse.

A young horseman who is in the habit of coming to break horses at my place in Central Queensland each year reported that he had just found a remarkable horse. This was while he had been breaking horses at Forest Hills, a place way back in the ranges. Being an enthusiast and greatly enamoured of horses he had probably seen a lot of wonderful horses in his time. He had probably broken more horses than any other man I can remember, but because of his custom of being enthusiastic about horses he had broken I did not take much notice.

Six months later he came through my place again, riding a mare, and I asked him where he had come from and where he was going. He was taking the mare to this remarkable stallion called Shiekie which he claimed was one of the greatest horses he had ever broken. He had already ridden 230 kilometres and had 150 more to go, and I was impressed that he would ride this distance just to breed her to this particular horse, so I decided to go along too. I allowed him time to reach his destination, then followed him to Forest Hills just to see this remarkable horse.

When I arrived, the grey stallion was standing in the paddock, emaciated and apparently sick. Someone had injected him with arsenic in the hope of curing him of the itch and he looked a picture of dejection. Nevertheless, we saddled him up and, although he had not been ridden from the time he had been broken, he performed magnificently. I agreed that he was indeed a remarkable horse.

I approached the owner but he would not sell. He did let me buy a half-share in the horse, upon which I put him in the truck, took him home and there nursed him back to health. When he was well rested and cured of his various sicknesses I took him for stock work and discovered that he was indeed remarkable. Taken out after mobs of horses we had not previously been able to muster, on account of their wild natures, their speed and their ability to elude us in the thick forest, Shiekie would stay on their tails. Crossing deep river beds, he would fly through the shallows and the currents and be up the other bank, still biting their tails. He would slide through the timber with a dexterity that I had never known before. He would always be there. If I were chasing a beast that was difficult to catch, Shiekie would put me on to his tail in a position where I was able to throw him, and when I jumped off to tie the beast, Shiekie would stand there, waiting.

Later in his life I took him to an exhibition given by Greg Lower, a great American who was holding schools to teach the arts of horsemanship to anyone prepared to listen. Lower immediately recognized Shiekie to be an exceptional animal and used him to demonstrate the various arts. He stated at that time that if he had Shiekie in America he could win almost any class he entered in the field of action.

I gave him then to a man named Corvey, a great horsemaster who was in the top echelon of those who were prominent in the show-rings of Australia. At the same time I allowed my daughter Mary to become Corvey's student, and she stayed with him two years learning the art of horsemanship. Corvey took Shiekie to the Sydney Royal Show and he excelled in a most difficult class, the Arabian Stallion under Saddle. I was very proud to see Shiekie win in a class which required high degrees of skill in dressage.

Shortly after that, Erica took him to a Cumberland show for action, in Sydney, where he was in competition with quarter horses and other action breeds. To my practised eye he was the most exceptional horse at that large function. By this time his fame had spread far and wide, and horsemen came long distances to put their legs over the saddle and feel the excellence of his action.

He had excelled as a working stock-horse. He was tops as a runner after brumbies in the bush and a chaser after wild cattle in thick scrub. He had stood motionless and behaved to perfection in the Sydney Showgrounds and won the highest accolade in his class. He had been favoured as a demonstration horse by Greg Lower, one of the greatest horsemen I have seen. Shiekie's great dignity of presence, his ability in action and his superb performance as a dressage horse all made him an exceptionally versatile champion.

When the hundred-mile Quilty race was first mooted in Sydney, a crossing of the Colo River was mooted as one of the obstacles. On the northern side the Colo banks are steep and sometimes bordered by quicksand. On the second occasion the race was run the Colo was in small flood. I decided that it might be wise to test the river to see if riders could cross without danger, and I took Shiekie in to swim him across. Halfway, we encountered a huge sunken snag of some great tree that had been washed down, and Shiekie became entangled in the branches. That was almost a disaster for both of us, but because of his spirit and his ability he freed himself and was able to take me back to the banks. So the hazard in the Quilty was not used because of the obvious risks, but I treasure the memory of his great effort there.

Like many other grey horses he was subject to melanoma of the skin, and towards the end of his life he was cursed with the melanoma on his nose. Veterinary advice was that the operation would not be ultimately successful and, as he had lived a long and useful life, I decided to put him down. In preparation for his burial I had a huge hole excavated close to the house. Taking him to the edge of the hole I told him with due respect that this was the end of the road. With many tears and deep sorrow I covered him with rich red soil which I had carted for the purpose, and above him planted a camphor laurel tree to be his memorial.

With experience it is possible to select a good type of horse for almost any purpose. I have always loved beautiful horses, and watched with interest a type which makes the best racehorse. I had done some study in the breeding of successful horse lines. A few years ago near Toowoomba I saw a man riding a magnificent chestnut mare and I stopped to pass the time of day with him and ask about her breeding. He told me that her name was Shady Meadows, and that she had successfully passed her trials, but unfortunately, just as she was ready to race, she had lost an eye by walking into a tree point and therefore was disqualified. When I asked if he would be interested in selling her, he laughingly but quite forcibly told me he would not part with her. He liked her. She was good to ride and he would use her to breed.

During the next year I chanced to meet the same man again and asked him about Shady Meadows. She had contracted tetanus, a disease from which few horses recover. She had lain at death's door. When the veterinarian had finally given her up she had been lying on the ground for twenty-one days, and her hip was worn quite through. She had a deep sore there for a long time. I saw the vet, and he told me he had left the mare for dead, believing that she would not recover. She did recover, but she still was not for sale.

Several months later I met the same man again and he told me that Shady Meadows had continued to encounter misfortune. She had come in contact with a poisonous plant known as Johnson grass. This poison had put her down for the second time, and again she was left for dead. But this time she had lost so much weight and was in such poor condition that when I asked her owner if she were for sale he immediately brightened and said, 'Yes, of course she is for sale, but I don't think she is worth a lot of money now.'

I offered him $500 and he accepted. So, with some difficulty, I led the mare home and treated her carefully. In due course she did recover.

For her first foal I had put her to a famous horse, and she lost the foal because of a foolish mistake I had made in grazing her on green young wheat, thinking I would give her a good pasture. This, of course, is a serious mistake in an equine pregnancy. For the next foal I put her to a horse called Stupormundi, owned by Bob Carmichael, a friend of mine. Two years later, when the foal was growing, I put her to another famous racehorse, Straight Arrow.

The foal from Stupormundi grew up and we called her after her mother, but at four years of age she showed no promise. Her docile attitude and her general apathy were so marked that we gave her the nickname of 'Dopey'. She was a very lovable animal, but she showed no inclination whatever to be a galloper. She was registered with the Thoroughbred Stock Book.

A young man called Bill Ford came by one day and asked if I had any horses that might be suitable for racing. I told him I had this one thoroughbred mare who was from a good mother, but I could not guarantee the qualities of the sire. He asked me if I would be prepared to let him try the mare and take her and train her, because he had a love of horses and had a great ambition to race some. He was a teacher of technology at the local high school. His great passion was racing but he could not afford to waste money.

Bill took her to an old, wise and experienced trainer, Gordon Neale, of Toowoomba. An old man, Gordon had no other horses in the stable but he took a fancy to the mare and he renamed her 'The Long Run', perhaps because she was the last horse that he would train, and perhaps because of the long run that he himself had had in training, and perhaps because of the great odds against this mare becoming a great racehorse.

Within a short time he had prepared her for the trials, which she won, showing considerable ability. From the maidens she went on to the improvers and then through all the classes a youngster must win before she can become one of the open runners. During her long career as a racehorse her list of winners has overshadowed her unplaced efforts and she has been responsible for four records in her racing career, three of which she still holds: the 1660-metre Mundamba course record of 1.39.6; the Eagle Farm 1400-metre Encourage class record of 1.22; and the Gold Coast 1600-metre Graduation Class record of 1.36.5. Her time of 1.22 at Eagle Farm would win most races of that class anywhere. The Long Run had sixty race starts for seventeen wins, eight seconds, nine thirds and five fourths. In May 1984 she came home at the end of her racing career and will be put to stud to the best horses I can find.

Her sister, Shady Ella, has shown much promise. She won her first maiden and we have great hopes for her. I took her to Gordon Neale for training. He put a buckjumper on her and she bucked him off and hurt him. She bucked another rider off and hurt him badly, and they said she was unridable. Then Leo O'Keefe gave her some quiet station work before I put her to a bush trainer and after that she won her first race. She's very good.

This is the extent of my racing career, but I have no doubt that I will have great pleasure in breeding these two mares to the stallion of my choice, because I think there is a lot of potential in a horse of the right breeding that looks like a galloper. There is also something to be said for my belief that horses should not be raced too young.

About 1947 I bought polo ponies from a great old trainer named Skene. His stables were in New South Wales and his ability made him one of the surest sources of supply for trained polo ponies. On one occasion he presented me with Stella, a mare of very unusual conformation. She had almost everything wrong with her that a well-conformed horse has not. She was thin to the point of emaciation, and of the type that I did not consider would ever get fat. But she had a wild, eager look in her eye, and Skene offered her to me, saying that although she might not be an oil painting she had very exceptional ability.

This she was to prove, for at the end of her polo life I was asked to play in a State side on the Melbourne Showgrounds. It was quite an occasion, for on the night of the last match 80 000 people were present, a huge crowd for a showground exhibition. The Victorian State side included a mare which had been awarded the championship for the best polo horse at the Show, and by coincidence this mare was my opponent in the matching side. I knew from the speed and extraordinary ability of my queer-looking chestnut mare that I would have no difficulty with the proclaimed champion. Naturally I set out to prove my mount's ability.

When the ball was going in the opposite direction she would turn with such speed as to be already headlong after it before the others had turned, and before long she had put on eight goals. When I returned to the centre of the ring Alec Creswick (later Sir Alec) said to me, 'My boy, that will be enough! This is a local side you are playing!' But I was not warned and, a few minutes later, at full gallop, the proclaimed champion fell dead alongside. I realized then that I had galloped the mare to her death. With great humiliation I decided that this was the last match that I would ever play, for in trying to prove that my mare was the greatest I had caused the death of her opponent.

The lights of the showground were put out, and the mare which had died in her tracks was pulled from the ground. I unsaddled. The mare was never ridden again, nor did I ever play polo again. The old mare died on a lonely watercourse in Central Queensland. I was not present and I did not see her die. It was one of my regrets that I neglected her at the last moment, but I treasure her memory as one of the great horses I have owned and loved.

In the hunting field one learns to trust the horse which carries one, and I have experienced the pleasure of having had some such trustworthy horses. In a field which sometimes exceeds eighty galloping horses, all racing to a fence where not everyone can get across the limited space, I have known the joy of an absolute confidence that my horse was totally secure. If it was not possible to reach the wooden barriers I knew that he would cross the barbed wire. If the crowd was thick and the going was rough, I knew that my horse would not stumble. This is a very great pleasure. Not all the horses that I have owned have given me the same sense of security; not all have possessed this particular strength of limb, or this peculiar ability to recover under any circumstances, and in the hunting field I have taken many falls.

The late Sir Alec Creswick once loaned me his favourite charger for a hunt with the Melbourne Hunt Club. The occasion was a memorable one, for the field was quite large. More than a hundred horses assembled for the meet and they were hunting behind a pack of experienced hounds. Since I was a guest of Sir Alec and riding his best horse I felt obliged to stay with the field wherever it might go, and Erica, who was with me, had a similar incentive.

For his part, Sir Alec probably felt that he had to put on something of a special exhibition, and when the fox crossed the railway line, instead of going to a safe place to cross, Sir Alec headed straight for the double barbs and the railway line and the ditches. Crossing the high, railway barbed wires, with the hazard of the rails themselves and then the ditch, and then the other high barbed fence, was in itself a considerable hazard, but Alec showed no hesitation. He went straight for the barbed wires. As his guest I felt I had no option but to follow, as did Erica. She was riding a wild, almost uncontrollable horse that was being groomed for a race.

So we followed Sir Alec, and with us came a little girl on a pony, a most exceptional pony. At the end of the hunt there was only Sir Alec, the little girl on the pony, and Erica and myself, out of a field of more than a hundred horses. I remember this as being one of the wildest rides I have known, and I remember with great affection that great man and brilliant horseman, Sir Alec Creswick.

It was a ride reminiscent of another great gallop that I had following George Day, the manager of the Chalet at Kosciusko in the days when the brumbies were picked from the alpine wilds. George had gathered the men from the Snowy Mountains for one great brumby chase. This was the heyday of the great Kosciusko riders, with George, in my opinion, the greatest of them all.

George had lent me his favourite horse, but being inexperienced I did not have the pleasure of bringing home a brumby. I was empty-handed when the others were leading their brumbies back towards the Chalet. One rider was missing, and because I was empty-handed I was asked to go back and find him. When we had last seen him he was flying at the tail of the brumby herd around the top of the mountain across the valley from Kosciusko.

When I found him he was crawling down the mountain, having broken his leg. One of his eyes had been knocked out when he was thrown, and was hanging against his cheek. He was in desperate shape.

Another kind of racing called endurance racing is, I believe, the best way to test certain horses. The thoroughbred business has its inevitable way of weeding out the bad from the good, but most other breeds do not have a comparable method of selection. Because of this I asked my old friend Tom Quilty, the owner of several cattle stations and a great old horseman, to give a gold cup as a yearly trophy, or a trophy in perpetuity, for an endurance race. To claim it, competitors would ride 100 miles (160 km) in one day and thus prove they could endure and their horse could do the distance. Tom gave the money, $20 000, and the Quilty Cup was produced, a magnificent trophy, containing more gold than the Melbourne Cup.

I called a well-attended meeting in the old Australia Hotel on the corner of Martin Place in Sydney, and people came from several States. The meeting settled on a course in the Blue Mountains back of Sydney, beginning and finishing at the old Hawkesbury Racecourse. It has been run as an annual event ever since.

The Royal Society for the Prevention of Cruelty to Animals tried desperately to stop this ride, but it has continued for seventeen years now and to date no horses have been killed because of the strict veterinary control. R.J. Rawlinson, a top veterinarian from the Sydney School of Veterinary Medicine, took charge. The event established the standards by which these rides would be conducted. The parameters of safety were set, the heart rate at which a horse would be considered to be unfit, the breathing rate, and everything to do with the physiological state of the horse. Much good was done, and much knowledge gained.

I have had great pleasure in breeding and training for these Hundred Mile Gold Cup rides, also in riding in them, and I have had some success. My stud has provide winners or place-getters in most of the major endurance rides of Australia, so that I have learned a great deal about what to expect from a horse and have been instrumental in establishing the guidelines by which future races will be conducted.

I've been delighted to see fellows who have believed they have a good horse bring it from the far Outback and win the Quilty. One bushman-drover has won it twice, and several others have been successful. One year Erica was very keen to win. We raced to the lead together, kept together and, when we came to Bowen Mountain near the end, we slid down that. Another challenge the event suggested was to ride the hundred miles in ten hours, which had never been done. We galloped the last 200 metres to the finish and Erica beat me by half a second, the pair of us finishing in just over the ten hours. That was the first time a woman had won the race and Erica was very pleased. However, I was more than satisfied with the result, as I won the Fittest Horse Cup.

At sixty-nine years of age I was very proud to take my old horse Granite over the finishing line in the Warwick to Gold Coast race, a 120-mile (193 km) ride, and in the past five years I have been placed four times in the Longreach and Winton ride, which is 150 miles (250 km). I am sure that this distance riding has helped to keep me fit and well. Now, towards the end of my life, I very much need some exercise, and these races have provided the motivation.

Young people training a horse for such a ride should take it along carefully until it can cover five miles (eight kilometres) in thirty minutes. When it can do this without excessive strain on the heart, showing a quick recovery and not sweating, it will be ready for a major distance. We feed a very simple diet: bran, wheaten chaff and oats, along with enough lucerne hay to provide the necessary roughage. An excess of oats seems to be a serious disadvantage. This diet, of course, is different from that used to bring a racehorse to galloping condition.

When the Longreach and Winton ride begins each July, our entries have been in training for many months. People from all walks of life become competitors, and the race is a major effort for them all, but it also takes a long and intensive application to train a horse to run such a distance without overstrain. In the course of such a training we discover that a horseman must cover many many miles before he is sufficiently athletic to keep up a good pace over the distance without being affected physically or suffering permanent damage. We persist until horses which, at the beginning of the regimen, sweated heavily become capable of galloping sixteen kilometres without raising any sweat at all. Horses that would have raised their heart-beat rate to one hundred to the minute can run 22.5 kilometres uphill in proper condition, with the heart-beat rate coming back into the low forties. Six weeks before the race we have several animals trained to this peak and ready to run.

One of the horses which perhaps has made the fastest time for the long distance, faster than any horse I have ever known, heard of or read about, was a horse which had previously been tied up with azoturia. From this it does not appear that azoturia makes for serious irretrievable muscle damage, contrary to the opinion of many veterinarians. All I can say is that I have run horses which have had it, and they have been winners despite having been previously tied up many times.

I have raced horses many times, been successful in endurance rides, played polo and taken part in the hunting scene, trained and bred horses for dressage and had many years experience with jumpers, besides taking a lifetime interest in stockhorses, having bred, broken, trained and used them. Looking back on that lifetime association I claim some right to speak about the way horses are bred, fed and trained.

I believe that the famous Australian Waler that was exported to India for so many years was a cross-breeding of the thoroughbred, the pony and the Arab, with a dash of the heavy cold-blooded horse. The Australian stock horse, now an established breed, probably originated from the same cross-breeding. The thoroughbred and the Arab provide the elegance but all are responsible for some of its qualities. The action of the feet must be straight, the chest must be deep, and the neck long and elegant. Anybody who goes in for a lifetime of breeding, though, must take chiefly into consideration the characteristic temperament, for nobody will be bothered with horses that are too wild or too frightened.

The Australian saddle, created, designed and produced in this country, is one of the finest pieces of horse furniture made and used anywhere in the world. I have had some experience with American saddles of all types. I know the English hunting saddles, and something of the saddles of Asia such as were used by the troops of Genghis Khan. I know the patent saddles of the American cavalry and the saddles produced for the Australian cavalry. Among all these the Australian stock saddle stands supreme, and among the Australian stock saddles are some which excel.

A few specialists brought the production of the Australian saddle to a fine art in the last century. The American saddle is much too heavy and too wide in the seat. The English saddle is quite useless for riding young horses, where one has to cling tight to stay aboard. The old American cavalry officer McLellan produced a fine type of cavalry saddle but the production was extremely difficult.

A rider must learn to ride on a loose rein. This requires strict control of stomach and back muscles, and is developed by much experience, good balance and continued riding, but it is better for the horse and produces a better rider.

I have had close association with those who have introduced patent methods of breaking horses, such as the swift one-day method, but I can say with confidence that only time and patience will eventually produce a quiet and reliable horse. A horse cannot be made thoroughly quiet and thoroughly reliable in one day or even one week. Some horses, of course, are naturally quiet but those which take some discipline to bring into usefulness cannot be made thoroughly reliable in a short time.

My father would have been as delighted as I am to see the way an affinity with horses has continued to mark the family. The Rockybar children of course grew up with them, particularly in the year we spent in the big forest at Wongongora, and the other times we were on the road with cattle.

Peter's education was completely in the hands of his mother, who used textbooks and other material supplied by the government, until he was ready for high school. He reached a proficiency in most subjects covered by the schools, sufficient anyway for him to get a pilot's licence after he left.

Peter went on to fly commercially, at one time running the mail from Tennant Creek on the northern Borroloola run. At another period he worked as a flyer for a cattle company in western Queensland. Several times he flew my own plane for me and I found him careful and meticulous. He had two crashes which could be ascribed to bad luck. Once his mates on a muster were finding it difficult to get some wild cattle into the mob. Peter kept circling lower and lower to help keep the cattle in hand and finally hit a bull head on and smashed the plane. This was foolishness, of course, but a tribute to his courage because few people will ever fly low enough to hit a bull head on when they are mustering cattle.

He got into trouble again by flying into a deep valley to wave his wings at some friends picnicking there. Trying to get out of the valley, he found the hazards too great, and his wing and airscrew hit a pylon of the electric power line, cutting off some of the airscrew. By revving the engine very high he managed to get enough elevation to land on the Toowoomba airfield. The airscrew is still hanging on the wall of the aero club there. The accident was born of inexperience, but few people have hit a power line in such a manner and survived.

A friend from the west of Queensland also told me of the time Peter ran short of petrol and landed on a road, using the lights of a big truck moving along the road to land in front of it. The truck, of course, pulled up behind him.

Peter's next move was to Adelaide, going to school there to study the manufacture of various articles we produce. His school card reveals him as a diligent student, one of the best in his group.

His sister Mary had an education similar to Peter's and a similar aptitude for learning. She was sent to Brisbane to finish at a high school and university, but she wrote to her mother to say that being as she hoped a horsewoman, she did not feel it necessary to have more education. I think she would have run away from school. Consequently we sent her as apprentice to a man named Corvey, a famous horseman of his time who was showing horses. She stayed with him a couple of years to learn dressage and driving, and drove many successful hackneys in Royal Show events. She also had success showing hacks, and her horsemanship was of a high standard.

She was selected Carnival Queen for the Toowoomba Carnival of Flowers from among a large group, and the honour brought her a year of activity promoting Toowoomba, travelling and meeting people. The following year she was Miss Rodeo Australia, a title competed for by girls connected with the sport throughout Australia. For this her ability as a horsewoman counted, as well as her looks and her ability to meet people and handle the necessary promotion. She was accounted one of the most successful rodeo queens we have had.

She married Stuart Neil, an experienced horseman who plays polocrosse for Queensland, and they took on the running of the large shop we have in Toowoomba. It had been a big old warehouse of 10 000 square feet (929 square metres). I had rebuilt the interior, intending that Angus Scobie, one of the sons of the famous whip-tailor from out near the beginning of the Birdsville Track, should take it over, but Angus died. Stuart and Mary are making a success of it and also keeping their eyes open for a property. Like Mary and Stuart, the youngest one, Michael, is also a polocrosse enthusiast, and from a very early age showed a distinction that persuaded me he would carry on our traditions of horsemanship. Besides that he had a grip on cultural affairs and shone in mathematics. He studied to become expert with the computer and in book-keeping, and with these interests I think he might eventually become the man we look for to take over the financial affairs of the company. With the expertise of his brother Dene to help him he could become an accomplished account executive. He also promises to develop the wisdom and judgment required to run a large establishment. Still single, and enjoying the discovery of life, he lives with his half-sister Diana, a pointer to the integration of the two families.

In 1983, while I was absent, the board of the company voted $250 000 for advertising, which annoyed me when I considered that a lot of this money would go to advertising firms and, in my opinion, result in little of value. Certainly our name would appear in many papers and some slick script-writer would put over something of the story of what we had to sell, but I have no hesitation in saying I think this is a waste of money.

When the question of allocating money for advertising came up at the next meeting, John Swain, the chairman of directors, had gone to live in France permanently, and I had taken the chair. The sales manager and the secretary were firm that we should send out printed leaflets to our customers. I felt that this was also a waste of money and, knowing that the majority of the board would back me, I put a strong case forward that we should print an old-fashioned catalogue.

The ones we used to put out were valued in the bush, where most people love catalogues. Stockmen particularly like to see the gear they use illustrated and described. Almost since our business really started we have issued catalogues of the goods we sell, and the average man in the bush has found them of interest. I confess that I like catalogues myself.

When our decision was made the advertising manager and the secretary asked, in a cynical way, 'But who is going to produce it?' The impression was that they did not have time and there was nobody else to do it. I took up the challenge and suggested that I would do the job myself. After the meeting I was delighted when Dene came to me and said, 'Look, Dad, I think Michael and I could produce this catalogue, and if you put Mike to work on it I will help him.' This pleased me because it was the first real out-going gesture I had had from Dene since taking over the board.

Michael immediately took up the challenge, gathering the old material from the printers, classifying it and getting the prices. The work proceeded at a good pace, though those who had promoted other forms of advertising, for what purpose I cannot tell, rated the whole procedure down. But I am convinced that catalogues are the backbone of the mail-order business, and we went ahead. In the past catalogues were produced painfully, because a lot of work goes into them. Artists and photographers were paid to get pictures for them. I have never lost the romance of the catalogue and I feel that it will always be the basis for our business. So it was in the past and so, eventually, it will be in the future. I am looking forward to something very special this time because Mike is laying his future on the line in this production, and Dene is helping him.

This accounts for all my living children. I am proud that they are all good citizens and that they have all set to work to earn their own livings. I am proud indeed that they are all workers and have all shown interest in literature as well as more mundane affairs. If I have in any way neglected them it has not shown through, probably because of the love and care their mothers gave them. They are a credit to that love and care, but in my own inept way I have tried to provide a background which would be one of stability.

I have been accused of neglecting to give my children religion. I read once that a student of Confucius questioned him about his belief. Confucius said he wished he did not have to speak, and could remain silent. The student asked, 'Sir, how then could we learn your wisdom?'

Confucius said, 'My son. Heaven never speaks.' If then the voice of Heaven is the wind and the storm and the sunshine and the bright stars and the beauty of Nature, then this, perhaps, is the voice that they have heard.

A short time ago an old prospector asked me to visit the western side of the Carnarvon Ranges and took me by a roundabout way through the dark valleys and the high crags to a lonely place where a spring bubbled out of the earth. Near the spring a bark hut of the old-fashioned type, genuine in every respect, stood exactly as the pioneers had left it, except that it had had much attention and did not look neglected. The old man carefully showed me the spotlessly kept interior, obviously maintained by someone who loved it. There were no roads going by in this lonely place, and yet it looked as though someone came regularly and cared for it with great affection.

The mystery of the beautiful spring in this dark valley and the bark hut intrigued me, and on occasion when I visited someone in that area, a vast area covering several hundred square kilometres, I mentioned the bark hut and the spring away back in the dim recesses of the Carnarvons, but nobody seemed to know about it. Then in May this year I was staying with some drovers and their family on a trip only about 300 kilometres to the west of that area. Talking about various happenings that night, I mentioned the hut and the way it was kept and the beautiful spring beside it. The drover's wife looked up to me with something of amusement in her eyes, a beautiful look, something I found hard to understand until she said, 'I was born in that hut, and we have kept it like that.' People make pilgrimages to Mecca, and others make pilgrimages to the Ganges, and some go to Jerusalem, but this family makes pilgrimages over these unmade roads and lonely tracks to visit the place which is sacred to them above all.

I like the idea of a place which is unknown and inaccessible to the world, where a person can go and worship solitude and loneliness and remembrance.

Another such place and another such person is situated in the Gammon Ranges in South Australia. About 1930 I chanced upon a hut so lonely and so inaccessible I doubt whether any people went by. The old woman who lived there was entirely mad, but she had all the things about her which meant so much and for which she lived. I had heard the tale of a mad woman living alone in the Ranges and when I met her, although the madness looked out of her eyes, I realized that it was a different kind of madness. It was the look of those who live alone, of those who have no other communication than with nature, of those to whom God is the hills and the rain and the clouds, the birds and wild animals, and I know that for them they have chosen the better path.

Another such lonely person was a woman who had emigrated, by herself, to Australia, a woman who was born in London within the sound of Bow Bells. She had gone to work in the Outback of western Queensland and married a young, well-dressed Aboriginal, holding him to be a very special person who, I suppose, represented all that was best in Outback Australia.

People living far away in the Outback in those days were subject to what was known as the Barcoo rot, a deficiency disease common among old-time sailors, or those who live in places where there is nothing but salt meat and no fresh vegetables. This young man died young of the Barcoo rot, but not before he had fathered two half-caste children. Before he died he took her to the only place he knew, which was the tribe from which his people came. They of course were still living in semi-civilized circumstances.

This woman, mourning the man she loved so much and intensely loyal to his children, resolved to stay with the tribe and raise her family. When I met her she must have been one of the lonely people of the world. She had little in common with the tribespeople, but they cared for her in a very gentle manner, giving her her share of the spoils of the chase. She had little else to keep her and lived as they did, entirely without sustenance other than that which the tribe supplied. She taught the boys the best she knew, but of course her knowledge was limited. I think of her living in her small wurlie, for that was all it was, as one of the great people of the world. She had faced an entirely alien world by her own choosing for the sake of her children, and raised them there without any comforts whatsoever, no water except that which she carried herself from the spring, no house except the wurlie the Aborigines had built her, no rag to cover herself except that which they had given her, which they themselves had probably gotten second-hand. She was intensely private, and I felt that nothing I could do for her at that time would have made her any happier than she was.

Chapter Sixteen

My property at Rockybar in the Auburn Valley was on the fall of the Auburn and Dawson Rivers. Nearby, a little more than 300 kilometres away, which is of course a relatively short distance in the bush, I had a neighbour, David Briggs, an American with an outgoing personality. His closest associate and friend was Greg Lower, another American who had brought his horses with him when he emigrated to Australia. These were the collection of a lifetime, and he is happy to tell any number of good stories about the way one or other of the breeds he had collected came into his possession.

Greg was a professional horseman of high calibre. His mother wanted him to be a doctor, but when she found him set on being a horseman she said, 'Well, Greg, if you must be a horseman, be a good one.' He has fulfilled his life's ambition and became one of the finest horsemen I have ever known.

Greg brought to my attention that Australia was badly served in the allocation of judges for various horse sports. The Royal Agricultural Societies had no really organized system of establishing the merits of the judges in the various classes. It seemed to him important that this question be discussed.

Other matters were also important to me. For example, I thought it would be a grand idea to establish a trail for riders down the east coast of Australia, using the high rocky range which extends, more or less, from Cooktown to Melbourne. In America the Mormon Trail, the Appalachian Wilderness road, the Redwood Trail and others were established early in the country's history, and it seemed to me that if something were not done to establish a trail it would become too late, because of other encroachments on the suitable land.

Establishment of a research organization in veterinary matters was another desideratum of the horse business. I would also have liked to see something in the form of an exposition where all breeds could show their best horses and explain the merits of that strain. To these ends, Greg Lower recommended that David Briggs might be a useful associate, and the three of us together set in motion the establishment of a Horsemen's Congress.

We organized the Congress from Rockybar, quite remote at that time, but possessed at least of a telephone, a battered typewriter and a weekly mail service. I sounded out the key people in the breed societies and others who might be interested. We wanted to investigate the economic side of the horse business, using as a basis the racing establishment. We obtained co-operation from the Australian Jockey Club in all States without exception, and they agreed to help with the economic survey.

This was handled by Mary Nunn, at that time a teacher in economic history at the University of Queensland, and comprised the assembly of all data concerning the racing business: the number of trainers, the number of horses in their establishments and the weekly cost, the cost of jockeys, the cost to the breeding establishment of their racecourses, various other costs sustained by the breeding establishments, and the recording of the numbers of breeding establishments in Australia.

The chairman of the Brisbane Amateur Turf Club, Dr C. Uhr (later Sir Clive), agreed to be the principal speaker at the Congress, talking on the economics of racing. We received co-operation from such breed societies as the Arabian, the Quarter-horse, the Ponies. In fact all the different horse-breeding associations and the Pony Clubs offered support and agreed to present the best of their animals at a 'red carpet' exhibition which we had proposed should be held at Gatton, the town 100 kilometres west of Brisbane, where an agricultural high school and college was established at the end of last century. It was incidentally the site of a cattle-station taken up about 1840 by Dr Uhr's pioneer ancestor.

For the Congress we took over the whole of Gatton College, using their extensive boarding facilities and their kitchens for the many presidents and their secretaries. We hired two huge marquees and set them up with a connecting area, building a platform on which the horses could be exhibited and a podium for the speakers.

A week before the Congress opened David Briggs announced that he had to go to the United States, where his father was seriously ill. This left the running of the congress to me, because Greg Lower was sick and unable to attend. Representatives came in their hundreds and each section was handled at the highest level. The show manual involved a lot of scholarly enquiry, but appeared with well-researched data. Sir Wallis Ray opened the congress and the chairman was John Nash, a highly professional radio and television personality.

The veterinarians who were there in force wholeheartedly supported the raising of a research fund and establishing a research branch. Top executives from every branch of the horse business attended, and Congress research did establish that ours was a billion dollar business, probably second only to the motor car in terms of money.

To establish the riding trail project we had asked an energetic young horseman, Dan Seymour, to bring along two pack-horses and, with saddles which I supplied, to be ready to head out from Gatton to Melbourne, and then from Melbourne back to Cooktown, when Congress should give its approval. This is exactly what happened. Dan set out looking for the trail, reached Melbourne and returned, then went on to Cooktown and returned, spending two valuable years on the task.

On his return from America David Briggs expressed deep regret that he had not been able to attend the Congress, and mentioned that he had again visited the American Stockmen's Hall of Fame, known also as the Cowboy Hall of Fame. He was an associate at Gatton of Hugh Sawrey the artist, and put the case to him that the Australian people should endeavour without delay to put together the record and the history of the founding of Australia by her stockmen, and to record the traditions of Outback Australia.

In view of the success of the Horseman's Congress Sawrey made contact with me immediately to suggest that we call a meeting of those interested. He suggested the names of several friends who might form the nucleus of a committee. I think his first selection was Ranald Chandler, who had been compere at the wedding of Bob Katter, the member for Kennedy in the Federal Parliament. Chandler, Katter, Sawrey and I met, with Katter's recently married wife Joy acting as secretary.

We first of all had to establish a corporation which would take charge of the whole operation. To this end we invited several prominent Australians to join us in the project: Dame Mary Durack-Miller, famous for her many books on Outback Australia; Ranald Chandler, prominent cattle-man; Bob Dodd, a soldier of distinction; Bruce Yeates, a prominent and respected physician. Rupert Murdoch, the publisher, became our Number One Foundation Patron.

At the second meeting we decided to write to every town and city in Australia that might possibly provide a venue for the building. We sent letters over a wide area, to Alice Springs, Perth, Rockhampton, Canberra and many other centres. The sites suggested to us were so numerous that it took two years to inspect them and absorb the propaganda from each area. I had my own plane and pilot, and no place that made a submission was neglected. Some of these places nominated wonderful sites; for example Rockhampton offered a section of twenty hectares in their gardens, one of the finest gardens in Australia. Canberra offered Black Mountain. Alice Springs was interested. Cloncurry and Longreach and many other centres suggested that we inspect what they had to offer, and we did so.

During this time our legal representatives, Cannon and Peterson in Brisbane, negotiated with the Commissioner of Corporate Affairs, the idea being to set up a corporation so that those who contributed would do so on a tax-deductible basis. This also took months; the matter had to be carefully considered and those associated with it vetted by the Commissioner. Then the Corporation was set up and registered in all States, and an office established.

So the project of the Hall of Fame was duly launched with many prestigious names on the Board, people whose achievements had made their names household words. But after the company was incorporated and the whole project theoretically on its way we seemed to bog down, in part because it takes a lot of money to circulate thousands of people with any kind of information. The newspapers and other media had been a great help. They had used me as a front-runner and given me a lot of publicity but it was not enough to keep it moving. I decided to do something about it.

We selected Longreach for the site because it represents the drier parts of Australia, a region where conditions are very lonely and harsh. Although it has bitumen roads and electricity it remains otherwise very much as it was, and there visitors can envisage what life was like without roads, telephones or electricity or any of the facilities which make living easier today.

I wanted the building to be of stone, something of the local background, a material linking the past and the present. Architects have very seriously opted for concrete and steel but I have been quite adamant in my resistance and I believe the Hall of Fame will rise mostly in local sandstone. This will make it necessary for me to spend much of the 1980s on the building, and although I am reaching an age that will limit the amount of work I can do, I am still able to build the corners and help where experience might be necessary. Younger men can be taught to do the bulk of the work.

I would like to remain active enough to retain a hand in the choice of what will be put before the public within its walls and its presentation. It is important that the next generation should know how our forefathers lived in this land, what they thought, what they did and how they did it.

I would like their condition of life to be presented in such a way that those who look can come away with a good understanding of the houses (or lack of houses) from which they pioneered the country, the atmosphere in which they lived and the tools they used. I would like Australians to know and appreciate the efforts which developed the stock-routes, the great cattle highways which led from water to water across the dry and desolate stretches. Down these tracks the battlers toiled day and night, minding their cattle and taking them, often enough, more than a thousand kilometres to watered country.

These pioneers developed a life of their own. They became a people apart, a group unique when seen against the general community. They had their own language, their own words, their own ways.

Their methods of handling themselves and their cattle and horses were developed under the driving guidance of necessity, and these methods became traditional in their time. Horses were hobbled out at night, saddles were placed on the ground in certain ways, camps were set up in such a manner that if cattle rushed they would still be safe from the stampede. The salt beef and damper the drovers ate was not a selection of choice; it became routine because they were the only foods that could be carried over the long dry stretches. Damper was easy to make; salt beef carried well in the packs.

The stockwhip was the extension of a man's hand. He used it as a symbol of his trade, but he also used it when a beast became a nuisance and had to be corrected. A man's hand on the bridle gave evidence of his experience, and it took many years of practice before the amateur could copy the way he sat in the saddle.

The hat he wore sheltered him from the fierce sun. The cut of his trousers was that most suitable for his work. His boots were made easy to get on, because of the need for fast action if cattle rushed in the night. His belt carried his knife, his matchbox and his watch, and often it denoted the way in which he intended to work. A lot of young fellows who considered themselves active stockmen wore a belt of knee hobbles of a special type, which could also be used to tie a beast down. Many stockmen still wear such belts.

The way a man shod his horse, or how he made his camp at night, indicated his experience. The way a boss drover looked after his horses' backs and girths betokened his efficiency in caring for his animals. A top stockman had a top plant of horses. Great stockmen did not become great through hearsay; they became top men because they were good at the job, because they were respected by others, because they were careful, because they were good horsemen, cared for their stock and looked after their men. As in every other profession, there were not many top men.

We want to record the life and times of such great men. In the Stockman's Hall of Fame we want to demonstrate the interpretation of their beliefs and their ways of life. Every generation has its heroes, and I have no doubt that there will be some whose life and times remain unsung, but still, while memory remains and the records are with us, I find it important that these records should be kept and cherished.

In 1980 I packed up my goods, left my horse stud and my garden in other hands and set out to Longreach, the site we had chosen for the Hall. It had been the crossroads of the droving era, situated on a magnificent waterhole on the Thompson Creek and populated by people who still valued the traditional ways. The shire, under the chairmanship of Sir James Walker, was sympathetic and the sons and daughters of the pioneers still living at Longreach got behind the project. In a short time they had raised tens of thousands of dollars—we were on our way.

I had my son John with me when we arrived on the site, a barren stretch on the eastern side of the town, just a gibber paddock. We had enlisted the help of architect William Durack to sketch out a building which would serve as both Information Centre and caretaker's cottage, and he made this contribution gratis. I had decided that some very spectacular move would have to be made to bring the project to the notice of the Australian public.

I had decided not to live in an elaborate set-up in Longreach or to go to a motel, but rather to camp on the spot and devote all my activities to the single purpose of erecting this building. The idea was to seek out and use local materials such as stone, timber and sand, and to use local labour if it were available.

The site was an ancient alluvial plain, the ground a sort of clay mixture which became boggy when wet, expanding to such a degree that the foundations could not possibly be established in it. We decided to gather old sleepers which had been discarded alongside the railway line, and with a truck we picked up as many of them as we could. John disturbed a Downs tiger snake with one of the first but the gathering of sleepers went well thereafter. We soon built them into something that kept out the wind, and when we covered this with a tarpaulin we had a reasonably comfortable camp. It became immediately popular. Stockmen coming into town for the weekend reckoned that this was a suitable place to camp because I always had plenty of firewood, supplied by Ranald Chandler. Sir James brought an occasional case of rum. The stock contractors and the ringers found this a pleasant place to spend the weekends, and I was very glad to have their company.

We discovered a local source of sandstone thirty-two kilometres from the site and proceeded to cart it. Hagen Machinery in Toowoomba had built me a machine for cutting it that suited my requirements. It weighed seven tonnes and I trucked it to Longreach and set it on a concrete slab and began to cut the stone. Since the first construction would be a talking point I made a great effort to get the foundations down to rock. It took several months to find bed-rock at four to five metres. On the bed-rock we poured a slab of concrete using a lot of steel reinforcing so that the completed building would stand a good chance of remaining free of cracks in spite of the drifting black soil.

The stonework was heavy and I needed help. One day a drover went past with his horses and called to say 'good-day'. I asked whether he was interested in a job. He said yes, as he was not droving at the time, but he needed a place to put his horses. I suggested that the 45-hectare paddock where we were building the Hall would be ideal and he agreed and took the job.

This turned out to be the beginning of an interesting relationship. Bob Sadler turned out to be one of the best working mates I have had. He was a typical drover, he had grown up on the road and he talked the language I understood. In the morning he would be there at six o'clock, kicking me awake where I slept in my swag. And then again as the sun sank at six o'clock he would still be there—he worked a twelve-hour day. His wife or daughter would bring morning and afternoon tea to us. I have a very special regard for Bob Sadler. He was a little uncouth and had one of the toughest of mentalities, having arrived at some harsh conclusions during his life on the road, but beneath was a warm and friendly personality, a loyal mate, a hard-working man and a friend I could trust absolutely.

I was expounding on his virtues one day to one of the locals who complained that, just the same, he was uncouth. I explained this to my helper and he asked me what 'uncouth' meant. I told him it meant putting elbows on the table and, seeing that we had no table, this of course did not matter.

Longreach is close to Barcaldine where the great shearers' strike of 1891 occurred and where the foundations were laid for the Australian Labor Party. The first meeting to establish the Party was held under the tree at Barcaldine, and the feeling that began in those days still runs strong there. A great deal of bitterness developed between the station-owners and the shearers, and anyone who knows of those battles between the shearers, the owners and the police would realize that it takes many generations before such animosity dies out.

One day, when I was laying the first of the stones of the western wall, a young man came and sat on a stone nearby and, without speaking, waited for me to finish what I was doing.

When I looked up he said, 'I am one of the newly-elected members of the Longreach Shire Council, and I belong to the Labor Party. I am sorry to have to tell you that today, in the council meeting, when the council nominated to support the Hall of Fame building, I voted against it.'

I raised my eyebrows. 'Why?'

'Well,' he said, 'the Hall of Fame is a silvertail project and in deference to the people who elected me I feel I cannot support you.'

This led to some discussion as to what constituted the various classes of society. When he discovered that I had a long association with the political credos of the various parties, that I had read and understood the works of Karl Marx and that I understood, far better than he did, the constitution of the Labor Party and could quote in detail the various bills the Labor Party had passed, he began to realize that I was perhaps less of an enemy than he had at first thought.

A fortnight after this he brought me two old leather chairs he had found in the dump. They were old chairs, individual in design, hand-made with leather seats—just the thing. He suggested I would find them useful in the camp, which I did. But more than that I was pleased to think that he had in some way buried the hatchet and was prepared to be friendly.

A solidly established relationship thus developed, and as time went by we discussed how he might work, as it were, with a foot in both worlds. I suggested that as a councillor he had a responsibility to the people of Longreach in other ways than that of serving the Hall of Fame. He asked what would be the help I needed that would also fit in with his political aims. I suggested that he should appeal to the government to back a project of building a larger water supply on the Thompson River.

This appealed to him immensely and he lent his weight whole-heartedly to this cause, because, as we agreed, in time to come there would be no city unless the water supply were much improved. And owing to his, and other help, the State council finally did allocate funds to the establishment of a better water supply. This of course was fundamental to the establishment of Longreach as a city, and also to the future of the Hall of Fame.

My friend Bob was politically ambitious, and within twelve months he had stood for the Federal Senate. Unfortunately for him the Labor Party placed him number five on the ticket, making it impossible for him to win. I told him that, though he hadn't succeeded in becoming a senator, I could possibly help in finding something else which would bring him into contact with the Labor Party in the city, and he took a job in our establishment in Brisbane. It has been a firm friendship and a fine alliance.

About this time my son Peter decided that for the time being he had had enough of flying those lonely mail-runs in the north for Tennant Creek Airways, and he came down to help us. He had the potential to be an excellent stonemason. He was meticulously careful in the placement of the stones and in the way he sorted them so that their graining and pattern were more pleasing to the eye. He was much more practical in this than I. So we battled on. The walls were thick and we had a lot of material to shift.

About midway through the project a young man named Cyril Darl came along and announced that he was something of a specialist with the axe and the adze, and that he would be pleased to help by cutting the woodwork, such as the door- and window-frames and the beams. He would cut the timbers on the coast, adze them to requirements and send them by rail. I did not really believe he would do as he said, but was convinced with the arrival of a wagon-load of timber weighing several tonnes.

These were beautifully cut from the hardwood trees of the coast. They were straight and smooth and fitted to perfection. One of the main beams was just on twenty metres long and weighed two tonnes. We had a crane unload the timbers from the trucks, and brought them to the site where we oiled them and stacked them straight so they could dry and season and become ready for use. Cyril Darl had proved to be one of the most experienced adze men I have met. He loved his work, he loved the timber and he supplied us with all the material we needed.

About this time I had a telephone call from a person I did not know, telling me he had some cedar trees and was prepared to cut enough cedar to do all the rest of the building for the Hall of Fame. I told him that I did not know there were such large quantities of cedar left in Australia. I thought the tree was just about extinct. He told me that he had been keeping these trees for just some such project, where their value would be appreciated, and he could think no better placement for them than the Hall of Fame.

Hugh Sawrey, the founding father of the Hall of Fame, came with his son John to help with the building, and John proved a willing assistant, mixing the mortar and helping with the stones. I'm afraid we worked him mercilessly. It was 'John this' and 'John that' all day long and he never complained, working magnificently through the long day, keeping up the supply of mortar. One day I asked him if he ever thought he'd like to build a stone building for himself. He said, in a subdued voice, 'I'd like to do that; but I'd get a boy to mix the mortar.' He made his point.

A heterogeneous flow of people, of all political colours and social standings, came to watch us work. Ita Buttrose, a prominent figure in the media who had come to open the local show, called to see us. She declined our invitation to leave a footprint or a handprint in the wet cement but took a trowel, drew a heart in it and wrote 'Ita loves R.M.' which I interpreted as an expression of support and confidence, and therefore valued.

The priest and the nuns from the local Catholic school came to visit us. Encouraged by their company I promised to visit church, which I did regularly while I was there. I have never been christened in any church, but I have had a lasting association with the Catholics. I have always been concerned that there is such bitterness emanating from the more extreme members of the various sects. I feel I could kneel with the Moslems on a prayer mat and quite comfortably call on the same God.

Longreach was my home through that cold winter and on into the burning hot summer. When the walls were topped and the big adze-cut ceiling beams lifted into place my friend Hagen flew over from Toowoomba with his son to put the iron roof on. It was a hot windy day, and he tells me the job was the hottest he ever had. For the floor we selected a parcel of marble that had come from the old government quarries at Marble Bar and put it down by hand with the help of Bob Sadler. After polishing it proved a magnificent addendum.

We discovered that if we were to expect State or Federal Government support we had to launch the project through the Institute of Architects. The Australian Institute of Architects advertised a competition, the prizes for which were put up by our organization. Since the project was reckoned to cost several million dollars the competition was quite keen and elicited eighty-odd submissions from around Australia and around the world. The Institute nominated the judges and these three gentlemen selected as the winner a young man from Sydney named Feiko Bauman.

We had hoped, of course, that the architect and the supervisors would be sufficiently impressed with the building we had completed to make use of a complementary design and materials in the main building of the Hall of Fame, but this was not to be. We were to discover that young architects know nothing but concrete and steel, and we had a long and bitter struggle to persuade the authorities that the massive stone walls we had built were more suitable and more aesthetically pleasing than concrete and steel.

I discovered that the old senior architect in the Department of Public Works was himself a stonemason from way back, and he understood the position thoroughly, so that at least I was sure of a sympathetic hearing. The matter is now settled our way, and if necessary I shall do the stone walls myself if I can persuade the architects and others interested to allow me to carry on with this work.

I would have liked the Hall of Fame to be more allied to the old-fashioned type of pioneer buildings, but young architects believe it necessary for their professional reputations to provide what they consider to be the modern look. At least, if I have my way, the interior will be filled with records of those who have made this country from the grass roots, the people who endured the rigours of pioneering and who made the traditions of this country that we respect so much.

The press baron Rupert Murdoch had taken the position of Number One Patron of the Hall of Fame and, with the help of his managing director, Ken Cowley, as treasurer, we made valuable and important contacts. Through Cowley I met the Prime Minister and we have strong promises from both Federal and State leaders of Federal and State backing.

With the project still in the making we have been gathering the records of pioneer families. It has always been a matter of deep concern to me that the history of old friends and famous old stockmen and horsemen should be lost, so we are making a concerted effort before it is too late. We will preserve all we can of the records of those who did so much to establish the Australian tradition.

The stories of the great stock-routes of Australia are being written now: the Canning route from the Kimberleys to Perth; the Murrunji from Hall's Creek to Newcastle Waters and on to Queensland across the treeless downs. Every year for the best part of a century big herds of cattle moved from Queensland to Wodonga in Victoria. The Overland route across the Gulf is a legend, and the desert sands of the Birdsville

Track hold the bones of tens of thousands of cattle caught in the sand blizzards of the area. The Strzelecki Track was tackled only by brave men and outlaws. Each of these cattle highways joining the pioneer cattle empires to markets or fattening lands demanded epic effort for its traverse, and the stories thereof will provide material to make the American Wild West look tame.

The Hall of Fame has occupied me from 1972 to 1983, a period of ten years during which some of our main supporters have passed on: Bob Dodd, who did much of the early work, and Dr Bruce Yeates, who helped with political co-operation. One man who travelled all these many miles and was present at almost every meeting through the years was Ranald Chandler. After Longreach was selected for the site Sir James Walker joined the board.

But the preliminaries are now complete; details of the work to come have been established in intent, and the Hall of Fame will be built. For me this is a crowning achievement and in future my contribution will be on a different basis. I will be more interested in making sure that the histories of the people who should be recorded there are adequately presented. The building is to be a cathedral to enshrine the memories of the unsung among the great stockmen of the nation.

I like to think of the spirits of these people as living on, having in their lifetime sown seeds which develop to produce again in the world which comes after. I think of Churchill, who warned against building a state of society in which industry has no reward. I think of Ben Chifley who crusaded so hard to establish that government is money, and money is government. I think of the martyrs, who gave their lives in vain for causes they believed in, and of the great old pioneering bushmen who also gave their lives. Unknown and unheralded, they left behind them a tradition of struggle. Men long since dead, their spirits live on, and perhaps will go on forever. Could this be everlasting life?

I'm impressed by Henry Wadsworth Longfellow's great lines:

> Lives of great men all remind us
> We can make our lives sublime
> And, departing, leave behind us
> Footprints on the sands of time.
> Footprints, that perhaps another,
> Sailing o'er life's solemn main,
> A forlorn and ship-wrecked brother
> Seeing, shall take heart again.

If these people who are dead left nothing else but one great line of poetry, one great memory of achievement, one thing that made the world the better for their having lived, one great moment of music, one kind word which helped another along the way, one act of charity which resurrected another life, one inspiration for a child, then they impose a duty on those of us who are the receivers of help. We should see that the seeds of hope and worth and beauty prosper, and we should remember the sower.

Those who qualify for the Hall of Fame gave their lives for an ideal. Turning their backs on every comfort in life, they set out to pursue the wider horizon willingly, even eagerly, accepting that their lives ahead would be lives of toil, adventure, hardship, danger and daily confrontation with the problems associated with pioneering. The drovers who qualify are those who took large numbers of cattle over long distances, sleeping under the stars, risking their lives when the cattle rushed, accepting that lack of water or a sandstorm might wipe them out, taking pleasure in a good delivery and then turning round and going back for the next mob. The roughriders qualify for the Hall of Fame, men well known who excelled in the extraordinary pursuit of riding unridable horses. We extol the virtues of our writers, our painters, our singers, our musicians; we should also pay a tribute in permanent form to those horsemen who set the great traditions of horsemanship.

This need to excel in some act of courage seems to be an inheritance from ancestors way back. No doubt cavemen demonstrated their courage facing up to the giant animals which lived on earth. For millions of years, perhaps, men have done something similar to prove themselves. The age in which we live seems exceptional in this regard. We have seen men risk their lives to go to the moon, men set out to cross the oceans on rafts or to challenge its depths, and we honour them for keeping alive this tradition of courage, inspiring the next generation to still greater adventure. Who knows but the next challenge may be the exploration of the universe.

During the Christmas holidays I drove several hundred kilometres to spend the season with my boys. I had occasion to do a lot of thinking on this long journey, and now and then I stopped to make note of what I considered I should tell them. First of all that they must never hate, and that they should be trustworthy. No other law seems to be so binding. These qualities demand a commitment, but they will enrich anybody who weaves them into a life pattern. The rewards are limitless, and could be forever.

Something which has become almost my credo of faith is the concept of freedom, freedom to sit by a running brook and listen to the birds and watch the wonders of the flowers. This calls for no commitment to either Heaven or earth. One must have time that is distinct from the limited encircled hours of a place hemmed in by walls and dominated by the clock. Freedom is the first priority for success and happiness, and I lay this down as a cardinal rule for those who follow me.

I also prefer to believe in the inevitability of fortune, luck, accident, predestination or the encompassing Hand of God. All are but names for the same thing. Nevertheless you are confined by the laws I have mentioned. With freedom one finds many worlds to conquer, an unlimited tally of them. The knowledge of the earth, the knowledge of history and literature, the knowledge of music, of government, of social problems, a knowledge of the living environment. Almost anybody can build a cottage on a stream as long as company is not something they demand, or money, or luxury. I think of the world's millions cooped up in cities, living in an iron-clad cage, dictated to by civilization, but bowed, most of all, under the weight of the traditions of the past.

I think one of the saddest, and probably one of the most momentous, declarations ever made to the world was uttered by the Man who said: 'How often would I have gathered my children together, as a hen doth gather her brood under her wings, and ye would not.'

The all-governing question of course is: can a person live without wealth? Can one live a full and satisfying life without the advantages that come from wealth? One can, as long as the struggle for necessary money does not become a total commitment. One should select, devise, seek out some means of economic survival and set the parameters within which one can achieve that which is hoped for, wished for, or necessary.

Money absorbs too much of our lives. The country does have a balance of payments problem, but this is a political responsibility. What is vital is that the individuals of this small nation owe the moneylenders something close to a hundred billion dollars. Our debt for this incredible amount demonstrates either that we live above our means, or that we do not receive enough for the goods or services we produce. The truth of the matter lies halfway between, and the condition will not be curable until the nation controls interest rates and credit through the Reserve Bank. I have talked about this vital subject with leaders of industry, commerce and banking, people such as Menzies who, I believe, understood the dilemma better than any other leader we have had. When Chifley tried to implement a nation-wide solution through his Banking Act of 1945, the crusade financed by the money-lending institutions defeated him. I remember it well and have a copy of the Act with me. Surely someone will be brave enough to tell the truth about the iniquity of high interest rates. Young people cannot build houses with money at 12 to 15 per cent. High inflation is given as the reason for the high level of interest rates, but if it is controlled now, and it could be, the poor borrower is still stuck with the 12 to 15 per cent interest on the house or debt.

Civilizations of the past have faced this problem and some at least have done the right thing and made usury a criminal act punishable by death. That has been the price paid by the money-lenders of China who have died in our time. I saw this evil in China and am brutally glad that the festering sore of *control by loan* has been rooted out, even if only temporarily. Starvation in time of drought and the severing of families resulted from this corruption practiced by the usurers of rural China.

I watched the Soviets' handling of the Orthodox Church with an equal satisfaction, for the oppression of the Church in Russia was absolute and it went hand-in-hand with the control by the Tsars. I could say that the Church in Australia has a stabilizing influence but I do not forget that the Church was guilty of a century-long Inquisition, and that in some countries religion has been 'the opiate of the people'. Nor is it arguable that 'the traditions of the past weigh like an Alp on the brains of the living'. Here, of course, we are almost equally affected.

Jesus has cast long shadows on history, and I suspect that He is badly represented. I sometimes wonder if Marx and Mao were not His instruments in freeing many slaves. I subscribe sincerely to the Father–Son concept, in which wrong-doing brings its own penalties, which the beneficent Father forgives. I like the idea of being a child of God; it carries no label, bears no stigmas. I have read carefully but I find no irksome dogmas in the simple statement: 'If the Son therefore shall make you free, you shall be free indeed.'

My mother was a pious woman, father silent about religion, so silent I suspected him to be anti. But Mother did teach us the Lord's Prayer. At the dinner Dame Mary Durack-Miller gave in celebration of the re-opening of Argyle homestead I was sitting next to the United States Ambassador. At a lull in the conversation he turned to me quietly and, looking seriously into my face, he asked, 'Have you got any religion?'

It stopped me a bit. 'I can recite the Lord's Prayer,' I said.

'Good enough,' he answered and left it at that.

A bit of Dad's attitude rubbed off on me, so that when I came to be married I would not enter a church and I never did until much later when it did not seem to matter any more. Then I attended a Catholic convention of sorts with Tom Quilty, who seemed to think that this meeting might be good for me. It was in a huge hall filled with tables, controlled by a priest on a raised platform. Tom and I were relegated to a table with two old ladies. Each group had to talk together on a designated subject and then the leader had to speak into a microphone a priest held into his face. Our subject was 'Sin'. The two old ladies did not look as though they knew much about it, and Tom was not letting on. It was not a brilliant foursome. When the mike came our way Tom, being the leader, had it thrust into his face and with some facility he shifted it across to me. I was dumb for a moment, then with the brilliance of self-preservation I said, 'Our Father which art in Heaven forgive us our trespasses as we forgive others.' The mike passed on and so ended that brief contact with organized religion.

On Good Friday the bells ring out round the world, the radio is blaring choir music, wonderful sentiment. But—if the Man Jesus were to step inside my door or come knocking, would I know Him? A man of the road, with straw, perhaps, from some lonely haystack still clinging to His uncut hair, garments creased and road-stained. Would I welcome Him? I might. What would He say to me, looking through my facade of respectability into my soul? If it were what He said to the rich young man: 'Sell all that thou hast and give it to the poor and thou shalt have treasure in Heaven; and come, follow Me,' I would not recognize Him or abide by His words. Remember that He was a man of the road, poor and hunted by the police. I am torn by the tragedy of it all. How do I follow Him? How would I know God if I saw Him? I shall look for Him among the uncouth, the sorrowful, the have-nots. Maybe He will be there. And will He know me?

A fearsome struggle has been mounted around the world. The armament manufacturers have slowly improved their weapons, inventing machines which can devastate large areas of an enemy's country. I do not think that these weapons such as hydrogen bombs will be used till the battle for the skies has been won. I believe that the technology now being devised for use beyond the stratosphere will ultimately dictate who will control the world. The battle for men's minds continues. Certain individuals have been slowly gaining control of the media. Their influence is vast; their intentions, I hope, honourable.

While dedication to the war machine has robbed the Russian people of their development and they have been kept in poverty, China is devoting much of her energy to raising her standard of living. China has ceased to send out propaganda and is devoting her time and energies now to setting an example to the world. The Chinese have gone some distance in freeing their people from the thralldom of money and the bondage of ignorance. They have improved the productivity of their land. We do not hear now of great famines in which millions die whenever there is a shortage of rice. Great rivers are being harnessed and power stations set up all over the country.

In Australia I have watched young and ardent revolutionaries grow old. Some I knew fifty years ago have lived their lives hoping, and have died still believing that revolution is on the way. That is not likely, because Australians are rich in what really matters, a plentiful food supply, abundant raw materials and ample space in which to live. Our political system is good and the only real bondage we suffer is that of money. This is not incurable, and I find it shameful that this country's thinkers have not devoted more time to dissecting and explaining the relevant theories, which in the last fifty years have caused two vast revolutions and changed the life-style of half the world's people.

I am sympathetic with Marx in his belief that the dictatorship of the proletariat would eventually change things, but this belief does not apply to Australia. The evils of our society can be changed politically and without bloodshed, as many people are beginning to understand. Marx believed that the course of history was changed by such factors as the wealth or poverty of people, the place in which they lived, the climatic conditions. These have profoundly influenced the life-style of people but they have not always been vital factors in political change. The great religious revivals had an important bearing on the life-style of the British and other European nations. In the United States the mixing of different cultures had a major influence on American thought. The Roman Church had a very great influence on the people of Italy, Spain and South America.

Some claim that certain European peoples have been priest-ridden into poverty. I do not believe this. I believe that people are poor in places where the land is poor and I do not think this can be drastically changed by religious belief. Certainly, though, a national character exerts great influence on a capacity to prosper. The saving habits of the early settlers in America created the wealth which, when it was invested, made capital for the development of the nation. This was real money, differing greatly from the money now created by government and by inflation. To have a lasting effect the savings of the people should be available to them in something tangible, such as gold. The manipulation of savings by paper money, such as was caused by Keynesian theory, will eventually lead to financial chaos.

One often wonders what made such frail and seemingly insignificant people as the Vietnamese fight so desperately against the people of wealth and might in France and America. When they set out to change their circumstances with ideas, as they did in those particular times, their dedication carried them through.

The courage and determination of a few individuals have certainly been able to change the world. In my time there were men like Ho Chi-minh, who led his people from slavery to victory, and Mao Tse-tung, who fought the whole might of several empires. Others who swayed the course of history in the past included Mahomet the Arab and Jesus the Jew, who continued to lead through the centuries, so that one cannot look to material reasons alone for change. Karl Marx's theory of surplus profit played an important part in changing the world in my lifetime, but I doubt if this theory holds water. It is an effect rather than a cause.

The sages nod their heads when I speak of truth, confident like all men that their own beliefs are the truth. My advice is for everyone to eliminate all dogmas and see for themselves what remains. The advice 'Seek and ye shall find' is probably the best. I cannot guarantee what you will find but at least the seeking will be good for you.

You don't have to shave your head, wear yellow robes or become a monk. You don't have to isolate yourself and leave the company of your fellows—this, it seems to me, is cowardice—you simply have to go about your work in the ordinary manner, facing the problems that everyone else faces, doing such work as other people do, living as your fellows do throughout the world. You will learn patience through your irritation with them, you will learn kindness in seeing their misery and you will learn tolerance when you realize that 'the whole world marches to the tune of sobs and sighs'. All the lessons that have been learned throughout history are stored somewhere in the recesses of our minds. We call some intuition, some commonsense. Some individuals recognize them more easily than others, or have a more immediate access to them. If we look deep inside our own intuitions we will find wisdom there to guide us on our way.

Somewhere along the line every responsible person does some social thinking about religion, or takes sides in the political struggle. I must confess to having been too confused for the most part all my life and to having not made serious allegiances, first because of the struggle to get out of the mud, then later because of involvement in mining, tea planting, cattle raising, printing, horse breeding and a host of interests so absorbing that I have been content to let the other fellow rant about religion and fight for the top spot in power.

In May 1984 I flew over to Alice Springs for the inauguration of what I hope will become an annual event, a championship in broncho branding. 'Broncho branding' is the elemental way of catching calves in the Outback, by concentrating the cattle herd in the smallest possible area. The rider, working quietly, ropes his calf, pulls it out against a gapped log barrier, or a forked tree, or a hook tied to a tree, and brands, castrates, earmarks and perhaps inoculates it. With closer settlement the process has given way to branding with a calf cradle, but the old method is more interesting for the man on the land, especially as some riders take great pride in being handy with a greenhide rope. During this meeting at Alice Springs the point was truly made that three calves can be handled in two minutes, which is as fast as or faster than the cradle method, so perhaps broncho branding may be on the way back. I hope so.

In Townsville on the way to the championships I met Ken Warrener, now the manager of the vast Newcastle Waters Station. He told me that in future his bullocks will be walked to market and not trucked. The previous herd at Newcastle Waters has all been destroyed for the eradication of brucellosis and a new breeding stock of 25 000 cows put in. Their progeny will see the resumption of droving, a complete turn of the wheel. The bores on the stock-routes have been idle for a long time since the introduction of the road-train, but there is a big advantage to buyers in taking cattle that have walked to market. They have become used to people and are quiet, whereas the cattle travelled by truck have become wilder and wilder. The same thing happens to cattle that have been handled by helicopter; they become wilder, while horse-handled cattle get quieter as they lose their fears. So I hope to see more horse work and less use of 'copters and motor-cycles.

I was happy to see so much of our equipment used at the broncho-branding championships as Central Australia, of course, is its original home. Almost everyone at this large gathering was wearing our boots and trousers, and although we are pleased with the good sales we have in the cities, I am prouder that we retain the bush business.

While I was busy making the opening speech for the broncho-branding championships officials asked me if I would judge the whip-cracking contest. I have done this quite often, of course, and I have many ways of selecting the best. It is not enough for a competitor to crack the whip and make a large noise, for he should be able to crack it accurately. Its prime function is to discipline hard-to-handle cattle and it is not enough to wave the whip madly in the air, hoping that the noise will affect the animal. Sometimes it is necessary to lay the tip of the whip across the beast's loins without damaging it, so in judging I make a feature of accuracy. To this end I usually ask the competitor for specific results, like cutting the top off a cigarette in a man's mouth, or taking a coin from a man's hand, or cutting a cigarette paper held between the hands. These, of course, call for a degree of accuracy, because the tip of a whip which cracks the sound barrier can do serious damage to the hands of the person holding the paper.

Quite a number of the contestants were special in the way they could handle a whip but two were outstanding. I selected them to make special efforts to display their expertise. I held coins in my hand for each of them to see whether they could take them away. I must admit that on several occasions they missed the coin and hit my fingers without serious damage, but the effect was fairly painful. I hope that I did not show this visibly.

I made the final selection by placing a twenty-cent piece on my tongue, and advised the two of them that if either made a mistake he would be automatically eliminated. At that, one of them opted out and gave the prize to the other so I was saved the painful necessity of eliminating one because he had hurt my tongue!

In one such whip-cracking contest the two finalists were difficult to separate, and I finally made the decision by asking them to crack a twenty-cent piece, making it bounce so that it entered the neck of a milk bottle. Of course this is a very difficult feat, but one of them managed to do just that.

Some experts are in the habit of always carrying a whip in their hands and using it so much that they are adept in its use. It pleases me that this skill is so very much in evidence. The style and make of the Australian stockwhip is unique in the world, and we have had our specialists in its making, rising to a peak with Alex Scobie who raised his family and made his whips out there by the Birdsville Track. I have tried to keep this specialized art alive by doing the work myself and teaching those in our plaiting department, but there will not be many, if any, who reach old Scobie's degree of perfection. There will surely be a place for Scobie in the completed Hall of Fame.

It is no exaggeration that an expert using the stockwhip can literally cut strips from the hide of an animal. Not many would follow this cruel practice, but it is possible. We notice when buying hides from Argentina that the hind parts of many of the skins are badly lacerated by whip marks, so it is evident that the gauchos of South America do use this cruel weapon. I am pleased that few of the hides we buy in Australia are so marked.

My mother lived to the age of 103. She died on 15 January 1984. She was born in 1881 and drawing on the memories of her mother, who lived to be a great age, she was able to recall stories from the eighteenth century. Interestingly, we have personal records or connections with people who have information about life in Wales and Cornwall, whence came my grandparents and great-grandparents. The stories of their lives were passed on through my mother who has often told me of happenings in the Welsh mining areas and of the fishing folk of Cornwall.

Towards the end she did not see very well, and she could not read, and the music she heard on radio did not appeal to her. Yet when I rang her she came quickly to the telephone and her powers of comprehension were good. She treated me like the small boy she had known when I lived with her, but she did not live in the past. She retained a strong faith, and I think she continued to live in a promising future. I worked it out that she lived thirty-seven thousand, three hundred and eighteen days, and with her passing I cannot help thinking there is so little time and so much to do.

We gather over the Christmas period at Ian's place at Rockybar on the Auburn River, in the house he and I built so many years ago when he was getting married. It was a happy gathering this year. Ian, his wife Daphne and their four children, Mark, Danny, Sean and Kylie, were joined by Kerry and his wife Robyn and their two girls, Stephanie and Tracy, who all came over from Dingaroo. During Christmas Day the telephone was busy with calls from round the country from other members of the family. They are still a close-knit unit. I feel ashamed when I think of how much I have done to split this family; and yet proud to know they have remained a cohesive whole, joined by some bond which seems stronger than all others, the concept of family.

Sometimes I reflect, with perhaps a touch of unease, that I have taught this large family no religion, yet there seems among them a love of their fellows and perhaps this is transcendent. The poet Leigh Hunt put it precisely when he wrote of Abou Ben Adhem who woke one night to find an angel in his room, writing the names of those who love God in a book of gold.

> 'And is mine one?' said Abou. 'Nay, not so,'
> Replied the angel.—Abou spoke more low,
> But cheerly still; and said, 'I pray thee, then,
> 'Write me as one that loves his fellow-men.'
>
> The angel wrote and vanished. The next night
> It came again, with a great wakening light,
> And showed the names whom love of God had blessed,—
> And, lo! Ben Adhem's name led all the rest.

It is possible, quite possible, that religion cannot be transmitted by words.

Ian took me for a drive through the many kilometres of beautiful countryside after the wonderful rain of the 1983 season, and he proudly showed me the development. Many thousands of hectares had been painfully cleared by hand, stick by stick; the logs burned and the stumps rooted out and burned; and then the suckers of young trees springing up consistently cut until the land was clean.

'But Ian, you must leave something for your sons to do,' I could not help saying. He looked at me as if to say, 'Yes, but this is my task.' I am sure the task is too big for one generation.

I spent twenty years of my life clearing on that place and seemed to have made little impression, but Ian has done much more than ever I could have. Looking now across the open country to the horizon, I marvel at the transformation he and his family have made. I see the sleek cattle grazing in the pasture he has created and I realize that this part of my life has been worthwhile. Back at the house I took photos of the granite buildings with their carved, hand-adzed beams. They will stand for generations.

Mark is now in the second year of the engineering course at the university and Danny in his second year of law. I am sure that Danny will be a brilliant lawyer and Mark a brilliant engineer. Although they were home-taught in their early years both have proved to be scholars above average in ability, a great credit to Daphne, who laid the foundations of their schooling.

Sean looks like becoming a stockman. He shows a lot of interest in working and training the dogs, for working cattle and for breeding horses. He has that slow, solid, contented attitude, the love for the land, which I am sure will give him permanence on the property after his father Ian has left it. This year I made him a special plaited bridle and I think that probably, considering the great amount of work that went into it, he might even hang it on the wall. Somehow I hope he does.

I have been making the boys plaited watch pouches and now most of them have one. The watches may wear out but the pouches will last for generations. Probably three or four days' work goes into each of these pouches, which I give with great pride and pleasure, for they are my own exclusive handwork and probably unique. Every time I make one I think of the old friends like Brown, in that far-off country at Oodnadatta, who taught me my first plaiting, and Dollar Mick, the half-caste who made the first complete plaited watch pouches. These two were among the only ones I have known who could have made these.

So much for my story, the chronicle of my life. Perhaps when I have finished telling such tales I might recall the long, slow, slogging climb from bagman, swagman, bottom dog to white tie and tails at the Governor's parties on the lawns of Government House, and inter-national traveller . . . . What a waste of time, climbing to the pinnacle of success only to slide willingly down the long slope to a humble but happy campfire where I belong.

Index